▷ 高等职业教育
公共基础课系列教材 ◁

高职英语拓展教程 ▶▶▶▶

主　编：雷启莲　柏佩利　于洪波
副主编：陈　卓　代　欣　曾熙美　吕　燕　林雪梅　侯　博　李鹤艺
参　编：兰　漫　何　伟　曾仁菊　胡　君　马昌勇　熊绘新　王　芳
　　　　易小玲　韩　洋　龙帮源　姚志敏　罗　晗　李　茜　汤静怡
　　　　陈　敏　向志敏

GAOZHI YINGYU
TUOZHAN
JIAOCHENG

北京师范大学出版集团
BEIJING NORMAL UNIVERSITY PUBLISHING GROUP
北京师范大学出版社

图书在版编目(CIP)数据

高职英语拓展教程 / 雷启莲，柏佩利，于洪波主编. 北京：北京师范大学出版社，2024.
ISBN 978-7-303-30114-0

Ⅰ. H319.39

中国国家版本馆 CIP 数据核字第 2024RK0396 号

图 书 意 见 反 馈　zhijiao@bnupg.com
营 销 中 心 电 话　010-58806880　58801876
编 辑 部 电 话　010-58808077

出版发行：北京师范大学出版社　www.bnupg.com
　　　　　北京市西城区新街口外大街 12-3 号
　　　　　邮政编码：100088
印　　刷：三河市兴达印务有限公司
经　　销：全国新华书店
开　　本：889 mm×1194 mm　1/16
印　　张：17.25
字　　数：562 千字
版　　次：2024 年 9 月第 1 版
印　　次：2024 年 9 月第 1 次印刷
定　　价：48.80 元

策划编辑：易　新　　　　　　责任编辑：易　新
美术编辑：焦　丽　　　　　　装帧设计：焦　丽
责任校对：陈　民　　　　　　责任印制：马　洁　赵　龙

前 言

《高职英语拓展教程》落实立德树人根本任务，遵循素质教育规律，促进技术技能人才成长，培养德智体美劳全面发展的社会主义建设者和接班人。本教材以学科核心素养为导向，依据教育部《高等职业教育专科英语课程标准（2021年版）》，并结合专科学校英语教学的实际情况进行编写。

教育部《高等职业教育专科英语课程标准（2021年版）》确定，高等职业教育专科英语课程由基础模块和拓展模块组成。基础模块为职场通用英语，是各专业学生必修或限定选修内容，旨在奠定本阶段英语学科核心素养的共同基础，使所有学生都能达到英语学业质量水平一的要求，满足高等职业教育专科毕业要求。拓展模块为学生根据自身需求自主选择修习的内容，与基础模块形成递进关系，供不同专业、不同水平、不同兴趣的学生在完成基础模块后选修。拓展模块主要包括三类：（1）职业提升英语，为特定专业学生群体开设，满足特定专业学生完成职场中的涉外沟通需求；（2）学业提升英语，为有升学需求的学生群体开设，为本科学习或出国留学做准备；（3）素养提升英语，为满足学生的兴趣爱好和提升学生的个人素养而开设。本教材属于第二类，即学业提升英语。

为了帮助普通高等专科学校学生学业提升，我们组织了有丰富教学经验、多年从事专科英语教学、熟知专科学生英语学习特点的高校教师，依据最新修订的四川省普通高等学校专升本招生考试大纲的要求，精心编写了这本教材。

本教材借助重点知识概览，帮助学生构建知识框架，利用重点点拨帮助学生把握学业提升英语考试的重点和难点，提高应试技巧和能力。在编写过程中，我们力图为学生着想，既注重基础语法讲解，又注重读、写、译综合应用能力的提高，帮助他们克服学习和应试中的问题和困难，尽力使本教材具有基础性、实用性和针对性。

本教材分为三个模块，各部分内容具体如下。

模块一 基础知识强化

本部分主要讲解名词、代词、动词、数词、形容词、副词、冠词、连词、介词等词类的特点和用法，以及句子成分和基本句型介绍。其目的是帮助学生有重点、有针对性地掌握常用基础词汇类型和基本句型结构，打好坚实的语言基础。

模块二 重点语法梳理

本部分主要讲解时态、语态、非谓语动词、主谓一致、复合句以及一些特殊句型，以帮助学生搭建完整的语法知识体系，从而从容应对学业提升考试。

模块三 语言综合运用

本部分讲解阅读、翻译、写作技巧，着重培养学生的语言综合运用能力，帮助学生克服在阅读、翻译、写作中遇到的困难。

每章节之后附有"小试牛刀"和"学以致用"两部分练习，由易到难，所附练习题均经过精心编选，使学生在复习过程中做到学练结合。本教材配套有练习题库，帮助学生巩固所学语言知识，提升学生解题技巧。

本教材在编写过程中，得到了川南幼儿师范高等专科学校和四川幼儿师范高等专科学校领导和老师的大力支持，在此一并表示感谢。本书主编为川南幼儿师范高等专科学校雷启莲、柏佩利，四川幼儿师范高等专科学校于洪波；副主编为川南幼儿师范高等专科学校陈卓、代欣、曾熙美，四川幼儿师范高等专科学校吕燕、林学梅、侯博、李鹤艺；参编人员有川南幼儿师范高等专科学校兰漫、何伟、曾仁菊、胡君、马昌勇、王芳、易小玲、韩洋，四川幼儿师范高等专科学校熊绘新、龙帮源、姚志敏、罗晗、李茜、汤静怡、陈敏、向志敏。

本书配有题库，可以帮助有需要的同学进一步巩固练习所学知识，请联系 963187033@qq.com 邮箱索取。

由于水平有限，书中难免有不当之处，敬请读者批评指正，以便我们修订完善。

2024 年 9 月 6 日

目 录 Contents

模块三 语言综合运用

模块一　基础知识强化

第一章

词 汇

第一节　名词和代词

🔍 重点知识概览

名词和代词重点知识概览

词性	类别	备注
名词	专有名词	首字母须大写
	普通名词	
	可数名词	注意名词复数的变化形式
	不可数名词	不能与不定冠词"a/an"连用
	个体名词	是可数名词
	集体名词	集体名词表示整体是单数，表示个体是复数
	物质名词	是不可数名词
	抽象名词	没有复数形式
	名词所有格	在名词后加"'s"或"'"
代词	人称代词	主格作主语，宾格作宾语。
	物主代词	名词性物主代词相当于名词的作用 形容词性物主代词相当于形容词的作用
	指示代词	近指"this，these"，远指"that，those"
	疑问代词	
	不定代词	

知识梳理

一、名词(Nouns)

名词是表示人、事物或抽象概念的词。根据其意义、形态和功能的差异，名词可以进行如下分类。

1. 专有名词(Proper Nouns)和普通名词(Common Nouns)

(1)专有名词指的是特定的人名、地名、机构名等，其首字母通常大写。

Beijing is the capital of China.

北京是中国的首都。

Confucius is a great philosopher in ancient China.

孔子是中国古代伟大的哲学家。

The Mid-Autumn Festival is a traditional Chinese holiday.

中秋节是中国的一个传统节日。

The Analects of Confucius is a collection of Confucius' teachings.

《论语》是孔子教学言论的汇编。

The Communist Party of China is the ruling party of China.

中国共产党是中国的执政党。

(2)普通名词则表示某一类人、事物或抽象概念的名称，不具有特指性。

She is a *teacher*.

她是一名教师。

Friendship is one of the most valuable emotions in human life.

友谊是人类生活中最宝贵的情感之一。

Tea is a popular beverage in China.

茶是中国人喜爱的饮品。

Harmony is a core value in Chinese culture.

和谐是中国文化的核心价值观之一。

Respect for elders is a traditional virtue in China.

尊老是中国的传统美德。

> **重点点拨**
>
> ★名词所有格的构成及用法
>
> 名词所有格表示所属关系，通常在名词后加"'s"，如"John's book"(约翰的书)。
>
> 以"s"结尾的复数名词后只加"'"，如"the students' classroom"(学生们的教室)。

2. 可数名词(Countable Nouns)和不可数名词(Uncountable Nouns)

(1)可数名词是可以计数的名词，有单数形式和复数形式。

There are five *books* on the table.

桌子上有五本书。

Apples are rich in vitamins.

苹果富含维生素。

The *classroom* has five chairs.

教室里有五把椅子。

There are ten *students* in the class.

班里有十名学生。

I saw four *vehicles* on the road.

我在路上看到了四辆车。

(2)不可数名词是无法计数的名词，通常没有复数形式，且前面不能用不定冠词 a 或 an 修饰，但可以用 some，much，a little 等修饰。例如：

I need some *water*.

我需要一些水。

Knowledge is power.

知识就是力量。

I ate a lot of *bread* yesterday.

我昨天吃了很多面包。

They gave us some good *advice*.

他们给了我们一些好建议。

The *traffic* in the city is very busy.

这座城市的交通很繁忙。

3. 个体名词(Individual Nouns)、集体名词(Collective Nouns)、物质名词(Material Nouns)和抽象名词(Abstract Nouns)

(1)个体名词是指代具体、可数的事物的名词,可以是人、动物、物品等。

I have a new *cat* named Whiskers.

我刚得到了一只名叫胡须的猫。

(2)集体名词是指代一组人或事物的名词,这些名词通常表示一个整体而非单独的个体。

The audience applauded when the performance ended.

表演结束时,观众鼓掌。

(3)物质名词指代无法分为单独个体的物质或材料的名词,如金属、液体、气体等。

Water is essential for life.

水是生命之必需。

(4)抽象名词是指代概念、想法、情感等非物质事物的名词。

Love is the most powerful force in the world.

爱是世界上最强大的力量。

4. 名词所有格

名词所有格是英语中表示所属关系的一种语法形式,主要用来指明某物为某人所拥有或某物与某人有关联。名词所有格的变化形式主要包括-'s 所有格和 of 所有格两种,下面我将详细讲解这两种形式及其变化规则。

(1)-'s 所有格

在名词后加 's 来表示所有关系,是最常见的名词所有格形式。

单数名词:直接在词尾加 's。例如:Tom's book(汤姆的书)。

以-s 结尾的复数名词:只在词尾加 '(省略-s 后的撇号)。例如:teachers' books(老师们的书)。

不以-s 结尾的复数名词:词尾加-'s。例如:children's toys(孩子们的玩具)。

复合名词:在最后一个名词后加-'s。例如:editor-in-chief's office(主编办公室)。

表示共同所有:由 and 连接的并列名词表示共同所有时,只在最后一个名词后加-'s。例如:Jack and Mike's room(杰克和迈克共同的房间)。

表示各自所有:由 and 连接的并列名词表示各自所有时,每个名词后都要加 's。例如:Jack's and Mike's cars(杰克和迈克各自的车)。

特殊地点名词:如表示店铺、某人的家等地点时,-'s 后可省略名词。例如:the barber's(理发店)。

(2)of 所有格

使用介词 of 加名词来表示所有关系,通常用于无生

重点点拨

拟人化:有时为了修辞的需要,无生命的事物也可以用-'s 所有格来表示,使其具有生命或情感色彩。例如:the world's history(世界历史)。

时间、距离等:表示时间、距离、重量、价格、国家、团体或城市等的名词,有时也可用-'s 所有格来表示所有关系。例如:a day's work(一天的工作)。

命的事物或抽象概念。

无生命的事物：常用于表示无生命的事物的所属关系。例如：the door of the house(房子的门)。

抽象概念：也可用于表示抽象概念的所属关系。例如：the beauty of nature(自然之美)。

双重所有格：有时-'s 所有格和 of 所有格可以结合使用，形成双重所有格，用于强调所属关系或表示不特定的所属。例如：a friend of my father's(我父亲的一位朋友)。

5. 名词的数

(1)可数名词为可以计数的名词，有单数和复数两种形式。

单数表示一个人或事物。

I have *a pen*.

我有一支笔。

复数表示两个或两个以上的人或事物。

I have two *pens*.

我有两支笔。

(2)不可数名词为无法计数的名词，通常只有单数形式。

I need some *water*.

我需要一些水。

(3)名词有单数和复数两种形式。一般情况下，名词复数加 s 或 es。例如：

book—books；bus—buses

(4)但也有些名词的复数形式变化不规则，例如：

man—men；mouse—mice

(5)此外，还有一些名词单复数同形，例如：

sheep(羊)，deer(鹿)等。

> **重点点拨**
>
> ★名词复数的变化规则
>
> (1)一般情况下，名词后加"s"或"es"构成复数，如"book"变"books"。
>
> (2)以"s""x""ch""sh"结尾的名词后加"es"，如"box"变为"boxes"。
>
> (3)以辅音字母加"y"结尾的名词，先将"y"改为"i"再加"es"，如"family"变为"families"。

二、代词(Pronouns)

代词是用来代替名词、形容词或数词的词类，可以避免重复使用同一名词，使句子更加简洁明了。代词按其功能可分为以下几类。

1. 人称代词(Personal Pronouns)

人称代词用于代替人或事物，包括主格和宾格两种形式。主格用作主语，宾格用作宾语或表语。例如：

I am a student.

我是一名学生。

Give *me* the book, please.

请把那本书给我。

You look tired. Have you been sleeping well?

你看起来很累。你睡得好吗?

We need to buy some groceries.

我们需要买一些杂货。

He is a very talented musician.

他是一位非常有才华的音乐家。

2. 物主代词(Owner Pronouns)

物主代词是表示所有关系的代词，也叫人称代词的所有格。它分为形容词性物主代词和名词性物主代词两种。物主代词有人称和数的变化，第三人称单数的物主代词还有性别的

> **重点点拨**
>
> **1. 主格与宾格**
>
> (1)主格代词用作主语，如"I""you""he""she"等。
>
> (2)宾格代词用作宾语或表语，如"me""you""him""her"等。
>
> (3)形容词性物主代词修饰名词，如"my book"(我的书)。
>
> (4)名词性物主代词独立使用，后面不接名词，如"This book is mine."(这本书是我的。)。
>
> **2. 疑问代词和关系代词**
>
> (5)疑问代词用于提问，如"who""what""which"等。
>
> (6)关系代词用于引导定语从句，如"that""which""who"等。

变化。

(1)形容词性物主代词置于名词前，起修饰作用，表示某物属于某人。

My book is on the table.

我的书在桌子上。

Your idea sounds great.

你的想法听起来很棒。

(2)名词性物主代词相当于"形容词性物主代词＋名词"，可在句中作主语、宾语或表语等。

Mine is red，while yours is blue.

我的是红色的，而你的是蓝色的。

This pen is *his*，not *mine*.

这支笔是他的，不是我的。

3. 指示代词(Demonstrative Pronouns)

指示代词是用来指示或标识人或事物的代词。它们具有指定的含义，可以在句子中起指示作用，或用来替代前面已经提到过的名词。英语中的指示代词主要包括"this"(这)、"that"(那)、"these"(这些)和"those"(那些)。

(1)"this"用于指代在时间或空间上较近的人或事物。

This is my bag.

这是我的书包。

(2)"that"用于指代在时间或空间上较远的人或事物。

That is your book.

那是你的书。

(3)"these"用于指代在时间或空间上较近的多个人或事物。

These are my friends.

这些是我的朋友。

(4)"those"用于指代在时间或空间上较远的多个人或事物。

Those are their cars.

那些是他们的车。

4. 疑问代词(Interrogative Pronouns)

疑问代词是用于提问的代词，它们帮助我们在句子中询问关于人、事物或情况的具体信息。

(1)Who用于询问人的身份或姓名，在句中可作主语、宾语和表语。

Who is the new teacher?

新老师是谁？

(2)Whom用于询问动作的承受者，通常出现在介词后或作为动词的宾语。在正式英语中更常用，非正式场合常用 who 代替。

To *whom* did you give the book?

你把书给谁了？

(3)Whose用于询问所属关系，即某物属于谁。

Whose pen is this?

这是谁的笔？

(4)What用于询问事物、活动或职业等。

重点点拨

★物主代词

形容词性物主代词修饰名词，如"my book"(我的书)。

名词性物主代词独立使用，后面不接名词，如"This book is mine."(这本书是我的。)

重点点拨

1. 指示代词用于说话人比较熟悉的语境中，大家都知道指代的东西是什么。

2. 作主语时，指示代词可以指代人，但在作其他句子成分时，多指代事物。

3. 为避免重复，有时可用"that"或"those"来指代前面已经提过的人或事物；用"this"或"these"指代下文中将要提到的人或事物。

What is your favorite book?

你最喜欢的书是哪一本?

(5)Which 用于在有多个选择时进行询问,通常用于指定范围内的人或物。

Which color do you prefer,red or blue?

你更喜欢哪种颜色,红色还是蓝色?

(6)Where 用于询问地点或位置。

Where are you going?

你要去哪里?

(7)When 用于询问时间。

When will you arrive?

你什么时候到达?

(8)Why 用于询问原因或目的。

Why did you choose this university?

你为什么选择这所大学?

(9)How 用于询问方式、程度或状态。

How did you solve the problem?

你是如何解决这个问题的?

5. 不定代词(Indefinite Pronouns)

不定代词是一类不指明代替任何特定名词或形容词的代词。它们可以用来代替名词或形容词,以避免在文章中重复使用相同的名词,从而使句子更加流畅和自然。不定代词可以根据其功能和用法的不同进行分类。以下是一些常见的不定代词。

(1)one,ones:用来替代特定的可数名词或名词短语。

—I have two pens. —Can I borrow *one*?

——我有两支钢笔。——我可以借一支吗?

(2)some,any:表示数量或程度的不确定,其中 some 常用于肯定句,any 常用于否定句或疑问句。

Can I have *some* water, please?

请问我可以喝点水吗?

Do you have *any* books on history?

你有关于历史的书吗?

(3)all,both:表示全部或两个事物都包括在内。

All the students are required to attend the meeting.

所有学生都必须参加会议。

Both of my parents are doctors.

我的父母都是医生。

此外,还有 many,much,few,little,either,neither 等也是常用的不定代词。

> **重点点拨**
> 1. 不定代词后接动词时,通常用第三人称单数形式,因为不定代词被视为单数。
> 2. 修饰不定代词的词应后置。

易错盘点

1. 可数名词与不可数名词的误用

例句:He gave me a very good advice yesterday. (错误)

解析:句中的"a"要去掉,因为"advice"是不可数名词。正确表达为"He gave me very good advice yesterday."如果要强调一条,可用 a very good piece of。即 He gave me a very good piece of advice yesterday.

2. 名词复数的误用

例句：Computer，as we all know，has many possible use in different fields.（错误）

解析：句中名词"use"前的修饰语"many"是用来修饰复数名词的，所以"use"应改为"uses"。正确表达为"Computers，as we all know，have many possible uses in different fields."

3. 集体名词的主谓一致问题

例句：My family is watching TV.（错误）

解析：一些集体名词如看成一个整体，谓语动词用单数；如强调集体中每个个体的行为，则用复数的谓语动词。如果看电视是个体行为，应把"is"改为"are"。

4. 名词所有格的误用

例句：He went into a book's shop and bought a dictionary.（错误）

解析：一般表示有生命的东西的名词的所有格用 's，而此处适宜用名词修饰名词，改为"a book shop"。

5. 代词的误用

(1)代词与先行词的一致性问题

例句：He is one of those speakers who make his ideas perfectly clear.（错误）

解析：定语从句的先行词是"those speakers"，为复数，因此从句中的指示代词应为复数，应把"his"改为"their"。

(2)疑问代词的误用

例句：Whom do you think has left the lights on?（错误）

解析：放在疑问句特殊疑问词后的"do you think"等不参与句子成分，疑问词在句中作主语应用主格，作宾语用宾格。本句中缺的是主语，应把"Whom"改为"Who"。

(3)人称代词的宾格误用

例句：The boss pretended not to see John and I.（错误）

解析："John"和"I"在句中都作的是宾语，应把"I"改为"me"。

(4)物主代词的误用

例句：These books are mine；those in the bag are her.（错误）

解析："her"是形容词性物主代词，后面应该加名词"books"，或把"her"改为名词性物主代词"hers"。

小试牛刀

Correct errors in the following sentences.

1. She has two brother.

2. This is my friend，he is from Beijing.

3. They don't like they teacher.

4. I have many homework to do.

5. I saw her in the street yesterday，but I didn't speak she.

学以致用

Ⅰ. **Choose the right words to fill into the blanks，and change the form if necessary.**

The Mid-Autumn 1. _____ is one of the most important traditional festivals in 2. _____ . It has a long 3. _____ dating back thousands of years. During this festival families gather together to admire the bright full 4. _____ and eat delicious mooncakes.

Mooncakes are round，symbolizing reunion and completeness. 5. _____ often send mooncakes to their relatives and friends as gifts, expressing 6. _____ wishes for a happy life. This 7. _____ helps to strengthen the bonds between people and promotes harmony within the community.

The Mid-Autumn Festival not only celebrates the full moon but also carries forward the excellent 8. _____ of the Chinese nation. It reminds 9. _____ of our roots and encourages us to cherish our 10. _____ and friends.

A. history	B. China	C. culture	D. tradition	E. people
F. we	G. moon	H. their	I . family	J. festival

Ⅱ. Please mark and correct the 10 mistakes in the following passage.

Today I visited the museum with my brother and he friend. The museum in our city are very interesting, but this one is my favorite. There was a lot of people there, so we had to wait in line for a long time. Finally, we entered and saw many beautiful paintings and sculptures. My brother and me really liked the ancient statues. One of the statue was very big and impressive. Later, we went to the gift shop and bought some souvenir for our parents. They will love it, I'm sure. We also saw a movie about the history of the museum. It was real interesting. I can wait to visit this museums again.	1. _____ 2. _____ 3. _____ 4. _____ 5. _____ 6. _____ 7. _____ 8. _____ 9. _____ 10. _____

Ⅲ. Translate the following sentences into English.

1. 我们要继承和弘扬中华优秀传统文化。

2. 社会主义核心价值观是我们共同追求的价值目标。

3. 他总是乐于助人，是我们学习的榜样。

4. 每个人都应该承担起自己的责任。

5. 这本书是我的，不是你的。

6. 中华民族拥有五千年的文明历史。

7. 我们应该尊重每个人的选择和权利。

8. 他通过实际行动践行了社会主义核心价值观。

9. 同学们之间互相帮助，共同进步。

10. 中华文化博大精深，值得我们深入学习和传承。

第二节　动词

重点知识概览

动词重点知识概览

知识点	类别	备注
动词分类	行为动词	分为及物(*vt.*)与不及物动词(*vi.*)。及物动词后需跟宾语。
	连系动词	连系动词最大特征是跟形容词作表语：*link v.* ＋*adj.*
	助动词	与主要动词一起构成谓语。
	情态动词	肯定句:need/ dare ＋ to ＋*v.* 否定句:needn't /dare not ＋ *v.*
动词语态	主动语态:S＋ V. ＋...	
	被动语态： be ＋*v.* ed（by sb.）	
非谓语动词	不定式	"to＋*v.*"常表示未发生的动作。
	动名词	"*v.* ing"相当于名词作用。
	现在分词和过去分词	"*v.* ing/*v.* ed"相当于形容词作用。*v.* ing 分词表示事物状态或主动,*v.* ed 分词表示被动或完成。

知识梳理

一、动词(Verbs)的基本概念

动词是英语句子的核心,用于描述动作、行为、存在或状态的变化。动词在句子中充当谓语,是表达句子意义的关键元素。动词的形式多样,可以表达时间、语态、情态等多种语法意义。

二、动词的分类

1. 行为动词(Action Verbs)

行为动词也被称为实义动词,是具有实际意义的动词,用于描述具体的行为或动作。这些动词可以表达身体上的行动或思想上的活动。行为动词在句子中会根据人称和时态进行相应的变化。行为动词主要分为两类:及物动词和不及物动词。

及物动词(Transitive Verbs):这类动词后面必须跟宾语,句子的意思才完整。

I believe that the committee will *consider* our suggestion. (其中"consider"就是及物动词。)

我相信委员会将会考虑我们的建议。

Sam and Eric *ride* the bus to school each morning. (ride 为及物动词,后跟宾语 the bus。)

山姆和埃里克每天早晨坐公交车去学校。

Jane *wants* a horse for her birthday. (want 为及物动词,后跟宾语 a horse。)

简过生日想要一匹马。

Ian *reads* a chapter in his book each night. （read 为及物动词，后跟宾语 a chapter）

伊恩每晚读完书的一个章节。

不及物动词（Intransitive Verbs）：这类动词本身意义完整，后面不需要跟宾语。

The sun rises in the east. （"rises"是一个不及物动词，表示太阳升起的动作。这里不需要宾语，因为"太阳升起"是一个完整的事件，不涉及对某个物体的动作。）

太阳从东方升起。

She sleeps well at night. （"sleeps"是不及物动词，表示睡觉的动作。句子中"well"是副词，修饰"sleeps"，但"sleeps"本身不需要宾语。）

她晚上睡得很好。

The flowers bloom in spring. （"bloom"是一个不及物动词，描述花朵盛开的状态。句子中没有宾语，因为"花朵盛开"是一个自然发生的现象，不涉及对某个物体的动作。）

花儿在春天盛开。

2. 连系动词（Linking Verbs）

连系动词也称系动词，是用来辅助主语的动词。它本身有词义，但不能单独用作谓语，其后必须跟表语，构成系表结构，用以说明主语的状况、性质、特征等情况。连系动词在英语中起着连接主语和表语的作用，以描述主语的性质、特征或状态。

(1)状态系动词：表示主语的状态，常用的状态系动词为"be"。

They *are* teachers.

他们是教师。

She *is* a talented musician.

她是一位有才华的音乐家。

(2)持续系动词：表示主语继续或保持一种状况或态度，如"keep""remain""stay"等。

He always *keeps* silent at meetings.

他开会时总保持沉默。

(3)表象系动词：用来表示"看起来像"这一概念，如"seem""appear""look"等。

He *looks* nervous.

他看起来很紧张。

He *seems* tired after a long day at work.

工作了一整天后，他看起来很疲倦。

(4)感官系动词：描述通过感官感知到的主语特征，如"feel""smell""sound""taste"等。

This kind of cloth *feels* very soft.

这种布摸起来很柔软。

The soup *tastes* delicious.

这汤尝起来很美味。

变化系动词：表示主语变成什么样，如"become""grow""turn"等。

He *became* happy after that.

自那之后他就开心了。

(5)终止系动词：表示主语已终止动作，主要有"prove""turn out"，表达"证实""变成"之意。

The rumor *proved* false.

这谣言证实是假的。

3. 助动词（Auxiliary Verbs）

助动词是协助主要动词构成谓语的词，它们帮助构成时态、语态、疑问句和否定句等。助动词具有语法意义，但除情态助动词外，一般没有具体的词汇意义，不可单独作谓语。助动词主要分为以下几类。

（1）基本助动词：be，do，have。它们没有词汇意义，只有语法功能，如协助构成进行体、完成体、疑问、强调、被动等。

be：用于构成进行时和被动语态。

He *is* studying.

他正在学习。

The book *was* written by him.

这本书是他写的。

do：用于构成疑问句和否定句，加强语气。

Do you like college life?

你喜欢大学生活吗？

I *do* not like coffee.

我不喜欢咖啡。

have：用于构成完成时态。

He *has* finished his homework.

他已经完成了作业。

（2）情态助动词：如 will，shall，can，may，must 等，它们有词汇意义，后接动词原形，用于表达情态或语气。

will/would：表示将来时态或过去将来时态，表意愿或预测。

I *will* go to the party tomorrow.

我明天会去参加聚会。

They *would* have gone to the beach if it had been sunny.

如果天气晴朗，他们本来会去海滩的。

can/could：表示能力、请求或猜测。

I *can* swim.

我会游泳。

Could you help me with this?

你能帮我这个忙吗？

半助动词：在功能上介于主动词和助动词之间，如 be about to，be going to 等。

be about to：表示即将发生的动作。

I *am about to* leave.

我即将离开。

be going to：表示打算或计划做某事。

They *are going to* travel.

他们打算去旅行。

4. 情态动词(Modal Verbs)

情态动词是英语中一种特殊的动词，它们本身具有一定的词义，但不能独立作谓语，需要与动词原形一起构成谓语。情态动词用来表示说话人对某一动作或状态的看法或主观设想。

（1）表示能力或可能性 can/could(表示请求，语气更委婉)

I *can* speak three languages.

我会说三种语言。

Could you pass me the salt，please?

请你把盐递给我好吗？

(2)表示许可或请求 may/might

May I come in?

我可以进来吗？

(3)表示义务或必要性 must(必须，主观)，have to(不得不，表示客观)

You *must* finish your homework.

你必须完成作业。

I *have to* go to the doctor today.

我今天必须去看医生。

(4)表示推测 must(肯定推测，语气最强)，may/might(可能，might 语气最弱)

He *must* be the manager，because he is wearing a suit.

他一定是经理，因为他穿着西装。

She *may* not come today.

她今天可能不会来。

(5)表示意愿或将来 will/would/shall，shall 主要用于第一人称

I *will* help you with your project.

我会帮你完成你的项目。

Shall we go for a walk?

我们去散步好吗？

三、动词的时态

时态是动词的一种形式，用来表示动作发生的时间和方式。英语中有多种时态，每种时态都有其特定的用法和表达方式。

1. 一般现在时

表示经常性、习惯性的动作或普遍真理。

The sun *rises* in the east every day.

太阳每天从东方升起。

She *works* hard every day.

她每天都努力工作。

Water *boils* at 100 degrees Celsius.

水在 100 摄氏度时沸腾。

I *always* take a walk after dinner.

我晚饭后总是散步。

They *usually* meet for coffee on Fridays.

他们通常在星期五一起喝咖啡。

2. 一般过去时

表示过去某个时间发生的动作或状态。

I *saw* a movie last night.

我昨天晚上看了一部电影。

She *worked* hard yesterday.

她昨天工作很努力。

They *visited* their grandparents last weekend.

他们上周末拜访了他们的祖父母。

The concert *started* at 8 p. m.

音乐会晚上 8 点开始的。

> **重点点拨**
>
> 动词时态的正确使用是英语表达中的关键，要根据时间状语和上下文来确定使用哪种时态。

He *forgot* his umbrella at home.

他把雨伞忘在家里了。

3. 一般将来时

表示将来某个时间将要发生的动作或状态。

I *will* meet you at the airport tomorrow.

我明天会去机场接你。

She *is going to* study abroad next year.

她打算明年出国留学。

They *won't* come to the party tonight.

他们今晚不会来参加派对。

The project *will be* completed by the end of the month.

这个项目将在月底前完成。

He *promises* to call me later.

他答应稍后给我打电话。

4. 现在进行时

表示现在正在进行的动作或状态。

I *am studying* for my exam right now.

我现在正在学习准备考试。

She *is cooking* dinner in the kitchen.

她正在厨房做晚饭。

They *are playing* football in the park.

他们正在公园踢足球。

The train *is arriving* at the station.

火车正在进站。

He *is watching* TV in the living room.

他正在客厅看电视。

5. 过去进行时

表示过去某个时间正在进行的动作。

I *was reading* a book when you called me.

你打电话给我时，我正在看书。

She *was studying* for her exam last night.

她昨天晚上正在为考试复习。

They *were playing* in the garden when it started to rain.

开始下雨时，他们正在花园里玩耍。

The concert *was starting* when we arrived.

我们到达时，音乐会正要开始。

He *was working* on his project when the phone rang.

电话响时，他正在做他的项目。

6. 现在完成时

表示过去发生的动作对现在仍有影响或结果。

I *have finished* my homework already.

我已经完成了作业。

She *has lived* in this city for ten years.

她在这个城市已经住了十年。

They *haven't seen* each other for a long time.

他们很长时间没见面了。

The train *has left* the station already.

火车已经离开车站了。

He *has written* several books on history.

他已经写了几本关于历史的书。

四、动词的语态

语态表示主语与谓语之间的关系。英语中主要有两种语态：主动语态和被动语态。主动语态表示主语是动作的执行者，而被动语态则表示主语是动作的承受者。

1. 主动语态

主语执行动作。

The boy *kicks* the ball.

这个男孩踢球。

She *writes* beautiful poems.

她写美丽的诗歌。

They *built* a new house last year.

他们去年建了一所新房子。

The teacher *explains* the lesson clearly.

老师清楚地解释了这一课。

He *drives* carefully on the highway.

他在高速公路上小心驾驶。

2. 被动语态

主语承受动作。

The ball *is kicked* by the boy.

球被男孩踢了。

The poems *are written* by her.

这些诗是她写的。

A new house *was built* by them last year.

去年他们建了一所新房子。

The lesson *is explained* clearly by the teacher.

这一课被老师清楚地解释了。

The car *is driven* carefully by him on the highway.

他在高速公路上小心驾驶着汽车。

> **重点点拨**
> 被动语态常用于描述客观事实或强调动作的承受者，使用时要注意主谓一致和时态的正确性。

五、非谓语动词

非谓语动词是指在句子中不作谓语的动词形式，包括不定式、动名词、现在分词和过去分词。这些形式可以在句子中担任不同的成分，如定语、状语、补语等。

1. 不定式

动词不定式表示具体的、一次性的动作，常用作目的状语、定语或宾语补足语。

I want *to travel* around the world.

我想环游世界。

He decided *to quit* his job.

他决定辞职。

She hopes *to become* a doctor in the future.

她希望将来成为一名医生。

They agreed *to help* us with the project.

他们同意帮助我们完成这个项目。

I offered *to drive* them to the airport.

我提出开车送他们去机场。

2. 动名词

动名词具有名词性质，常用作主语、宾语(包括介词宾语)。

Swimming is good exercise.

游泳是很好的锻炼。

He enjoys *reading* books in his free time.

他喜欢在空闲时间读书。

She avoids *eating* fast food.

她避免吃快餐。

They considered *buying* a new car.

他们考虑买一辆新车。

I am interested in *learning a* new language.

我对学习新语言感兴趣。

3. 现在分词和过去分词

现在分词和过去分词用作定语、状语、补语等，表示主动、正在进行或完成的意思。

The *smiling* girl waved at us.

那个微笑的女孩向我们挥手。

He sat there, *staring* out of the window.

他坐在那里，盯着窗外。

The book *written* by him is very interesting.

他写的那本书非常有趣。

She felt *excited* about the upcoming trip.

她对即将到来的旅行感到兴奋。

They were *surprised* to see us there.

在那儿见到我们他们很惊讶。

> **重点点拨**
>
> 动词的非谓语形式在句子中扮演重要角色，要注意它们的功能和用法，以及与其他词类的搭配。

易错盘点

1. 主谓不一致

谓语动词要与主语在人称和数上保持一致。当主语是单数时，谓语动词也要用单数形式；当主语是复数时，谓语动词用复数形式。同时，要注意一些特殊的主语，如集合名词、不定代词等。

错误例句：They was very happy.（was 应为 were）

正确例句：They were very happy.

2. 时态误用

在使用时态时，要注意动作发生的时间和方式，选择合适的时态。同时，要避免在不需要使用进行时或完成时的情况下误用这些时态。

错误例句：I am having a headache yesterday.（am having 应为 had）

正确例句：I had a headache yesterday.

3. 语态误用

在使用被动语态时，要注意动作的执行者和承受者，确保语态的正确使用。同时，要避免将不及物动词用于被动语态。

错误例句：The accident was happened yesterday. （happen 是不及物动词，它表示某事发生，但不涉及动词的执行者，因此无被动语态）

正确例句：The accident happened yesterday.

4. 情态动词误用

情态动词表示说话人的态度或推测，要根据语境选择合适的情态动词。同时，要注意情态动词后接动词原形的规则。

错误例句：I mustn't to go there. （must 后接动词原形，去掉 to）

正确例句：I mustn't go there.

5. 非谓语形式误用

非谓语动词在句子中不能单独作谓语，要根据句子的结构和语境来选择合适的非谓语形式。

小试牛刀

Fill in the blanks with the correct forms of the verbs.

1. The Great Wall _____ (build) many centuries ago to protect China from invaders.

2. Every year, millions of tourists _____ (visit) the Terracotta Warriors in Xi'an.

3. Chinese people _____ (celebrate) the Mid-Autumn Festival by eating mooncakes and admiring the full moon.

4. The Belt and Road Initiative _____ (promote) economic cooperation between China and other countries.

5. Confucius' teachings _____ (influence) Chinese culture and society for thousands of years.

学以致用

Ⅰ. Read the following passage and fill in the blanks with the correct forms of the verbs provided.

The Dragon Boat Festival, also known as Duanwu Festival, 1. _____ on the fifth day of the fifth month of the lunar calendar. It is a traditional Chinese festival with a history of over 2,000 years. During the festival, people often 2. _____ dragon boat races and eat *zongzi*, a kind of glutinous rice dumpling wrapped in reed leaves(芦苇叶).

The origin of the festival 3. _____ back to the Warring States period. It is said that the festival 4. _____ from the legend of Qu Yuan, a patriotic poet who lived during that time. After his country was defeated, Qu Yuan 5. _____ himself in the Miluo River on the fifth day of the fifth month. To prevent his body from being eaten by fish, the local people 6. _____ *zongzi* into the river. Since then, people have 7. _____ the Dragon Boat Festival to commemorate Qu Yuan and his patriotism.

Nowadays, the Dragon Boat Festival not only 8. _____ as a reminder of China's rich cultural heritage but also 9. _____ unity and cooperation among people. During the festival, families and friends often get together to make *zongzi*, 10. _____ the delicious food, and watching exciting dragon boat races.

| A. observe | B. drown | C. promote | D. trace | E. celebrate |
| F. serve | G. throw | H. enjoy | I. originate | J. hold |

Ⅱ. Please mark and correct the 10 mistakes in the following passage.

Yesterday，I decided go to the movies with my friends. We choose a new action movie that just released. When we arrived to the cinema，we buy our tickets and went inside. The movie started，but unfortunately，I forget to bring my glasses. I decided to go back and get it. After I returned，the movie already begun. I sat down quickly and watched the movie. Later，when the movie ended，my friends and I decided making a stop at the snack bar. We buy some popcorn and sodas before we leave. It was a great evening，but I wish I hadn't forget my glasses.	1. _____ 2. _____ 3. _____ 4. _____ 5. _____ 6. _____ 7. _____ 8. _____ 9. _____ 10. _____

Ⅲ. Translate the following sentences into English，using the words provided.

1. 我们应该尊重传统文化并传承下去。（respect，inherit）

2. 中国政府致力于推动全球经济发展。（commit，promote）

3. 青少年应该树立正确的价值观和人生观。（establish，view）

4. 中国的航天事业取得了巨大的成就。（achieve，accomplishment）

5. 我们要努力学习，为实现中国梦贡献力量。（strive，contribute）

6. 中国的四大发明对世界文明产生了深远影响。（exert，influence）

7. 我们要坚持走和平发展道路，推动构建人类命运共同体。（adhere，promote）

8. 中国的传统文化博大精深，值得我们深入学习和传承。（extensive，profound，deserve）

9. 我们要弘扬爱国主义精神，为祖国的繁荣昌盛贡献力量。（promote，patriotism，contribute）

10. 中国政府积极推动绿色发展，保护生态环境。（promote，protect）

第三节　形容词和副词

🔍 重点知识概览

形容词和副词重点知识概览

类别	知识点	备注
形容词 *adj.*	位置	通常位于名词前,修饰名词; 以"a-"开头的形容词常置于名词之后。
副词 *adv.*	位置	可位于句首、句中或句尾,取决于修饰对象和语境。
形容词和副词的 比较结构	原级	常见形式:"(not so)/as+*adj./adv.*＋as "
	比较级	能修饰比较级的词语:a little, a bit, a few, much, rather, far
	最高级	形容词最高级前加定冠词"the";有范围的限定。

📖 知识梳理

一、形容词(Adjectives)

形容词是用来描述名词的词,提供关于名词的更多信息,比如颜色、大小、形状等。形容词通常位于它们所修饰的名词之前。

1. 形容词的种类和功能

根据功能和形式,形容词可以分为描述性形容词、数量形容词、指示形容词、疑问形容词和所有格形容词。在句子中,形容词主要充当定语、表语、补语或状语。

2. 形容词的位置

形容词一般位于名词之前,但在某些情况下也可以放在名词之后,尤其是在使用形容词短语时。

She has a pair of *bright* big eyes.（描述性形容词）

她有一双明亮的大眼睛。

Some students in the class haven't finished their homework yet.（数量形容词）

班里有一些学生还没完成作业。

This apple looks very sweet.（指示形容词）

这个苹果看起来很甜。

Which difficulties do you have that need my help to solve?（疑问形容词）

你有哪些困难需要我来帮忙解决吗?

I like *my* new book.（所有格形容词）

我喜欢我的新书。

3. 形容词的比较级和最高级

形容词有原级、比较级和最高级三种形式。比较级用于两者之间的比较,最高级用于三者或三者

> **重点点拨**
>
> 形容词通常位于名词之前,而副词则根据所修饰的词类而位置不同。修饰动词时,副词通常位于动词之后;修饰形容词或其他副词时,可位于其前或其后。

以上的比较。

Today's weather is *better than* yesterday's.（比较级）

今天的天气比昨天好。

She is *the smartest* student in the class.（最高级）

她是班上最聪明的学生。

This book is *more interesting than* that book.（比较级）

这本书比那本书更有趣。

The Great Wall is one of *the most famous* historical sites in China.（最高级）

长城是中国最著名的古迹之一。

Diligence is *more important than* talent.（比较级）

勤奋比天赋更重要。

二、副词（Adverbs）

副词主要用于修饰动词、形容词、其他副词或整个句子，表示时间、地点、程度、方式等。

1. 副词的种类和功能

副词可以分为时间副词、地点副词、程度副词、方式副词等。

在句子中，副词主要充当状语。

2. 副词的位置

副词的位置相对灵活，可以放在句首、句中或句尾，具体取决于修饰的对象和语境。

I went to the Forbidden City *yesterday*.（时间副词）

我昨天去了故宫。

He has worked *here* for many years.（地点副词）

他在这里工作了很多年。

She likes Chinese traditional culture *very much*.（程度副词）

她非常喜欢中国的传统文化。

He walked into the classroom *slowly*.（方式副词）

他慢慢地走进了教室。

Fortunately, I caught the bus in time.（结果副词）

幸运的是，我及时赶上了公交车。

3. 副词的比较级和最高级

和形容词一样，副词也有原级、比较级和最高级三种形式。

He runs much *faster* than before.（比较级）

他跑得比以前快多了。

Among all people, he sings the *best*.（最高级）

在所有人中，他唱得最好。

She arrived at school *earlier* today than yesterday.（比较级）

她今天比昨天更早到校。

He performed the *most outstandingly* in this competition.（最高级）

在这次比赛中，他表现得最出色。

Studying diligently will always yield *more than* studying lazily.（比较级）

勤奋地学习总会比懒惰地学习收获更多。

重点点拨

在使用比较级结构时，要确保比较的对象是可比较的，避免逻辑上的错误。例如，"I am taller than him." 应改为"I am taller than he is."以保持句子结构的平衡和准确性。

重点点拨

在具体语境中，要注意形容词和副词的词义差异以及固定搭配的使用。例如，"hard"作为形容词时表示"坚硬的"，作为副词时表示"努力地"；而"hardly"则是一个副词，表示"几乎不"。因此，在使用时要根据语境选择合适的词语。

三、形容词和副词的比较结构

1. 原级比较结构

原级比较表示两者在某方面(不)相同或(不)相近。肯定结构为"as＋形容词/副词原级＋as"，否认结构为"not as/so ＋ 原级 ＋ as"。

She speaks English *as well as* her teacher.

她的英语说得和她的老师一样好。

This room is *as big as* that one.

这个房间和那个房间一样大。

My sister and I are *as tall as* each other.

我和我妹妹一样高。

This movie is *not as good as* the last one we saw.

这部电影不如我们上次看的那部好。

His knowledge of English is *as deep as* hers.

他的英语知识和她的一样深厚。

2. 比较级比较结构

在英语中，形容词和副词的比较级用于比较两个事物的性质或状态。通过比较级，我们可以描述一个事物比另一个事物更具有某种性质或状态。

(1)形容词和副词比较级的构成

规则变化：

· 单音节和部分双音节词：在词尾加"er"，如"tall"变为"taller"(更高的)，"fast"变为"faster"(更快的)。

· 以"e"结尾的词：在词尾加"r"，如"nice"变为"nicer"(更好的)。

· 重读闭音节词且词尾只有一个辅音字母：先双写该辅音字母，再加"er"，如"fat"变为"fatter"(更胖的)。

· 以"辅音字母＋y"结尾的双音节词：将"y"改为"i"，再加"er"，如"happy"变为"happier"(更快乐的)。

· 多音节词和部分双音节词：在词前加"more"，如"beautiful"变为"more beautiful"(更美丽的)。

不规则变化：

部分形容词和副词的比较级变化是不规则的，需要单独记忆，如"good/well"变为"better"(更好的)，"bad/badly"变为"worse"(更坏的/地)。

(2)形容词和副词比较级的用法

A ＋ be ＋比较级 ＋ than ＋ B：表示"A 比 B 更……"。

She is *smarter* than him.

她比他更聪明。

which/who is ＋ 比较级，A or B?：用于询问两者中哪一个更……。

Which is *bigger*, the elephant or the tiger?

大象和老虎，哪一个更大？

the ＋比较级，the ＋ 比较级：表示"越……，越……"。

The more you read, *the wiser* you will be.

你读得越多，就会越明智。

比较级 ＋ and ＋ 比较级：表示"越来越……"。

重点点拨

比较级前可用 much、far、a little 等词修饰，以增强语气。例如："much taller"(高得多)。在比较级中，为了避免重复，常用 that 或 those 代替前面提到的名词。例如："The weather here is warmer than that in Beijing."(这里的天气比北京的天气暖和)。

It's getting *colder and colder* outside.
外面越来越冷了。

3. 最高级比较结构

在英语中，形容词和副词的最高级用于描述三个或更多事物中某一事物性质或状态的最高级别。通过最高级，我们可以明确指出哪一个事物在某一性质或状态上达到了最高点。

(1)形容词和副词最高级的构成

规则变化：

· 单音节和部分双音节词：在词尾加"est"，如"tall"变为"tallest"(最高的)。

· 以"e"结尾的词：在词尾加"st"，如"nice"变为"nicest"(最好的)。

· 重读闭音节词且词尾只有一个辅音字母：先双写该辅音字母，再加"est"，如"fat"变为"fattest"(最胖的)。

· 以"辅音字母＋y"结尾的双音节词：将"y"改为"i"，再加"est"，但这类例子较少见，一般多音节形容词直接使用"most"来表示最高级。

· 多音节词：在词前加"most"，如"beautiful"变为"most beautiful"(最美丽的)。

不规则变化：

部分形容词和副词的最高级变化是不规则的，如"good/well"变为"best"(最好的)。

(2)形容词和副词最高级的用法

①the ＋ 最高级 ＋ 名词：表示"最……的……"。

She is *the smartest* girl in her class.
她是她班上最聪明的女孩。

②which/who is ＋ the ＋ 最高级，A，B or C?：用于询问三者或超过三者中哪一个最……。

Which is *the biggest*, the elephant, the tiger, or the lion?
大象、老虎和狮子，哪一个最大？

③序数词 ＋ 最高级：表示"第几最……"。

The Yellow River is *the second longest* river in China.
黄河是中国第二长的河流。

④one of the ＋ 最高级 ＋ 名词复数：表示"最……之一"。

He is *one of the most popular* teachers in our school.
他是我们学校最受欢迎的教师之一。

易错盘点

一、比较级的易错点

1. 比较级构成错误

· 规则变化的形容词和副词在构成比较级时，需要遵循一定的规则，如加"er"或"more"。有学习者会在使用比较级时将"tall"的比较级"taller"误写为"more tall"，或将"beautiful"的比较级"more beautiful"误写为"beautifuler"。

· 对于不规则变化的形容词和副词，如"good"变为"better"，而非"gooder"，需要特别注意。

2. 比较对象不一致

· 在使用比较级时，比较的对象应该保持一致。例如，不能说"My bag is bigger than your."而应该说"My bag is bigger than yours."以保持比较对象的一致性。

3. 遗漏或误用"than"

· 比较级后面通常要跟"than"来引出比较的对象。遗漏"than"或者误用其他词汇都会导致句子意义不清或语法错误。

4. 比较级前的修饰语错误

· 比较级前不能使用"very""quite"等词修饰，而应使用"much""even""a little"等来表示程度。例如，"He is much taller than me."而不是"He is very taller than me."

二、最高级的易错点

1. 遗漏定冠词"the"

· 在使用最高级时，前面必须加定冠词"the"。例如，"She is the smartest girl in her class."而非"She is smartest girl in her class."

2. 未明确比较范围

· 在最高级的使用中未明确比较范围，往往会导致句子意思模糊或产生歧义。例如，"This is the most beautiful flower."这个句子没有明确指出"最美丽的花"是在哪个范围内进行比较的。可能是在整个花园里，也可能是在某个特定的花束中，或者是与世界上所有的花相比。可改为"This is the most beautiful flower in the garden."或者"Among the flowers at the flower show, this one is the most beautiful."

3. "one of ＋ 最高级"后名词单复数形的误用

· 当使用"one of the ＋ 形容词最高级 ＋ 名词复数"结构时，需要注意名词要用复数形式。例如，"She is one of the most talented singers."而不是"She is one of the most talented singer."

小试牛刀

Fill in the blanks with the correct forms of the words.

1. The _____ (high) mountain in this area is over 5,000 meters.

2. She sings _____ (beautiful) than her sister.

3. He works _____ (hard) in his class.

4. The weather today is _____ (bad) than yesterday.

5. I feel _____ (happy) when I am with my friends.

6. She is _____ (smart) student in her class.

7. They arrived _____ (early) than expected.

8. The movie was _____ (boring) one I have ever seen.

9. He spoke in a _____ (loud) voice.

10. The food tastes _____ (delicious) when it's hot.

学以致用

Ⅰ. Read the following passage and fill in the blanks with the correct forms of the words provided.

It was a sunny day in Beijing. Xiao Li, a young Chinese student, walked 1. _____ the Forbidden City, admiring the ancient buildings and feeling the 2. _____ of Chinese culture. Suddenly, he noticed a foreign couple looking 3. _____ in front of a palace. They seemed to have lost their way.

Xiao Li approached them 4. _____ and asked if they needed help. The couple explained that they were looking for the Hall of Supreme Harmony but got lost. Xiao Li smiled and said, "Don't worry, I'll show you the way."

As they walked, Xiao Li 5. _____ explained the history and architecture of the Forbidden City. The foreign couple listened 6. _____, nodding and asking questions occasionally. They were 7. _____ by Xiao Li's knowledge and enthusiasm.

Soon, they arrived at the Hall of Supreme Harmony. The couple thanked Xiao Li 8. _____ and praised him for his kindness and helpfulness. Xiao Li felt 9. _____ to represent Chinese culture and hospitality to foreign visitors. He realized that being 10. _____ and friendly was not only a virtue but also a responsibility when representing one's country.

A. profoundly	B. through	C. helpful	D. impressed	E. confused
F. proud	G. friendly	H. attentively	I. richness	J. patiently

Ⅱ. Please mark and correct the 10 mistakes in the following passage.

Yesterday，I went to the new shopping mall in town. It was amazing huge，with various stores selling different items. I saw a beautifully dress in a fashion store and tried it on. It fitted me perfectly and looked lovely on me. Then，I walked into a bookstore where the books were neat placed on the shelves. I found a interesting book about space exploration and bought it. After that，I had a delicious lunch in a restaurant which served tast food. The atmosphere there was real cozy，and the staff were friendliness and helpful. I had a greatly time there and felt happily when I left.

1. _____
2. _____
3. _____
4. _____
5. _____
6. _____ 7. _____
8. _____ 9. _____
10. _____

Ⅲ. Translate the following sentences into English.

1. 这本书很有趣，我读了一遍又一遍。

2. 她唱得如此动听，以至于所有人都为她鼓掌。

3. 他工作非常努力，经常加班到深夜。

4. 这道菜尝起来很美味，我很快就吃完了。

5. 她在比赛中表现得非常出色，赢得了观众的热烈掌声。

6. 他非常友好地向我打招呼。

7. 这部电影相当无聊，我看了一半就睡着了。

8. 她总是准时到达，从不迟到。

9. 中国的嫦娥五号成功返回地球，这是中国航天事业的又一重大突破。

10. 兵马俑是令人赞叹的世界文化遗产之一。

第四节　连词和介词

🔍 重点知识概览

连词重点知识概览

类别	连接两者的关系	具体连词	备注
并列连词	并列关系	and，both … and …，not only … but also …，as well as，neither … nor …等	1.在否定句中,用 or 连接并列成分,表示对各成分都否定。 2."祈使句＋and/or＋陈述句"为固定结构,当前后是顺承关系时,则用 and,当前后是转折关系时,则用 or。
	选择关系	or，either … or …，whether … or …等	
	转折关系	but，while，however 等	
	因果关系	for，so 等	
从属连词	名词性从句（主语、宾语、表语以及同位语从句）	that，if，whether，because，what，who，whom，which，how，why，where，when，whatever，whoever，whomever，wherever，whenever，however 等	边际从属连词: (不属于从属连词,但其作用相当于从属连词) even if，just as，if only，the moment，the minute，the instant 等。
	副词性从句（状语从句）	when，while，as，after，before，until，till，since，as soon as 等	
		where，wherever 等	
		because，since，as 等	
		if，unless，as long as 等	
		in order that …，so that …等	
		so … that …，such … that …，so（that）…等	
		as，as if，as though 等	
		although，though，even if，even though 等	
		than，as 等	

介词重点知识概览

类别		具体介词	备注
表示时间		in, on, at, since, for, during, till/until, by, from 等	不用介词的情况： 1. 在含有 today, yesterday, tomorrow 的时间状语前； 2. 在含有 last, next, this, that, these, those, every, one, some, all 等词的时间状语之前； 3. 在含有 here, there, home, back, abroad 等副词前, 不加介词。
地点方位		in, on, at, to, over/under, above/below, in front of/in the front of, inside/outside, behind/at the back of, near, between…and… / among, on the right of/ on the left of , in the middle of 等。	
方式手段		by, with, in 等	
其他	除了……	but, besides, except 等	
	关于	about, on 等	
	像, 作为	like, as 等	
	动作方向	across/through, along/down, to/towards, into 等	
	表示材料	of, from, in 等	
	表示原因或理由	for, at, from, of, with, by 等	
介词短语	介词＋名词		
	介词＋代词		
	介词＋动名词		

> 重点考查题型：词汇与语法结构、选词填空、完形填空、短文改错、句子翻译

知识梳理

一、连词(Conjunctions)

连词是一种虚词，通常不重读，连词起连接的作用，不单独充当句子中的成分，我们可以根据它所起连接作用的不同，分为并列连词和从属连词。

(一)并列连词(Coordinating Conjunctions)

并列连词用来连接平行的词、词组和分句，从而构成平行或并列结构。按照连接的词与词、短语与短语、句子与句子之间的关系，可以分为以下四种。

1. 表示并列关系的并列连词：and, both … and …, not only … but also …, as well as, neither … nor … 等。例如：

We are singing *and* they are drawing.
我们在唱歌，他们在画画。
Both you *and* I are doctors.
我和你都是医生。
Her younger sister is *not only* good at History, *but also* good at Chinese.
她的妹妹不仅历史好，语文也很好。
She is a talented photographer *as well as* being a

> **重点点拨**
> ★and 连接的对象可以是两个，也可以是多个。当 and 连接三个以上的对象时，通常前面的对象之间用逗号隔开，最后两个对象用 and。例如：
> My hobbies are singing, dancing, playing football and swimming.
> 我的爱好是唱歌、跳舞、踢足球和游泳。
> ★在否定句中，用 or 连接并列成分，表示对各成分都否定。例如：
> He does not like red or yellow.
> 他不喜欢红色和黄色。

musician.

她不但是一位音乐家而且还是个天才的摄影师。

Lucy likes *neither* dancing *nor* drawing.

露西既不喜欢跳舞也不喜欢画画。

2. 表示选择关系的并列连词：or，either…or…，whether…or… 等。例如：

Do your homework quickly, *or* you will have no time to have a rest.

快点做作业，否则你就没有时间休息了。

Either her mother *or* her father cooks meals at home.

要么是她妈妈，要么是她爸爸在家做饭。

They haven't decided *whether* they will go to London *or* New York.

他们尚未决定是去伦敦还是去纽约。

3. 表示转折或对比关系的并列连词：but，while，however 等。例如：

His mother won't be there, *but* his father might.

他母亲不会去那里，但他父亲也许会去。

I like swimming *while* he likes playing tennis.

我喜欢游泳，而他喜欢打网球。

They all tried their best. *However*, they lost the game.

他们都已尽力，然而还是输掉了比赛。

4. 表示因果关系的并列连词：for，so 等。例如：

He worked hard to memorize the words, *so* he passed CET4.

他努力背单词，所以他通过了英语四级考试。

It's morning, *for* the birds are singing.

早晨了，鸟儿在歌唱。

> **重点点拨**
>
> ★"祈使句＋and/or＋陈述句"为固定结构，当前后是顺承关系，则用 and，当前后是转折关系，则用 or。例如：
>
> Wait for a moment and you will see the result.
>
> 稍等片刻，你就会看到结果。
>
> Turn off the heat or the food will burn.
>
> 把火关了，不然食物会烧焦的。

（二）从属连词（Subordinate Conjunctions）

从属连词用于连接有主次之分的句子，也可以看作是引导词引导主从复合句。根据引导句子类型的不同可以分为：引导名词性从句的从属连词和引导状语从句的从属连词。

1. 引导名词性从句的从属连词：that, if, whether, because 等。例如：

Whether he'll come is still unknown.

仍然没人知道他是否要来。（引导主语从句）

I don't think *that* you should stay another week.

我认为你们不该再待一星期。（引导宾语从句）

The result is that he won the boys' 1,500 meters race.

结果是他赢得了男子 1,500 米赛跑冠军。（引导表语从句）

2. 引导状语从句的从属连词

（1）时间状语从句

引导时间状语从句的从属连词主要有：when, while, as, after, before, until, till, since, as soon as 等。例如：

When the teacher came into the classroom, I was talking with my deskmate.

当老师走进教室时，我正在和我的同桌说话。

It began to rain outside *while* we were running on the playground.

当我们在操场上跑步时，外面开始下雨了。

They talked about their old times *as* they walked along the beach.

他们沿着海边散步，边走边聊着往事。

Wait here *until/till* I come.

在这里等到我来。

I have lived in Beijing *since* I was ten.

我自 10 岁起就一直住在北京。

As soon as we get home, go to have a shower.

我们一到家你就去冲个澡。

（2）地点状语从句

引导地点状语从句的从属连词主要有：where, wherever 等。例如：

I live *where* there are hot springs.

我住在有温泉的地方。

Wherever he goes, his dog follows him.

无论他去哪里，他的狗都跟在他后面。

（3）原因状语从句

引导原因状语从句的从属连词主要有：because, since, as 等。例如：

You can't eat too many sweets *because* you're overweight.

你不能吃太多的甜食，因为你超重了。

Since all of you come here, I will tell you the whole thing.

既然你们都来了，我就把事情原原本本地告诉你们。

As your negligence, we have to redo the report.

由于贵方疏忽，我们不得不重做报告。

（4）条件状语从句

引导条件状语从句的从属连词主要有：if, unless, as long as 等。例如：

If you wish to go, please go.

如果你想去，就去吧。

We can't get out of this forest *unless* someone comes to help us.

除非有人来帮助我们，否则我们无法走出这片森林。

You can play basketball *as long as* you stay in your school.

只要你待在学校，你就可以打篮球。

（5）目的状语从句

引导目的状语从句的从属连词主要有：in order that…，so that… 等。例如：

In order that/So that you can arrive there on time, you should take a taxi.

为了能按时赶到那里，你们应该乘坐出租车。

重点点拨

从属连词按词形可分为三类：

★简单从属连词

由单个单词充当，如：before, after, although, but, if, lest, as, once, since, than, that, when, where, until, unless 等。

★复合从属连词

由两个或两个以上单词构成，w 如：

so that, in order that, as long as, for fear, no matter who, as if, even if 等。

★关联从属连词

由两个关联词构成的从属连词，如：although…yet…，as…as…，

such … that …，hardly … when…，

no sooner…than… 等。

重点点拨

so that 在目的状语从句和结果状语从句中的区别：

★意义区别：

在目的状语从句中的意思为以便、为了；在结果状语从句意义为：结果是、所以。

★用法区别：

1. 目的状语从句里常带有情态词 can, could, may, might 等；结果状语从句中没有情态动词；

2. 目的状语从句 so that 后的动作还没发生，是一种目的；结果状语从句 so that 后的动作已经发生，是一种结果。

In order not *to* disturb the children's sleep，he worked in the office all night.

为了不打扰孩子们的睡眠，他整晚都在办公室工作。

(6)结果状语从句

引导结果状语从句的从属连词主要有：so…that…，such…that…，so（that）…等。例如：

I was *so* careless *that* I forgot to write my name on the paper.

我如此粗心，以至于忘了在试卷上写上我的名字。

Sanya is *such* a wonderful place *that* tourists around the world like to go there for holidays.

三亚是如此棒的一个地方，以至于来自世界各地的游客都喜欢去那里度假。

The teacher explained very clearly *so that* we all understood.

老师解释得非常清楚了，因此我们都懂了。

(7)方式状语从句

引导方式状语从句的从属连词主要有 as，as if，as though 等。例如：

You should do *as* I do.

你应按我做的去做。

He walked about *as if*/*as though* he had lost something.

他到处打转，好像丢了什么东西。

(8)让步状语从句

引导让步状语从句的从属连词主要有：although，though，even if，even though 等。例如：

Although he lost a leg, he kept on studying.

尽管他失去了一条腿，仍然坚持学习。

Even if/*Even though* he ran as fast as he could，he was caught up with by the bad guys.

尽管他竭尽全力地奔跑，还是被坏人追上了。

(9)比较状语从句

引导比较状语从句的从属连词主要有：than，as 等。例如：

India has a larger population *than* China now.

印度现在的总人口比中国的多。

The foreigner speaks Chinese *as well as* Chinese people.

这个外国人汉语说得和中国人一样好。

Some people think that planes now are not *so* / *as* safe *as* trains（are）.

有些人认为现在飞机没有火车安全。

二、介词（Prepositions）

介词是虚词，在句子中不单独充当句子成分，必须与名词或相当于名词的其他词构成介词短语，才能在句子中充当成分。介词短语可以在句子中作定语、状语、表语和宾语补足语。例如：

The boy *under* the tree is my son.

树下的男孩是我的儿子。（作定语）

I put the coat *on* the bed.

我把外套放在床上。（作状语）

He came *from* Columbia University to study in our school for a year.

他来自哥伦比亚大学，到我们学校进修一年。（作表语）

Help yourselves *to* some cakes.

> **重点点拨**
>
> ★边际从属连词，此类词本身不属于从属连词，但其作用相当于从属连词，多为副词加连词、连词加副词或名词词组，如 even if, just as，if only，the moment，the minute，the instant 等。
>
> The moment I saw her, I fell in love.
>
> 我一看到她，就坠入了爱河。

请随便吃些蛋糕。(作宾语补足语)

(一)介词的位置

介词的位置分为置于宾语之前和置于宾语之后两种。

1. 介词一般位于名词短语之前

介词通常用来修饰名词、代词等，因此在句子中名词短语通常会放在介词的前面，例如：

They are studying *in* the classroom.

他们正在教室里学习。

Please put the book *on* the shelf.

请把书放在架子上。

2. 介词也可以放在名词短语之后

当介词所修饰的名词短语较长，或为了更好地突出中心词，介词也可以放在名词短语后面，例如：

The man *under* the tree is my father.

树下的男士是我的爸爸。

The boy *in* blue is my son.

穿蓝色衣服的是我儿子。

3. 介词也可以置于句首或句末

在句子中为了强调介词所指代的内容，介词也可置于句首或句末，例如：

With you, I feel very happy.

和你在一起，我觉得很开心。

I know a lawyer whom we can believe *in*.

我认识一个我们可以信赖的律师。

(二)介词的分类

1. 表示时间的介词

in, on, at, since, for, during, till/until, by, from 等。

(1)in 用在年份、月份、世纪、季节、上午、下午、晚上等词前。例如：

He was born *in* the 1770s.

他出生于 18 世纪 70 年代。

I will come back *in* a month.

我一个月后回来。

(2)at 用在时刻、中午、晚上、深夜或某些词组中。例如：

at seven o'clock 在 7 点；at noon 在中午的时候；at night 在晚上；at midnight 在午夜时分；at the age of… 在……岁的时候。

(3)on 在表示具体的某一天的时候，后面接具体的日期、星期、节假日或上午、下午、晚上，同时也可用于有形容词修饰的某天等。例如：

on the afternoon of May 10

在 5 月 10 日下午

on a rainy day

在一个下雨天

on Monday morning

重点点拨

介词按词形可分为五类：

★简单介词

由一个不可分割的单词构成，例如：about, at, in, on, by, during, after, of, off, as, before, to, till 等。

★复合介词

由两个单词组合在一起的介词，例如：into, onto, outside, inside, throughout, within, without 等。

★双重介词

由两个介词结合在一起使用，例如：as for, as from, except for, from among, from behind, outside of 等。

★分词介词

由动词的分词转变而来的介词，例如：considering, regarding, including 等。

★短语介词

相当于介词作用的短语，例如：according to, along with, because of, in case of, in charge of, instead of 等。

在星期一上午

(4)for/since：for 接时间段，since 接时间点。例如：

Those old men haven't seen each other *for* over thirty years.

这些老人三十多年没见过面了。

My grandfather has lived here *since* 1994.

我祖父自 1994 年以来就一直住在这里。

(5)by 表示"在……之前，最迟……之前"，常与完成时连用。例如：

I had already left *by* the time he got home.

他到家时，我已经走了。

(6)from 在表示"从……到……"的意思时，常与 to 或 till 连用，构成 from… to/till… 词组。例如：

The dentist will be free from Monday to Friday.

这个牙医星期一到星期五有空。

2. 表示地点方位的介词

(1)in，on 与 at

in 表示在国家、城市等大地方或某空间内，还可以表示"在……里"；on 表示"在……上"；at 用于小地方之前。例如：

in France 在法国　　*in* China 在中国　　*on* the road 在路上　　*at* the bus stop 在公交车站　　*on* the table 在桌上　　*at* home 在家

(2)in，to 与 on

这三个词均表示在不同的方位。in 表示在某范围之内；to 表示在某范围之外；on 表示与某地相邻或接壤。例如：

Vietnam is *on* the south of China.（接壤）

越南在中国的南边。

Guangdong is *in* the south of China.（在……范围之内）

广东在中国的南部。

China lies *to* the west of America.（在……范围之外）

中国位于美国的西边。

(3)over/under 与 above/below

over 和 above 均有"在……的上面"的意思，其中 over 强调在"正……上方"，而 above 仅表示"在上方"，不一定是正上方。此外，above 还能代表温度、海拔等"高于……"；over 则可以指"越过、翻越"。over 和 under，above 和 below 互为反义词，后者的意思指的是"在……下面"。例如：

There is an old stone bridge *over* the pool.

池塘上有一座古老的石桥。

There are two chairs *under* the table.

桌子下面有两把椅子。

The temperature is *below* 0℃.

温度在 0℃ 以下。

The eagles are flying *above* the forest.

老鹰在森林上空飞翔。

(4)in front of 与 in the front of

in front of 意为"在……的前面（物体外部）"，前后所指内容不在同一范围内，in the front of 意为"在……的前面（物体内部）"，前后所指内容在同一范围内。例如：

Lily is *in front of* Tom, but James is behind me.

莉莉在汤姆的前面，但詹姆斯在我的后面。

Teacher's desk is *in the front of* the classroom.

老师的桌子在教室的前面。

(5)其他表示地点方位的介词或介词短语

inside/ outside 在······里面/外面　　　　behind/ at the back of 在······后面/后部

near 在······附近　　　　　　　　　　　　between…and… / among 在······之间

on the right of/ on the left of 在······右/左边　　in the middle of 在······中间

3. 表示方式手段的介词

(1)by 表示用某种方式，后跟动名词或名词，如表示乘坐某种交通工具时，by 后不接冠词，但是用 in 时要用冠词。例如：

He improves his English *by* reading English books.

他通过读英文书来提高英语水平。

I went there *by* taxi.

我乘出租车去的。

(2)with 表示用某种工具，而且在名词前要用冠词；on 表示"以······方式"，多用于固定词组；而 in 表示用某种语言。例如：

He wrote the letter *with* computer.

他用计算机写了这封信。

We talked on the telephone *in* French.

我们用法语在电话里交谈。

(3)in 表示用某种材料、语言、声调等。例如：

Can you say it *in* French?

你能用法语说它吗？

4. 表示"除了······之外"but，besides 与 except

but 有"除······之外"的意思，常常和表否定意义的词连用，当 but 前有动词 do 或其相关形式时，but 后需要跟动词原形；except 表示"除······之外(不再有)"，表达的意思是从整体中除开 except 后跟的事物，前面常用 all，every，any，no 等词；besides 指的是"除······之外(还有)"，表达的意思是在原有基础上加上 besides 除开的事物，其前常用 another，any，other，a few 等词。例如：

You can do nothing *but* wait.

除了等你们什么也做不了。

All the students went to the park *except* Lucy.

除了露西，所有的学生都去公园了。

I have a few good friends *besides* Lily.

除了莉莉之外，我还有几个好朋友。

5. 其他一些介词的用法

(1)表示动作方向的介词：across/through，along/down，to/towards，into 等。

across/through 两者都表示"穿过"，across 表示从空间表面穿过，through 表示从空间内部穿过；along/down 表示"沿着，顺着"；to/towards 意为"向，朝着"；into 意为"进入"。例如：

He walked *across* the street.

他步行穿过街道。

The hikers wanted to go *through* the forest on foot.

驴友们想徒步穿过森林。

(2)表示材料的介词：of，from，in 等。

of 表示成品可以看出原材料；from 表示成品已看不出原材料；in 表示用某种材料。要注意的是 in 指使用某种材料，材料前不加冠词，而 with 后接工具，工具前要加冠词。例如：

This coat is made *of* silk.

这件外套是丝绸做的。（看得出原材料）

Paper is made *from* wood.

纸是由木头制成的。（看不出原材料）

He painted *in* ink.

他用墨水作画。

The children painted *with* colored pencils.

孩子们用彩色铅笔作画。

(3)表示"关于"的介词：about，on 等。

about 表示关于某事或物的比较具体的情况或细节；on 则偏向于学术性的或比较正式严肃的事。例如：

Can you tell me something *about* that beautiful girl?

你能告诉我一些关于那个漂亮女孩的事吗？

It's a textbook *on* the history of China.

这是一本关于中国历史的教科书。

(4)表示原因或理由的介词 for，at，from，of，with，by 等，一般同其他的词构成短语来表达原因。for 表示"因为"时，常与 famous，thank，praise，sorry 等词连用；at 表示"因为"时常常指的是情感变化上的原因，翻译为"因听到或看到而……"；from 表示"因为"，时常指外在的原因，比如受伤、遭遇车祸、遇到意外等情况；of 常指内在的理由，如生病、饥饿等；by 也可表示"因为"，但多指外部的原因，尤其是无意识的情况下造成了某种结果的原因。例如：

I was quite surprised *at* what you said to me.

我对你对我说的话感到十分吃惊。

She was so excited *at* the news that she was going to study abroad.

她对自己要出国留学的消息非常激动。

No one died *from* the traffic accident.

没有人死于这次交通事故。

Some homeless animals die *of* hunger.

一些无家可归的动物死于饥饿。

My teacher was very satisfied *with* my thesis.

我的老师对我的毕业论文很满意。

She took my bag *by* mistake.

她错拿了我的包。

此外，because of 表示引起结果的直接原因，thanks to 指带来某种好的结果的原因，意为"幸亏，多亏"。例如：

Jack didn't go to school *because of* his injured arm.

杰克因为手臂受伤没去上学。

Thanks to Jane, I made great progress.

多亏了简，我取得了很大的进步。

重点点拨

★不用介词的几种情况

1. 在含有 today，yesterday，tomorrow 的时间状语前，不加介词。例如：

What are they going to do tomorrow?

明天他们打算做什么？

2. 在含有 last，next，this，that，these，those，every，one，some，all 等词的时间状语前，不加介词。例如：

We visited the Palace Museum last year.

我们去年参观了故宫博物院。

3. 在含有 here，there，home，back，abroad 等副词前，不加介词。例如：

Some visitors will visit here next month.

下个月将有一些游客来这里参观。

(5)表示"像，作为"的介词：like，as 等。

like 通常表示"像……一样"，事实上不是，可以构成短语 be like/look like；as 通常表示"作为"，事实上就是。例如：

The dog looks *like* a ball.

这只狗看起来像一个球。

She is famous *as* a painter.

她是一位著名的画家。

(6)接动名词的：to。

to 虽常用作不定式，但也可充当介词使用。用作动词不定式符号时，后面跟动词原形：to＋*v.*；用作介词时，后面跟名词、代词或动名词：to＋*n.*/pronoun/*v*-ing；在下列含有 to 的词组中，to 都是介词，在使用时应特别注意，如果它们后面跟动词，则用动名词形式。例如：pay attention to，make a contribution to，according to，get used to，prefer…to…，look forward to …等。

(三)介词短语

介词短语是指介词后跟宾语构成的短语，其常见构成形式有以下几种。

1. 介词＋名词，例如：

We need to be masters *of* time.

我们要做时间的主人。

I got some beautiful flowers *for* our school.

我为学校买了一些漂亮的花。

2. 介词＋代词，例如：

Knowledge is a treasure, but practice is the key *to* it.

知识是一座宝库，而实践是开启这座宝库的钥匙。

You can only succeed if you believe *in* yourself.

只有相信自己，你才能成功。

3. 介词＋动名词，例如：

I spend too much time *in* playing computer games.

我花太多时间打计算机游戏。

重点点拨

★介词和其宾语一起构成的介词短语，在句中可以作定语、表语、状语和补足语等成分。

1. 作定语(常置于被修饰词之后)

A friend in need is a friend indeed.

患难见真情。

2. 作表语

My English teacher is out of China this year.

我的英语老师今年不在中国。

3. 作状语

During the Spring Festival Lily lived at her grandma's house.

春节期间，莉莉住在她奶奶家。

4. 作补足语

I keep my mother's words in heart.

我把妈妈的话记在心里。

✎ **易混词辨析**

一、in charge of 和 in the charge of

两者都表示"负责、照顾"。

1. in charge of 主语常是人，常用 sb. be in charge of sth. 构成"某人掌管某物"的结构。例如：

I am *in charge* of the work.

我负责这项工作。

2. in the charge of 表被动、被掌管、被负责，in 还可以用 under 代替，常用 sth. be in the charge of sb.** 构成"某物由某人掌管"结构，主语通常是事或物。例如：

This class is *in the charge of* an experienced teacher.

这个班由一位经验丰富的教师负责。

The matter is *in the charge of* her and he is *in charge of* the matter.

这件事由她掌管，他负责这件事。

二、around 和 round

around 和 round 在作介词或副词时，基本可以互换，但在部分情况下，仍然存在区别。

1. 当两个词语作"周围、四周"解时，around 表示的是静止、静态的位置，而 round 既可以表示静态的位置，也可以表示动态的动作。例如：

The children stood *around* their teacher.

孩子们站在老师的周围。

The kindergartners were sitting *round* the table to have dinner.

幼儿园的小朋友们围着桌子坐着吃晚餐。

I guide the visitors in a circle *round* the building.

我领着游客绕着大楼转了一圈。

2. around 有"大约""在现场""避开、绕过"的意思。例如：

I will be there *around* ten.

我大约 10 点到。

The building was built *around* 1,000 years ago.

这座建筑是大约 1000 年前建造的。

There are *around* 30,000 students in our university.

我们大学大约有 30000 名学生。

I am sorry he is not *around*.

很抱歉他不在。

She managed to get *around* the issue somehow.

她设法避开了这个问题。

三、among 和 amidst

1. among 指的是三者及三者以上的同类事或物之间，其宾语一般是笼统数量或复数意义的名词或代词。among 的用法较为常见，主要用于日常交流和写作中；amidst 则偏向于指在某个地方的中间、被什么包围或在非同类人中间。它更多地用于正式场合，如法律文件和文学作品中，给人一种正式的感觉。

2. among 强调"处于易分辨的事物当中"；而 amidst 则偏向于指"处于不易分辨的混杂的事物中"。例如：

You can easily find him *among* the crowd.

你在人群中可以轻易地找到他。

The murder is *amidst* the crowd.

凶手隐藏在人群中。

3. among 多用于表示"处于友好的、美好的、善意的事物当中"；而 amidst 多用于表示"处于困难的、凶险的、敌对的事物当中"。例如：

I'm *among* my friends, so there's nothing to be nervous about.

我和朋友们在一起，所以没什么好紧张的。

Do you know you're *amidst* in danger?

你知道你正身处危险之中吗？

四、below，under 和 beneath

below，under 和 beneath 都可以用来表示"在……下"，但在实际使用时存在一定的区别。

1. 当我们表示在"在……下"是两者有接触、紧贴或一物覆盖在另一物上时，用 under，不用 below 和 beneath。例如：

The nurse puts the thermometer *under* my tongue.

护士把温度计放在我舌头底下。

The kid kept his mother's photo *under* the pillow.

这个孩子把他妈妈的照片放在枕头下面。

2. 当我们表示"在……下"是"在……脚底下"，即直接接触的地面时用 beneath，不用 below 和 under。例如：

That surfboard heaved *beneath* my feet.

冲浪板在我的脚下颠簸。

3. beneath 可以表示抽象的"在……之下"，即指一个人的地位、能力或声望等水平较低，而 below 和 under 则没有这种用法。例如：

All the people thought she was marrying *beneath* her.

所有人都认为她是下嫁。

4. below 和 under 均能用于表示工作上的职位高低关系，而 beneath 没有这种用法。例如：

All of us worked *under* a same boss.

我们都在同一个老板手下工作。

My designation was one position *below* him.

我的职位比他低一级。

5. under 可以表示依据，而 below 和 beneath 不可以。例如：

Under the law, you must send your child to school.

依照法律，你必须要让孩子上学。

6. under 可以表示"在……过程中"，而 below 和 beneath 不可以。例如：

Our college's new campus is still *under* construction.

我们学校的新校区还在兴建中。

The murder case is *under* investigation.

那个凶杀案仍在调查中。

7. under 可以指"由……造成，受……影响"，而 below 和 beneath 不可以。例如：

Our mood deteriorates when we are *under* stress.

当我们压力大时，情绪会变差。

五、be made from 和 be made of

be made of 和 be made from 都表示"由……制成"，主语均为制成物。

be made of 一般指从物品的外观上就能直接看出制作物品的原材料，而 be made from 是指从物品的外观上不能直接看出制作物品的原材料。例如：

Those bowls *were made of* wood.

那些碗是用木头制成的。

The soles *are made of* leather.

鞋底是皮革做的。

Red wine *is made from* grapes.

红葡萄酒是用葡萄做的。

Steel *is made from* iron.

钢是由铁炼成的。

小试牛刀

Choose the appropriate preposition and fill in the blanks.

1. Kids are often told not to play _____ fire and water.

2. They go abroad for their holiday _____ plane.

3. Paper is actually made _____ trees.

4. I don't agree _____ you because ten-year-old aren't serious enough _____ that age.

5. The supervisor is strict _____ us.

6. I know my mother cares _____ me.

7. China lies _____ the east of Asia and _____ the west of Japan.

8. _____ our surprise，she has passed the final examination.

9. Young people often wear red clothes _____ New Year's Day.

10. The boy is a foreign kid _____ blue eyes.

11. There are some gifts _____ you _____ my best wishes.

12. _____ Dragon Boat Festival，most people in our country don't need to go to work.

13. They are doing much better _____ the subject _____ my help.

14. Brazil is famous _____ its football and people there are very proud _____ their football team and football stars.

15. _____ the age of 10，he learned to play the violin and he succeeded _____ winning the gold prize this year.

16. _____ fact，he always comes up _____ special ideas.

17. The book must belong _____ Lily. It has her name _____ it.

18. _____ be honest, food that is bad _____ you can taste good.

19. _____ general，I'd like to stay at a place _____ a swimming pool or somewhere _____ the sea.

20. I'm all in favor _____ equal pay for equal work.

学以致用

Ⅰ. Choose the best answer from the four choices A，B，C and D.

1. I am flying to America soon. I will arrive _____ New York _____ the morning of April 8th.

    A. at；in   B. in；in   C. in；on   D. at；on

2. How does their son go to work，_____ foot or _____ bus?

    A. on；with   B. with；on   C. by；on   D. on；by

3. You look so tired. _____ working in your office, you should go home to have a good rest.

    A. Ahead of   B. In spite of   C. In front of   D. Instead of

4. The temperature will stay _____ ten in the morning，but it will fall _____ zero at midnight.

    A. on；at   B. up；down   C. over；under   D. above；below

5. —What's your report _____ , Professor Choose the best answer from the four choices A，B C and D. Lee?

    — Tomorrow you will know.

    A. by   B. of   C. from   D. on

6. There are many big oranges _____ that tree, and there are many birds _____ the tree, too.

　　A. on; in 　　　B. in; on 　　　C. on; on 　　　D. in; in

7. A beautiful girl got _____ the car and went _____ a building.

　　A. from; in 　　B. through; onto 　　C. out of; of 　　D. out of; into

8. If you are a person with good manners, you will never look down _____ people when they are _____ trouble.

　　A. on; in 　　　B. upon; in 　　　C. on; to 　　　D. upon; at

9. Chinese is spoken _____ the native language _____ most people in the world.

　　A. as; by 　　　B. for; by 　　　C. by; as 　　　D. by; for

10. Tommy waited _____ the bus stop _____ over half an hour.

　　A. in; at 　　　B. for; for 　　　C. at; for 　　　D. from; of

11. Playing _____ the sun isn't good _____ your skin.

　　A. under; for 　　B. in; for 　　C. in; at 　　D. under; at

12. Mrs. Wang got _____ the subway near the school and then she went to school _____ foot.

　　A. off; on 　　B. to; on 　　C. on; by 　　D. off; by

13. Exercise is good _____ our body, but _____ the same time we should avoid excessive exercise.

　　A. for; in 　　　B. for; at 　　　C. at ; at 　　　D. at; on

14. Some of us go to school _____ a bike _____ times.

　　A. by; on 　　　B. in; in 　　　C. on; at 　　　D. with; to

15. — How are you going to meet your sister at the high-speed railway station _____ Sunday morning?

　　—I'm going there _____ my car.

　　A. on; in 　　　B. on; by 　　　C. in; by 　　　D. in; in

16. Most of the young teenagers like playing computer games and chatting _____ friends _____ the Internet.

　　A. to; by 　　　　　　B. with; on

　　C. for; in 　　　　　　D. about; through

17. —What would you do _____ the lost book which you borrowed from your classmate?

　　—If I can't find it, I will pay _____ it.

　　A. about; for 　　B. for; to 　　C. with; to 　　D. with; for

18. —What did you get _____ your father _____ Father's Day?

　　—A fishing tackle.

　　A. for; on 　　B. for; in 　　C. to; for 　　D. to; at

19. These bowls are made _____ stone and the skirt is made _____ silk.

　　A. of; from 　　B. of; of 　　C. from; from 　　D. from; of

20. These pictures reminds the boy _____ the days when he lived _____ the small town with his grandfather.

　　A. on; in 　　　B. in; at 　　　C. of; in 　　　D. on; at

II. Please mark and correct the 10 mistakes in the following passage.

I went to see a film after supper. In my way to the cinema, I met an English woman, that had lost her way. I gave up the chance to see the film but took her to her hotel. While go there, I told her about great changes that had taken place here for the past few years and she had told me something about her country. Because I missed the film, I still felt very happy, so I had not only helped her out of trouble and practiced my spoken English. If I had not worked hard in English, I wouldn't have been able help her.	1. _____ 2. _____ 3. _____ 4. _____ 5. _____ 6. _____ 7. _____ 8. _____ 9. _____ 10. _____

III. Translate the following sentences into Chinese.

1. Study hard, or you won't catch up with your classmates.

2. My grandmother is very old, but she never stops learning.

3. Even if you have passed final examination, you should keep on studying hard.

4. They set off early in order that they might arrive there on time.

5. I'll have to stay here until my mother gets well.

6. We must not walk on the grass in the park.

7. The supermarket is in front of the bookstore and the library.

8. They were late for school because of the heavy rain.

9. You can't believe how terrible the fire is unless you see it with your own eyes.

10. The car accident happened on a hot summer afternoon.

IV. Translate the following sentences into English.

1. 没有你的帮助，我们就不能把工作做好。

2. 我对英语很感兴趣。

3. 最后我们想出了一个主意。

4. "Dust"在这里作名词用，意思是那些过去的不好的事情。

5. 比亚迪最新型汽车正在商场展出。

6. 今晚有什么电视连续剧？

7. 邮局就在这条街那一头的左边。

8. 在做面包的时候，我们用植物油代替了黄油。

9. 有人错拿了我的准考证。

10. 空调冬天的时候会在这里减价出售。

第五节　冠词和数词

🔍 重点知识概览

冠词重点知识概览

类别	用法	备注
定冠词 a/an	表示第一次提到的人或物前,意为"一个",相当于 one;泛指一类人或物	1.置于形容词后: (1)形容词为 such,what,many,half 等; 2.置于名词后:如果 rather 和 quite 与单数的名词连用;
	可用于抽象名词之前,将抽象名词的意义具体化	
	用于序数词之前,意为"又一个……,再一……",意义上等同于 another	
	用于表示"一份、一阵、一场"等	
不定冠词 the	特指某人或某物,或是双方都知道的事物;前文提到过的事物	常用于名词或名词修饰语前,但如果出现了 both,all,half,double,twice,... times 等词,要用在名词之前,这些词之后。
	表示世上独一物二的事物,也可用于自然界现象或表示方位的名词之前	
	与形容词连用表示一类人或事物;与复数名词连用,指整个群体	
	用在序数词和形容词最高级,及形容词 only,very,same 等前面	
	the+比较级,则表示"(两个中)更……的那一个"	
	用在表示山脉、河流、湖泊、海洋、名胜古迹、节日等专有名词的前面	
	用在某些由普通名词构成的国家名称、机关团体、阶级等专有名词前	
	用在表示乐器的名词之前	
零冠词	专有名词、头衔、职务前	不能使用任何冠词
	泛指的复数名词,表示一类人或事物时;不可数名词和可数名词表泛指时	
	学科、语言、三餐、球类运动及棋类游戏之前	
	在季节、月份、节日、假日、日期、星期等表示时间的名词之前	
	当 by 与火车等交通工具或通信手段连用	

数词重点知识概览

类别	用法	备注
基数词	表示年份、年代、年龄、时刻	1.基数词的替换词: couple/pair 2/俩 decade 10年 century 100年 dozen 12(打) fornight 2周 2.分数: 分子用基数,分母用序数词,当分子大于1分母加"s",分子在前面,分母在后面。
	表示顺序、编号和电话号码,数学运算	
	表示数量、度量衡、货币、概数、约数	
	"another+基数词"或"基数词+more"结构表示"再……""又……"	
序数词	表示编号、日期	
	"the+序数词"表示"第……次/个"	

重点考查题型:词汇与语法结构、选词填空、完形填空、短文改错、句子翻译

知识梳理

一、冠词（Articles）

冠词是虚词，不具有实际的意义，没有数和格的变化，不能单独使用，所以在句子中也不能担任任何成分，一般放置于名词之前，帮助说明其意义。英文中的冠词可分为不定冠词（Indefinite Articles）、定冠词（Definite Articles）和零冠词（Zero Articles）。

（一）不定冠词（Indefinite Articles）

不定冠词 a(an)与数词 one 属于同源，意义上相同，都表示"一个"。

a 用于辅音音素前，一般读作[ə]，而 an 则用于元音音素前，一般读作[en]。例如：

a boy 一个小男孩 　 a table 一张桌子 　 a pencil 　一支铅笔
a banana tree 一棵香蕉树 　 an American girl 一个美国女孩 　 an honest student 一个诚实的学生 　 an English book 一本英文书

1. 用于表示第一次提到的人或物前，意为"一个"，相当于 one。 例如：

This is *a* Schnauzer.
这是一只雪纳瑞犬。

That is *an* orange tree.
那是一棵橘子树。

I'd like to have *an* apple now.
我现在想吃一个苹果。

A Mr. Wang is waiting for you outside the office.
一位王先生在办公室外面等你。

2. 泛指一类人或物。 例如：

A lawyer should speak carefully.
律师应该说话严谨。

A teacher should be punctual and patient.
教师应该守时且有耐心。

3. 用于某些可数名词之前，用于表示频率、比率、速度等，意为"每一……" 例如：

Three pills *a* time, three times *a* day.
一次三片，一日三次。

We travels twice *a* year.
我们每年旅游两次。

4. 可用于抽象名词之前，将抽象名词的意义具体化。 例如：

It's *an* honor for me to be your sponsor.
我很荣幸能成为你们的赞助者。

My grandmother was *a* great beauty 50 years ago.
我的祖母 50 年前是个大美人。

5. 用于序数词之前，意为"又一个……，再一……"，意义上等同于 another。 例如：

I really like Beijing, so I decide to go there *a* second time.
我真的很喜欢北京，所以我决定再去一次。

重点点拨

★注意：我们这里所指的是

"a ＋辅音音素开头的单词"

"an ＋元音音素开头的单词"

要特别注意某些元音字母开头的单词，并不是元音音素开头，也有部分辅音字母开头的单词却是元音音素开头：

（×）an University
（√）a University
（×）an European country
（√）a European country
（×）a "M"
（√）an "M"

It's not terrible to fail once，you can try *a* second time.

失败了一次并不可怕，你可以再试一次。

6．用于表示"一份、一阵、一场"等。例如：

The children had *a* big dinner last night to celebrate Children's Day.

孩子们昨晚吃了一顿丰盛的晚餐来庆祝儿童节。

7．组成词组或某些固定搭配。例如：

a number of 大量	a few/little/bit(of) 少数，一点儿
quite a few 相当多，不少	a great many 很多
as a result 结果，因此	for a while 一会儿
have a try 试一试	half an hour 半小时
have a rest 休息	have a cold 感冒
have a good time 玩得开心	in a hurry 匆忙
in a mess 混乱	in a word 总之
many a 许多	give sb. a hand 帮助某人
come to an end 结束	once upon a time 从前

（二）定冠词（Definite Articles）

定冠词 the 与指示代词 this，that 同源，带有"这（那）个"的意思，但意义较弱，可以和一个名词连用，来表示某个或某些特定的人或东西。

> **重点点拨**
>
> 定冠词 the 用在辅音音素开头的单词前，读[ðə]，例如：the book；用在元音音素开头的单词前，读[ði]，例如：the orange；在需要强调的情况下，读[ði:]。

1．特指某人或某物，或是双方都明白或知道的人或物。例如：

The Encyclopaedia on the desk is mine.

桌上的百科全书是我的。

Do you know *the* old man in green?

你认识那个穿绿色衣服的老人吗？

Take *the* medicine right now.

现在马上把药吃了。

Turn on *the* light please.

请打开灯。

2．如果第一次提到某人或某物，第二次再次提起时，需要使用特指，用定冠词。例如：

There's a man in the room. *The* man is a doctor.

屋子里有位男士，他是一名医生。

He bought a pencil last night. I like *the* pencil.

他昨晚买了一支铅笔，我喜欢那支铅笔。

3．表示世界上独一无二的事物，也可用于自然界的某个现象或表示方位的名词之前。例如：

the sun/the sky/the moon/the earth/the world/the spring of 2000 等。

The sun rises in the east.

太阳从东方升起。

The earth is much bigger than *the* moon.

地球比月球大多了。

4．定冠词与形容词连用表示一类人或事物。例如：

the rich 富人　　the poor 穷人　　the living 生者　　the deaf 失聪者

The injured were rushed to the rescue room.

伤者被迅速送往急救室。

5. 用在序数词和形容词最高级前，也可以用在形容词 only、very、same 等前面。例如：

I live on *the* third floor.

我住在三楼。

He is *the* very man I've been looking for.

他正是我要找的人。

6. 当定冠词用在比较级前面：the＋比较级，则表示"(两个中)更……的那一个"。例如：

Of the two boys, he's *the* taller.

这两个男孩中，他个子比较高。

7. 与复数名词连用，指整个群体。例如：

They are *the* teachers of this school.

他们就是这所学校的老师。（指全体教师）

They are teachers of this school.

他们是这所学校的老师。（指部分教师）

8. 用在表示山脉、河流、湖泊、海洋、名胜古迹、节日等专有名词的前面。例如：

the Yangzi River/the Pacific Ocean/the Great Wall/the Summer Palace/the Sahara Desert/the Spring Festival

9. 用在某些由普通名词构成的国家名称、机关团体、阶级等专有名词前。例如：

the People's Republic of China 中华人民共和国

the United States 美国

the United Nations 联合国

10. 用在表示乐器的名词之前。例如：

She can play *the* piano and *the* guitar.

她既会弹钢琴又会弹吉他。

11. 用于姓氏复数前：the＋姓氏复数，表示一家人或者夫妻二人。例如：

The Greens are at home now.

格林一家现在都在家里。

12. 含有 the 的习惯用法

(1)"in the＋年份复数"表示"世纪年代"。例如：

in *the* 1990s 在 20 世纪 90 年代

(2)"hit＋sb.＋on/in＋the＋身体部位"表示"打某人某部位"。例如：

A football hit the boy on *the* head.

那个足球打到了小男孩的头。

(3)含有 the 的固定短语。例如：

in the day, in the morning(afternoon, evening), the day after tomorrow, the day before yesterday, the next morning, in the sky(water, field, country), in the dark, in the rain, in the distance, in the middle(of), in the end, on the whole, by the way, go to the theatre

(三)零冠词(Zero Articles)

1. 某些专有名词(如称呼、人名、街道名、城市名、国家名等)，头衔、职务、官衔前通常不用冠词。例如：

Mr. Green's daughter, Susan, lives in London.

格林先生的女儿苏珊住在伦敦。

> **重点点拨**
>
> ★外国的节日前不加定冠词，中国的节日如含有 festival 要加定冠词。如：the Spring Festival/the Dragon Boat Festival/Christmas Day Mother's Day, Labor Day

This is Professor Lee，headmaster of our university.

这是李教授，我们大学的校长。

China is a beautiful country in Asia.

中国是亚洲一个美丽的国家。

2. 泛指的复数名词，表示一类人或事物时，不用冠词。例如：

They are teachers.

他们是教师。

3. 不可数名词和可数名词表泛指时，不用冠词。例如：

Animal can't live without air.

动物没有空气就不能生存。

Dogs are helpful animals.

狗是有用的动物。

Red is Chinese people's favorite color.

红色是中国人最喜欢的颜色。

4. 学科、语言、三餐、球类运动及棋类游戏之前，不用冠词。例如：

She likes reading Japanese every morning，so she can speak it fluently.

她喜欢每天早上读日语，所以她能说得很流利。

I went to school after breakfast this morning.

今天早上我吃完早饭就去学校了。

He often plays basketball in his spare time.

他经常在业余时间打篮球。

He's great at chess.

他很会下象棋。

5. 在季节、月份、节日、假日、日期、星期等表示时间的名词之前，不加冠词。例如：

The workers in this factory work from Monday to Sunday.

这家工厂的工人从星期一工作到星期天。

6. 名词前已有指示代词、形容词性物主代词或名词所有格等修饰时，不加冠词。例如：

Every student likes English in our class.

我们班每个学生都喜欢英语。

7. 当两个或两个以上名词并用时，常省去冠词。例如：

I can't write without pen or pencil.

没有钢笔或铅笔，我就写不了字。

8. 当 by 与交通工具或通信手段连用，表示一种方式时，中间一般无冠词。例如：

by bus/by train/by car/by ship/by plane/by high-speed railway

send a message by letter/mail/radio/telephone/telegram

9. 部分个体名词的前面一般不使用冠词，如 school，college，prison，hospital，bed，table，class，town，church，court 等个体名词，直接置于介词后，表示该名词的深层含义。例如：

go to hospital 去医院看病

go to the hospital 去医院（不是去医院看病）

10. 某些特定的情况下序数词前不用冠词。

(1)序数词前有物主代词时。例如：

> **重点点拨**
>
> ★当 by 与交通工具或通信手段连用，表示一种方式时，中间一般无冠词，但某些情况也可用冠词，意义会发生变化。如：
>
> He seldom went out by bus，so I was surprised when noticing him on the bus.
>
> 他很少乘公共汽车出去，所以当我在公共汽车上看到他时，我感到很惊讶。

That is my second car.

那是我的第二辆车。

(2)序数词作副词。例如：

He came first in the race.

他跑步得了第一。

(3)在固定词组中。例如：

at first/first of all/from first to last

11. 在某些固定搭配中不用冠词。例如：

in surprise 惊奇地	on foot 步行	on holiday 在度假
at first 起初	at home 在家	at last 最后
at night 最后	at work 在工作中	by mistake 错误地
for example 例如	side by side 肩并肩	day by day 一天天
by accident 意外地	from beginning to end 自始至终	
day and night 日日夜夜	face to face 面对面	
hand in hand 手拉手	husband and wife 夫妻	
learn by heart 背诵	in fact 事实上	

(四)冠词的位置

1. 不定冠词位置

不定冠词一般位于名词或名词修饰语前，除了下列特殊情况外。

(1)位于 such，what，many，half 等形容词之后。例如：

I have never seen such *an* animal.

我从来没见过这样的动物。

Many *a* man is fit for the position.

许多人适合这个职位。

(2)如果名词前的形容词被 how，however，as，so，enough，too 等副词修饰时，不定冠词应放在形容词之后。例如：

so short *a* time 如此短的时间

too long *a* distance 太远的距离

(3)如果 rather 和 quite 与单数的名词连用，冠词要放在名词后面。但如果 rather 和 quite 前还有另外的形容词修饰，不定冠词放在名词的前后都可以。例如：

rather *a* cold day/*a* rather cold day

(4)在由 as 或 though 引导的让步状语从句中，当表语为形容词修饰的名词时，不定冠词要放在形容词后。例如：

Self-confident *a* woman though she is，she fears in a show of this magnitude.

虽然她是个自信的女人，但对这种规模的演出还是感到害怕。

2. 定冠词位置

定冠词常常用于名词或名词修饰语前，但如果出现了 both，all，half，double，twice，… times 等词，要用在名词之前、这些词之后。例如：

Both *the* boys were ill，so no one can take part in the performance.

两个男孩儿都病了，所以没有人能参加演出。

二、数词(Numerals)

(一)基数词

英语中的基数词是用来描述事物数量的。

1. 基数词的基本结构

(1)第一类：基数词 1～12(独立的单词)

one 一　　　two 二　　　three 三　　　four 四　　　five 五　　　　six 六

seven 七　　　eight 八　　　nine 九　　　ten 十　　　eleven 十一　　twelve 十二

(2)第二类：基数词 13～19(后缀-teen)

这一类基数词均以后缀"teen"结尾。十五和十八拼写上略有不同要特别注意。

thirteen 十三　　　　fourteen 十四　　　fifteen 十五　　　sixteen 十六

seventeen 十七　　　eighteen 十八　　　nineteen 十九

(3)第三类：20～90 均以后缀"ty"结尾。

此类基数词共有 8 个，均为十位整数。

twenty 二十　　　thirty 三十　　　forty 四十　　　fifty 五十　　　sixty 六十

seventy 七十　　　eighty 八十　　　ninety 九十

(4)第四类：几十几(十位整数-个位整数)

此类基数词属于合成词，均是使用十位整数加上个位整数，用连字符号"-"在中间连接，意思为"几十几"。例如：

twenty-one 二十一　　　　　forty-five 四十五

seventy-nine 七十九　　　　ninety-two 九十二

第五类：三位数或三位数以上的基数词

三位数或三位数以上的基数词，需在十位数之前(若十位数是"0"，则在个位数前)加连词 and。阿拉伯数字每三位数就需用一个千分号","隔开，从右往左数；所用的英语单词为：thousand(千)，million(百万)，billion(十亿)。英语中没有"万""千万"和"亿"的表达，可以用十进位法来推算。如：

1 万可用 10 千来表示，即 10,000＝ten thousand

1 亿即 100,000,000＝a hundred million

65,945＝sixty-five thousand, nine hundred and forty-five

108　a hundred and eight

321　three hundred and twenty-one

858　eight hundred and fifty-eight

1,427　one thousand four hundred and twenty-seven

9,018　nine thousand and eighteen

9,865,435　nine million, eight hundred and sixty-five thousand, four hundred and thirty-five

> **重点点拨**
> ★ 表确切数字时 hundred, thousand, million, billion 都只能用单数，但在合成中数词一般用复数，表示数以百计、数以千计、数以百万计泛指许多，常与 of 连用：Hundreds of…, thousands of…, millions of…, billions of…

2. 基数词的用法

(1)基数词可以在句了当中充当主语、宾语、表语、同位语等。例如：

Three of the students went to the playground.

三个学生去了操场。(主语)

I want *one*.

我要一个。(宾语)

My mother is *forty-one*.

我妈妈 41 岁。(表语)

Is there a room left for us *two*?

还有我们两个人的房间吗？(同位语)

（2）表示年份、年代

①年份用基数词表达，年份前用介词 in。例：

在 1998 年　in 1998（读作 in nineteen ninety-eight）

在 2008 年　in 2008（读作 in two thousand and eight）

年、月、日同时出现时，可以表达为月、日、年或日、月、年。如：

October 2nd，1999/2nd October，1999　1999 年 10 月 2 日

②年代用"in the＋基数词的复数"表示。如：

在 20 世纪 30 年代 in the 1930s（读作 in the ninety thirties）

（3）表示年龄

①直接用基数词（＋years old），表示"……岁"。如：

His father is *forty-one* years old.

他的父亲 41 岁。

②at the age of＋基数词。如：

She went to school at the age of *six*.

她 6 岁就上学了。

③in one's＋整十基数词的复数，表示"在某人几十多岁的时候"。

例如：

My brother went abroad *in his thirties*.

我哥哥在他 30 多岁的时候出国了。

（4）表示顺序、编号和电话号码

有编号的事物要用基数词表示顺序，但是基数词要后置。例如：

六年级二班　Class 2，Grade 6　　第四十一页　Page 41

2105 房间　Room 2105　　　　　　19 路公共汽车　Bus No. 19

Tel：9865466（读作 telephone number nine eight six five four six six）

（5）表示时刻

①顺读法：先时后分。例如：

It's *nine ten*.

现在是九点十分。

②逆读法：先分后时。

分钟不超过 30，（几点）过（几分），介词用 past。例如：

It's *five past eleven*.

现在是十一点五分。

差几分几点，相差的分钟数不超过 29 时，用 to。如：

It's *a quarter to* ten.

现在是差一刻十点。

（6）在数学运算中常用到基数词，"加"用 plus 或 and，"减"用 minus，"乘"用 times 或 multiplies by，"除"用 divided by，谓语动词用单数。例如：

1＋2＝3　　　One plus two is/equals three.

5－3＝2　　　Five minus three is/equals two.

2×5＝10　　　Two times/multiplies by five is/equals ten.

9÷3＝3　　　Nine divided by three is/equals three.

（7）表示度量衡通常用"基数词＋单位名词＋形容词（long，wide，high 等）"，或者"基数词＋单位名

重点点拨

★含有基数词的复合形容词

由基数词＋名词构成的合成词，当作形容词使用时，各部分之间用"-"连接，名词用单数形式。如：

The kid is 6 years old.

＝ The kind is 6-year-old.

这个小孩六岁。

The building is 500 hundred meters high. ＝ The building is 500-hundred-meter high.

这幢楼 500 米高。

词＋in＋名词（length，width，height，weight）"。例如：

two feet long ＝ two feet in length

ten meters high ＝ ten meters in height

(8)货币表达通常是用符号加基数词。如：

¥9.80 nine yuan eighty fen 9 元 8 角

£7.37 seven pounds thirty-seven pence 7 英镑 37 便士

$28.5 twenty-eight dollars fifty cents 28 美元 50 美分

(9)表示概数、约数。

①"大约"用 about，around，nearly 等，放在数词前面，"多于"用

more than 或 over，"小于"用 less than，"或……以上"用 or more，"或……以下"用 or less。例如：

He is *about* 50 years old.

他大约 50 岁。

We will arrive there *around* 5.

我们大约 5 点到达那里。

There are *over* 40,000 people at the Bird's Nest tonight.

鸟巢今晚有 4 万多人。

American-style coffee has 100 calories *less than* ordinary coffee.

美式咖啡的热量比普通的咖啡少 100 卡路里。

The Bird's Nest can hold 80,000 people *or more*.

鸟巢可容纳 8 万人以上。

②"左右"用 or so，放在数词短语后面。例如：

In the past fifteen years *or so*, she has changed a lot.

在过去 15 年左右的时间里，她改变了很多。

(10)"another＋基数词"或"基数词＋more"结构表示"再……""又……"。例如：

This pair of pants is too big. Can you bring me *another* two?

这条裤子太大了，你能再给我拿两条吗？

This ice-cream is so delicious，and I'd like *one more*.

这个冰激凌如此美味，我还想再吃一个。

> **重点点拨**
> ★基数词的替换词
> couple/pair 2
> decade 10 年
> century 100 年（世纪）
> dozen 12（一打）
> fornight 2 周

(二)序数词

1.序数词的构成

序数词是指表示顺序的数词。

(1)第一类(1st～3rd)

first(1st)第一　　second(2nd) 第二　　third(3rd) 第三

(2)第二类(4th～19th)

此类序数词是由"基数词＋th"构成。注意 fifth、eighth、ninth、twelfth 的拼写。

fourth (4th)第四	fifth (5th) 第五	sixth (6th) 第六
seventh (7th) 第七	eighth (8th)第八	ninth (9th) 第九
tenth (10th) 第十	eleventh (11th) 第十一	twelfth (12th)第十二
thirteenth (13th) 第十三	fourteenth (14th) 第十四	fifteenth (15th)第十五
sixteenth (16th) 第十六	seventeenth (17th) 第十七	eighteenth (18th)第十八
nineteenth (19th) 第十九		

(3)第三类(20th～90th)

这类序数词是把对应的十位整数基数词词尾变"y"为"i"，加上"eth"。

twentieth (20th)第二十　　thirtieth (30th) 第三十　　fortieth (40th) 第四十

fiftieth (50th) 第五十　　sixtieth (60th)第六十　　seventieth (70th) 第七十

eightieth (80th) 第八十　　ninetieth (90th) 第九十

(4)第四类(两位或两位以上的序数词)

这类序数词是将对应的基数词十位数保持不变，将个位基数词变成序数词。例如：

thirty-second (32nd) 第三十二　　fifty-third (53rd) 第五十三

twenty-seventh (27th)第八十七　　ninety-sixth (96th) 第九十六

two hundred and forty-first 第二百四十一

2. 序数词的基本用法

(1)表示编号。例如：

My seat is in *the second* row, number *two*.

我的座位在第二排，二号。

(2)表示日期。例如：

She was born on October *the fifth*.

她出生于10月5日。

(3)表示"第……次"做某事：It's the(one's) ＋ 序数词 ＋ time ＋ to do sth. 例如：

It's *my first* time to go abroad.

这是我第一次出国。

It's *the second* time for him to eat such food.

这是他第二次吃这样的食物。

(4)主要用作定语、表语，前面要加定冠词 the。例如：

I like *the first* dress, but my sister like *the second* one.

我喜欢第一件衣服，但我妹妹喜欢第二件。

(5)用于作文的过渡

first, firstly, first of all, first and foremost 首先

second, secondly(in addition, what's more)其次

third, thirdly(last but not least, finally, at last)第三/最后

(三)基数词和序数词的应用

1. 分数

(1)基本构成：分子用基数，分母用序数词，当分子大于1时，分母要加"s"，分子在前面，分母在后面。例如：

1/3　one third　　4/5　four fifths

当分子是1时，可以用 one 也可以用 a；

当分母是2时，可以用 half；

当分母是4时，可以用 quarter。

如：

1/5　a (one) fifth　　1/2　a (one) half

1/4　a (one) quarter　　3/4　three quarters

表示带分数时，应在分数之前加基数词和 and。如：

$3\frac{3}{4}$, three and three fourths

> **重点点拨**
> ★second to sb. /sth. 仅次于，例如：
> The danger of heart disease is only second to traffic accident. 心脏病的危险性仅次于交通事故。
> ★second to none 无人能及/行业领先，例如：
> Our invention is second to none. 我们的发明是首屈一指的。

(2)其他构成：基数词＋in/out of/over＋基数词。如：

1/10 one in ten　　　2/5 two out of five　　　3/7 three over seven

(3)个别表示分数的词：half, quarter

half 二分之一　　　　quarter 四分之一　　　three quarters 四分之三

2. 倍数

在英语中表示倍数时，一倍是 once，两倍是 twice，三倍或三倍以上用"基数词＋times"。

其基本用法结构如下。

(1)主语＋系动词＋倍数＋as＋形容词＋as＋比较对象

The car is *twenty times* as heavy as that bike.

这辆汽车的重量是那辆自行车的 20 倍。

(2)主语＋谓语 *vi*．＋倍数＋as＋副词＋as＋比较对象

Tom runs *twice* as fast as John.

汤姆跑得比约翰快两倍。

(3)主语＋谓语 *vt*．＋倍数＋as＋形容词＋宾语＋as＋比较对象

He eats *twice* as much food as I do.

他吃的食物是我的两倍。

(4)主语＋系动词＋倍数＋形容词比较级＋than＋比较对象

The car is *20 times* heavier than the bike.

汽车比自行车重 20 倍。

(5)主语＋谓语 *vi*．＋倍数＋副词比较级＋than＋比较对象

Tom runs *twice* faster than John.

汤姆跑得比约翰快两倍。

(6)the＋*n*．＋of＋主语＋系动词＋倍数＋that＋of＋the 比较对象

The weight of the car is *20 times* that of the bicycle.

汽车的重量是自行车的 20 倍。

(7)主语＋系动词＋倍数＋the＋*n*．＋of ＋the 比较对象

The car is *20 times* the weight of the bicycle.

这辆汽车的重量是自行车的 20 倍。

3. 小数

英文中小数的表达是将小数点读作"point"，小数点左边的整数按照基数词的读法，小数点右边的数字按照数字本身逐个读出即可。例如：

0. 45 zero point four five

89. 15 eighty-nine point one five

109. 219 one hundred and nine point two one nine

4. 百分数

百分数一般用"基数词/小数＋percent"表示，也可采用"％"。例如：

Ninety percent of the soldiers are against the plan.＝90％ of the soldier are against the plan.

90％的士兵反对这个计划。

重点点拨

★分数的主谓一致

如果名词是可数名词单数或不可数名词，谓语用单数。例如：

One third of the playground is covered with leaves. 三分之一的操场被树叶覆盖。

如果名词是可数名词复数，谓语用复数。例如：

One third of the students are boys. 三分之一的学生是男孩儿。

📖 **易错盘点**

一、"the＋形容词"结构

当"the＋形容词"表示一类人，其作主语时，谓语动词用复数。

当"the＋形容词"表示事物或抽象概念，其作主语时，谓语动词用单数。例如：

The poor get poorer and poorer.

穷人变得越来越穷。

The new is to take place of the old.

新生事物将代替旧事物。

二、冠词与形容词＋名词结构

1. 两个形容词都有冠词，指的是两个不同的人或物。例如：

My grandma raises a black and a white cat.

我奶奶养了一只黑猫和一只白猫。

The black and the white cats are my grandmother's.

这只黑猫和这只白猫都是我奶奶的。

2. 前一个形容词有冠词，而后一个形容词无冠词的时候，指的是一人或一物。例如：

My grandma raises a black and white cat.

我的祖母养了一只黑白相间的猫。

三、有定冠词和无定冠词的短语意义辨析

go to school 去上学（是学生）	go to the school 到学校去（不一定是学生）
go to university 上大学	go to the university 去大学
go to hospital 去看病（是病人）	go to the hospital 去医院（不一定是病人去看病）
go to bed 去睡觉	go to the bed 去床上（不一定是睡觉）
go to war 交战	go to the war 参军
at table 在吃饭	at the table 在桌子旁边
at school 在学校	at the school 在学校里
in hospital 生病在医院	in the hospital 在医院（不一定是生病）
in class 在上课	in the class 在班级里
in front of 在……（外部的）前面	in the front of 在……（内部的）前面
in control of 控制了（主动）	in the control of 被控制了（被动）
in future 从今以后	in the future 在将来
in person 亲自	in the person 以……资格，代表
in place of 代替	in the place of 在……地方
in possession of 占有，拥有（主动）	in the possession of 被……占有（被动）
in sight of 看得见	in the sight of 从……观点来看
in red 身穿红衣服	in the red 亏损，赤字
in view of 鉴于，由于	in the view of 按……的意见
in case of 万一	in the case of 就……来说，至于
out of question 不成问题，无疑	out of the question 不可能
take place 发生	take the place of 代替
by sea 乘船	by the sea 在海边
by day 在白天	by the day 计日，按日计
in church 在做礼拜	in the church 在教堂里

on earth 究竟，在世上　　　　　on the earth 在地球上

on fire 着火　　　　　　　　　on the fire 在火上，考虑中，在准备中

小试牛刀

Ⅰ. Fill in the blanks with appropriate articles.

1. _____ new study says that going to _____ bed late is harmful to our health.

2. Sun Yang is _____ excellent swimmer，I want to become _____ person like him.

3. April is _____ fourth month of the year. It's _____ very pleasant time of the year.

4. Every evening she spends _____ hour doing homework and then she goes to bed at ten.

5. What _____ useful dictionary it is!

6. _____ Children's Day is not _____ traditional Chinese festival.

7. —Have you seen _____ movie *Chosin Reservoir*?

　　—Yes. That is _____ educational film and it has become one of _____ most popular films in China.

8. The UK is _____ European country while Korea is _____ Asian country .

9. —How long does it take us to go to your school from the city centre?

　　—It takes us _____ hour to go to my school by _____ bus.

10. All the people in our school took part in _____ party. They are _____ teachers in our school.

Ⅱ. Fill in the blanks with appropriate numerals.

1. Children's Day is on the _____ of June.

2. There are _____ days in a week.

3. Three plus five is _____ .

4. My father is _____ (50)years old . This is his _____ birthday.

5. The ladder is _____ (3倍) as heavy as that box.

6. _____ (40%)of the students can take the entrance examination.

7. My apartment is on the _____ (9) floor.

8. _____ (60%) is equal to _____ (3/5).

9. He became the President in his _____ (50多岁的时候).

10. It's time for you to go to bed，it's _____ (11点40).

学以致用

Ⅰ. Choose the best answer from the four choices A，B，C and D.

1. I run long distance _____ .

　　A. every five days　　B. every five day　　C. every fifth days　　D. every fives day

2. Lucy is going to be _____ years old. She'll have her _____ birthday party tonight.

　　A. eleven；eleven　　B. eleventh；eleven　　C. eleventh；eleventh D. eleven；eleventh

3. December is the _____ month in a year.

　　A. twelve　　　　　B. twelfth　　　　　C. twentieth　　　　D. twenty

4. —Helen，it is the _____ time in _____ days that you've made such mistake.

　　—I'm so sorry. I won't do it again.

　　A. two；three　　　B. second；third　　C. two；third　　　D. second；three

5. I have no time to go with you for I've got _____ things to do today.

    A. a million   B. millions   C. a million of   D. million

6. It is reported that the earthquake has left about _____ people homeless.

    A. four thousand   B. four thousands   C. four thousands of D. thousands of

7. —What is 40％ of 100,000,000?

    —It is _____.

    A. forty million   B. five millions

    C. five hundred million   D. five billion

8. —Lucy，do you have the time?

    —_____.

    A. Yes，I have   B. Ten to eight

    C. Sorry，I'm so busy.   D. Little

9. —What are you going to be in the future?

    —I'm going to be _____ teacher like Zhang Guimei.

    A. a   B. an   C. the   D. /

10. Look！There are so many stars in _____ sky.

    A. a   B. an   C. the   D. /

11. _____ Greens did manage to send _____ Green to a technical school.

    A. /；/   B. An；an   C. The；/   D. The；an

12. _____ snow/Snow is white. The snow that covers the top of the Mount Emei is _____ a-mazing sight.

    A. The；the   B. The；/   C. /；an   D. /；the

13. Kids' ll wait for the bus at the gate of _____ school on _____ Children's Day.

    A. the；the   B. the；/   C. a；/   D. a；a

14. _____ students in our school are mostly from _____ north.

    A. The；/   B. The；a   C. /；the   D. The；the

15. The foreigners have _____ great love for _____ their own country.

    A. a；the   B. an；/   C. the；/   D. a；/

16. The man who is _____ can't even imagine a bit about what happened _____ of the last century.

    A. in the 30s；in the 80s   B. in his 30s；in 80s

    C. in his 30s；in the 80s   D. in the 30s；in 80s

17. About _____ of the ground _____ covered with grass.

    A. two fifth；are   B. two fifths；is   C. two fifth；are   D. two fifth；is

18. _____ of students in my college _____ going to the conference.

    A. Three fifths；is   B. Three fifths；are C. Three fifths；are D. Three fifths；are

19. —What _____ the population of China?

    —China has a population of 1. 4 _____.

    A. is；billion   B. are；billion   C. is；billions   D. are；billions

20. —Did you pay 1,000 yuan for the table?

    —No. I paid _____ for it.

    A. three times so many   B. three times so much

    C. three times as many   D. three times as much

Ⅱ．Please mark and correct the 10 mistakes in the following passage.

Two months ago, I went to abroad for further study. Before I left, I was given lot presents.	1. ＿＿＿＿＿＿＿＿＿
	2. ＿＿＿＿＿＿＿＿＿
Between them, there were two presents which really interested me. My sister bought me the book with color pictures about a body language and with words about customs of different countries in them. My brother gave me note which read, "My present has been put in your bedroom." When I hurried into a bedroom, I found a box, in which there was a electronic dictionary. I was very glad but a few surprised to receive these two presents.	3. ＿＿＿＿＿＿＿＿＿
	4. ＿＿＿＿＿＿＿＿＿
	5. ＿＿＿＿＿＿＿＿＿
	6. ＿＿＿＿＿ 7. ＿＿＿＿＿
	8. ＿＿＿＿＿ 9. ＿＿＿＿＿
	10. ＿＿＿＿＿＿＿＿＿

Ⅲ．Translate the following sentences into Chinese.

1. After the new technique was introduced, the factory produced twice as many cars in 2010 as the year before.

2. Millions of people around the world suffer from a painful addiction to biting their nails, which can be harder to quit than smoking cigarettes.

3. It is reported that a large number of people have been killed and the number has added up to nearly ten thousand.

4. The population in Japan is not very large, but it is reported that about twenty-five percent of the population are old people.

5. About 50 percent of the population of that country live on farms.

6. Our teacher often tells us, "Be an honest boy today and a useful man tomorrow."

7. Things of a kind come together; people of a kind fall into the same group.

8. What a happy life people in the small island lived at that time!

9. Europe and America are separated by the Atlantic Ocean.

10. I would like to have a room, the window of which opens to the south.

Ⅳ．Translate the following sentences into English.

1. 我感到有人拍了拍我的肩膀。

2. 长安是世界著名的"丝绸之路"的起点。

3. 青岛是一座美丽的城市，位于中国的东部。

4. 现在是早上 11 点了，但他还在睡觉。

5. 杭州是一座充满活力的城市，与许多国家和地区建立了贸易关系。

6. 我们的活动还需要两把椅子，你可以去 102 房间再拿两把。

7. 这个男孩这学期已经迟到 4 次了。

8. 每天有数千万人通过微信联系。

9. 里奥结婚时才 20 多岁。

10. 我们班有 60 名学生，3/4 的人喜欢足球。

第二章

句　法

第一节　句子的基本成分及结构

🔍 重点知识概览

句子的基本成分及结构重点知识概览

类别	组成	位置	备注
主语	由名词、代词、数词、不定式、动名词、名词化的形容词和主语从句等充当	一般放置在句首	句子唯一性原则：一个句子只能有一套主谓关系
谓语	中心词由动词充当	一般位于主语之后	
宾语	由名词、代词、数词、不定式、动名词、宾语从句充当。	位于谓语（及物动词）之后	
表语	由形容词、名词、代词、分词、数词、不定式、动名词、介词短语、副词及表语从句充当。	位于连系动词之后	基本句子结构： 1. S＋V（不及物动词）＋Ad.（状语） 2. S＋V（系动词）＋P 3. S＋V（及物动词）＋O 4. S＋V（及物）＋InO（间宾）＋DO（直宾） 5. S＋V（及物）＋O（宾语）＋OC（宾补）
补语	由名词、形容词、副词、不定式、分词、介词短语充当。	宾语补足语一般位于宾语之后	
定语	由形容词、名词、数词、名词的所有格、动名词、过去分词、副词、介词短语、不定式短语、定语从句充当。	前置定语：中心词之前 后置定语：中心词之后	
状语	由名词、形容词、副词、介词短语、分词短语、不定式、状语从句等充当。	句首、句中、句末	
同位语	由名词、代词、数词、介词短语、同位语从句充当。	一般位于被修饰的主语、宾语或表语之后	

重点考查题型：选句填空、选词填空、短文改错、句子翻译

知识梳理

句子是由词语根据一定的语法结构组合而成，是能表达一个完整意义的语言单位。句子成分可以分为：基本成分、修饰成分、独立成分、省略成分和连接成分五类。

英文句子最主要的主干部分由基本成分(主语、谓语、宾语、表语、补语)和修饰成分(定语、状语、同位语)组成。

一、主语(Subject)

主语是一个句子所叙述的主体，即动作的发出者。主语一般放置在句首，不能省略。只有在疑问句(主语不是疑问词)、倒装句、there be 句型中，主语要放置于谓语、助动词或情态动词后面。主语通常由名词、代词、数词、不定式、动名词、名词化的形容词和主语从句等充当。例如：

Jane is playing the violin.

简正在拉小提琴。(名词作主语)

He went out in no hurry.

他不慌不忙地出去了。(代词作主语)

One plus four is five.

一加四等于五。(数词作主语)

To see is to believe.

眼见为实。(不定式作主语)

Drinking alcohol is bad for your health.

喝酒对身体不好。(动名词作主语)

The young should respect the old.

年轻人应该尊敬老人。(名词化形容词作主语)

What she has said is not true.

她所说的不是真的。(从句作主语)

二、谓语(Predicate)

谓语即主语发出的动作或主语具有的特征和状态(即谓语动词)。谓语一般位于主语之后，中心词由动词充当，在人称和数上与主语保持一致。例如：

Time *flies*.

光阴似箭。

Every child here *needs* our help.

这里的每个孩子都需要我们的帮助。

All of the stories in the book *touched* me a lot.

书中所有的故事都深深打动了我。

What *happened*?

发生了什么？

The airplane *took off* at 11 o'clock in the morning.

飞机早上 11 点起飞。

You *can do* it if you try hard.

如果你努力的话，你就能做到。

We *will watch* the film.

> **重点点拨**
> ★ 在阅读句子的时候，首要任务就是要找到谓语。
> ★ 做谓语的动词有时态、语态和数的变化。
> ★ 谓语动词可能是及物动词或不及物动词。

我们将看电影。

They quickly *filled in* the form.

他们很快地填好了表格。

三、宾语（Object）

宾语即动作的对象或承受者，位于谓语之后。宾语一般由名词、代词、数词、不定式、动名词、宾语从句充当。例如：

Show your *passport*，please.

请出示护照。（名词）

My mother didn't say *anything*.

我妈妈什么也没说。（代词）

——How many do you want?

——I want *one*.

——你想要多少？——我想要一个。（数词）

I sent *the wounded* to clinic.

我把伤者送往诊所（形容词作名词）。

The police asked *to see my passport*.

警察要求看我的护照。（不定式）

I enjoy *walking* with you after dinner.

我喜欢和你一起晚饭后散步。（动名词）

Did you write down *what they said*?

你把他们说的话都记下来了吗？（宾语从句）

四、表语（Predicative）

表语用于说明或表述主语的身份、特征和状态，位置在系动词之后，一般由名词、代词、形容词、分词、数词、不定式、动名词、介词短语、副词及从句充当。例如：

Is it *mine*?

这是我的吗？（代词）

The weather has turned *hot*.

天气变热了。（形容词）

The speech is *exciting*.

这演讲激动人心。（形容词）

Five times seven is *thirty-five*.

5 乘 7 等于 35。（数词）

His job is *to repair cars*.

他的工作是修车。（不定式）

His hobby is *playing tennis*.

他的爱好是打网球。（动名词）

The air conditioner must be *out of order*.

空调一定是坏了。（介词短语）

Time is *up*.

时间到了。（副词）

The truth is *that he has never been to Shanghai*.

重点点拨

间接宾语 & 直接宾语

宾语分为直接宾语和间接宾语。

He gave me some books.

　　间接宾语　直接宾语

★当直接宾语位于间接宾语之后时，应在间接宾语前加介词 to，for 等。

He gave some books *to* me.

重点点拨

1. 不定式、分词作表语的区别

Our plan is to keep the affair secret. （主语和表语相等）

This beautiful village remains unknown to the rest of the world. （主语和表语不相等）

2. 不定式和动名词作表语的区别

His job is to paint the walls. （强调具体的、将要发生的、一次性的动作）

His job is painting walls. （强调的是抽象的、经常发生的、一般性的动作）

3. 现在分词和过去分词作表语的区别

This dog is frightening. （说明特征）

This dog is frightened. （说明状态）

事实是他从未去过上海。（表语从句）

五、补语 (Complement)

补语也叫补足语，用于补充说明主语或宾语的身份、性质、特征、状态或动作等。补语可由名词、形容词、副词、不定式、分词、介词短语和从句充当。补语分为主语补足语和宾语补足语两种。例如：

Lily was appointed *chairman of the Students' Union*.

莉莉被任命为学生会主席。（名词短语作主语补足语）

She was found *eating in the library*.

她被发现在图书馆吃东西。（分词短语作主语补足语）

His grandfather named him *Huanghua*.

他的祖父给他起名叫黄华。（名词作宾语补足语）

They painted the ship *white*.

他们把船漆成白色。（形容词作宾语补足语）

You mustn't force me *to do the work for you*.

你不能强迫我帮你做这个工作。（不定式短语作宾语补足语）

We saw him *entering the building*.

我们看见他进了那幢楼。（分词短语作宾语补足语）

The librarian found everything in the library *in good order*.

图书管理员发现图书馆里一切都井然有序。（介词短语作宾语补足语）

We will soon make our school *what your school is now*.

我们很快就会把我们的学校变成跟你们现在的学校一样。（从句作宾语补足语）

> **重点点拨**
>
> 主语补足语 & 宾语补足语
>
> 主语补足语即被动语态中的宾语补足语。
>
> We found her reading in the library. （宾语补足语）
>
> She was found reading in the library. （主语补足语）

六、定语 (Attribute)

定语是用于修饰或限制名词或代词的词、词组或从句。定语通常由形容词、名词、数词、名词的所有格、动名词、过去分词、副词、介词短语、不定式短语、定语从句充当。例如：

He is a *naughty* kid.

他是一个顽皮的孩子。（形容词）

His father works in a *silk* factory.

他的父亲在一家丝绸厂工作。（名词）

There are *60* women in our organization.

我们组织有60名女性。（数词）

Do you know *Mary's* sister?

你认识玛丽的妹妹吗？（名词的所有格）

She ate some *sleeping* pills.

她吃了一些安眠药。（动名词）

His *spoken* language is good.

他的口语很好。（过去分词）

I have got something *old* for you.

我有老物件要给你。（形容词）

The people *there* are very friendly to visitors.

那里的人对游客很友好。（副词）

The girl *with red scarf* is my sister.

戴红围巾的女孩是我的姐姐。（介词短语）

Mr Lee has the ability *to make his classes interesting*.

> **重点点拨**
>
> 前置定语 & 后置定语
>
> ★前置定语位于所修饰词之前。通常由名词、代词、数词、形容词、分词、动名词等充当。
>
> ★后置定语位于所修饰词之后。通常由形容词（短语）、副词（短语）、介词（短语）、分词（短语）、不定式（短语）、从句充当。

李先生有能力使他的课上得有趣。（不定式）

The book *that I bought yesterday* is so boring.

我昨天买的那本书很无趣。（定语从句）

七、状语（Adverbial）

1. 状语用来修饰动词、形容词、副词或句子。状语通常由名词、形容词、副词、介词短语、分词短语、不定式、状语从句等充当。例如：

Wait *a minute*.

等一下。（名词）

Young in years, he is old in experience.

他虽然年轻，但经验丰富。（形容词短语）

Light travels *most quickly*.

光传播得最快。（副词）

He has learned English *for ten years*.

他学习英语已经 10 年了。（介词短语）

She is in the classroom *making a model building*.

她在教室里面做模型建筑。（分词短语）

He is happy *to have passed the national college entrance exami-nation*.

他为通过了高考而高兴。（不定式短语）

Once you begin, you must continue.

一旦你开始，就必须继续下去。（状语从句）

2. 状语通常用于说明方式、原因、条件、时间、地点、让步、方向、程度、目的等。例如：

How about meeting again *at six*?

6 点再见面怎么样？（时间）

Last night he didn't go to the library *because of the heavy snow*.

昨晚因为大雪，他没去图书馆。（原因）

I shall go there *if it doesn't rain*.

如果不下雨，我就去那里。（条件）

Mr. Green lives *on the third floor*.

格林先生住在三楼。（地点）

She put the kitten into the basket *with great care*.

她小心翼翼地把小猫放进篮子里。（方式）

She came in *with a bunch of flowers in her hand*.

她手里拿着一束花进来了。（伴随）

In order to catch up with the others, I must work harder than them.

为了赶上别人，我必须比他们更努力。（目的）

He was so tired *that he fell asleep immediately*.

他如此疲倦，以至于立刻就睡着了。（结果）

She works very hard *though she is old*.

虽然她年纪大了，但她工作很努力。（让步）

I am taller *than he is*.

我比他高。（比较）

> **重点点拨**
>
> 状语的位置
>
> ★通常在句子基本结构之后，强调时放在句首。
>
> ★修饰形容词或副词时，通常位于被修饰的词之前。
>
> ★表示时间、地点、目的的状语一般位于句子两头，强调时放在句首，地点状语一般须在时间状语之前。
>
> ★一些表示不确定时间（如 often）或程度（如 almost）的副词状语通常位于 be 动词、助动词、情态动词之后，动词之前。

八、同位语（Appositive）

同位语是对句子中的主语、宾语或表语作出进一步的解释或说明。同位语与所修饰的成分处于语法上的同等地位，所以同位语不是修饰句子的主语（不同于定语）。同位语可以由名词、代词、数词、介词短语、同位语从句充当。例如：

This is my friend *Lily*.

这是我的朋友莉莉。（名词）

They *both* enjoy playing basketball.

他们俩都喜欢踢足球。（代词）

We *six* study in the same school.

我们 6 个在同一所学校上学。（数词）

This is the only one place left — *under the desk*.

这是唯一漏掉的地方——桌子下面。（介词短语）

The news *that he will come back* is true.

那个说他将会回来的消息是真的。（同位语从句）

易错盘点

一、句子唯一性原则

一个句子只能有一套主谓关系，当句子不能满足上述原则时，需要对句子进行以下处理。

1. 把其中一个谓语动词变成非谓语动词

如翻译句子：成功意味着要非常努力地工作。

该句中主语为 success，谓语为 mean，考虑到句子唯一性原则，将第二个谓语动词 work 处理为非谓语动词。即翻译为：Success means working very hard.

2. 对谓语动词进行某种关系化的处理

当一个主谓结构中出现不止一个谓语动词时，谓语动词间可以是某种并列关系，所以原则上必须有 N 减 1 个并列连词连接。例如：

She always calculated(and) measured (and) wrote and thought.

可以看到整个句子只有一个主谓结构，四个动词都是谓语，由三个 and 并列连接，叫并列谓语。一般情况下，前面的并列连词 and 可以省略，只留下最后一个 and，动词之间的并列关系不变。

3. 把其中一个句子变成另外句子的辅助或从属句关系，即变成主从复合句

例如：他坐在沙发上听音乐。

如翻译为：He sat on the sofa listen to music. 则违反了句子唯一性原则。所以我们将 listen to music 处理为伴随状态：He sat on the sofa listening to music.

再如翻译句子：我同意你刚才说的话。

应处理为主从复合句，翻译为：I agree with what you said just now.

二、句子成分分析

（一）五种基本句子结构

英语句子可以分为五种基本句型以及其扩大、组合、省略或倒装的句子。

1. S｜V(不及物动词)

The moon｜rose.

月亮升起了。

The universe｜remains.

宇宙长存。

注意：此结构中主语通常应当放置于句首，动词原形不能作主语。谓语通常跟在主语之后，必须是不及物动词(vi.)，后面可以跟副词、介词短语、状语从句等作状语。

2. S │ V(系动词) │ P

This │ is │ an English book. (n.)

这是一本英语书。

The breakfast │ smells │ good. (adj.)

早餐闻起来不错。

The problem │ is │ that they have no time to join our party. (表语从句)

麻烦的是他们没有时间来参加我们的派对。

注意：此结构中谓语动词是系动词，系动词因本身不能表达一个完整的意思，在后面须跟一个指明主语特征、状态、性质的表语构成复合谓语。

3. S │ V(及物动词) │ O

Who │ knows │ the answer?

谁知道答案？

He │ smiled │ his thanks.

他微笑地表示感谢。

He │ has agreed │ to help me.

他同意帮助我。

注意：此结构中谓语动词为及物动词(vt.)，该动作由主语发出，具有实际意义，但由于及物动词通常不能完整地表达意思，因此其后需要跟一个宾语，以此保证句子意思的完整性。宾语位于及物动词之后，构成宾语的代词必须是"代词宾格"，如：me, us, him, her, them 等。

4. S │ V(及物) │ InO(多指人) │ DO(多指物)

I │ ordered │ myself │ a new dress.

我给自己订了一条新连衣裙。

His grandmother │ cooked │ him │ a delicious meal.

他的祖母给他做了一顿美味的饭。

My sister │ brought │ me │ a novel.

我妹妹给我带来了一本小说。

注意：此结构中的及物动词可以跟两个宾语，一个为直接宾语(动作的承受者或结果，一般指物)，另一个为间接宾语(表示动作是为谁做的，一般指人)。

5. S │ V(及物) │ O(宾语) │ OC(宾补)

They │ painted │ the desk │ red.

他们把桌子漆成红色。

This │ set │ us │ thinking.

这使得我们要想一想。

I │ found │ the old building │ deserted.

我发现那幢旧楼无人居住。

注意：此结构中的动词是及物动词，但是由于只跟一个宾语不能完整地表达句子的意思，需要跟一个补充成分来补足宾语，以此来保证句子意思的完整性。

(二)定语和状语

英文中的句子不可能只用到基本句型的部分，大多数情况下句子除了基本句型的成分外，还会在这些成分的前面或后面添加修饰语(modifier)。修饰语既可以是单词(主要是形容词、副词和数词)，又可以是各种类型的短语(主要是介词短语、不定式短语和分词短语)。这些修饰语就是定语和状语。

I met my best friend Lily at the airport last night.　S | V | O

主 谓 定 宾 同位语 状

我昨晚在机场遇见了我最好的朋友莉莉。

She makes her mother angry.　S | V | O | OC

主 谓 定 宾 宾补

她惹她妈妈生气了。

小试牛刀

Analyze the following sentences and mark the names of the components.

1. She asked me to buy some food.

2. To catch the plane，we got up early.

3. My dream is to be a teacher in the future.

4. I have nothing to say on this topic.

5. The children were surprised.

学以致用

Ⅰ. **Choose the right words to fill into the blanks.**

Researchers have found that people who go to concerts，shows and museums can live longer than 1. _____ who do not. Experts from University College London have been examining the lifestyles of over 6,700 British people 2. _____ 15 years. They 3. _____ how often the people went out and what kinds of events they attended. They found that people over 50 years old 4. _____ regularly went to concerts were about 30 percent 5. _____ likely to die over the next 14 years. The researchers said the over-50s could extend their life 6. _____ engaging with the arts. In addition to living longer，concertgoers could also have more fun.

The UK Health Secretary Matt Hancock believes there could be a lot of 7. _____ in the research. He said the arts and culture could 8. _____ things like mental health，aging and loneli-ness. He 9. _____ announced plans for the UK's National Health Service to use the arts to help people live a healthier life. One researcher said，"Our results highlight the importance of 10. _____ to explore new social factors that affect our health."

A. studied	B. continuing	C. by	D. who	E. whose	F. improve
G. truth	H. ignored	I. recently	J. those	K. for	L. less

Ⅱ. Please mark and correct the 10 mistakes in the following passage.

I have been in college for 3 years. For the first time, I fail an Maths examination. I felt very sadly because Maths was one of my favorite subjects. My friends, Lily, tried to cheer me up, giving she full support to me. She listened to me careful and said to me, "Failure is the mother of success!" Then, with her encouragement, I felt more better and decided to try harder. In the following days, I am studied very hard and made great progresses. Encouragement is best way to help me feel better, face difficulties and moving on.	1. _____ 2. _____ 3. _____ 4. _____ 5. _____ 6. _____ 7. _____ 8. _____ 9. _____ 10. _____

Ⅲ. Translate the following sentences into Chinese.

1. His father bought him a new car as a reward last year.

2. His younger brother has wanted to be a soldier since he was a child.

3. My hometown is rich in sugar cane and is called "Sweet City".

4. The movie is so wonderful that I went to see it with my boyfriend yesterday.

5. Be careful what you say, for walls have ears.

6. He doesn't like to communicate with people, so that he has few friends.

7. Last week we had a survey on reading habits.

8. The Internet has changed our life, making our life more and more convenient and people closer and closer.

9. You can't always avoid difficulties in life, but you should face them bravely and try to solve them.

10. We need to consider not only the short-term interests of the school, but also the long-term development.

Ⅳ. Translate the following sentences into English.

1. 你的故事听起来很精彩。

2. 我认为这件衣服很贵。

3. 我不知道他昨天什么时候离开的家。

4. 她买了一件非常时髦的连衣裙。

5. 我的哥哥告诉了我如何使用这台相机。

6. 我把这本参考书推荐给了我所有的学生。

7. 他被选举为这个健康协会的负责人。

8. 吃是为了活着，但活着不是为了吃。

9. 你们这些学生请保持课堂的安静。

10. 你应当让你的父母了解你的想法。

第二节　句子的种类

重点知识概览

句子的种类重点知识概览

分类		构成	备注
按结构分类	简单句	主语＋谓语(S＋V)	可以有并列成分，如并列主语、并列谓语、并列宾语、并列定语。
		主语＋谓语＋宾语(S＋V＋O)	
		主语＋谓语＋宾语＋宾语补足语(S＋V＋O＋Oc)	
		主语＋谓语＋间接宾语＋直接宾语(S＋V＋Oi＋Od)	
		主语＋系动词＋表语(S＋V＋P)	
	并列句	并列连词连接两个分句	
	复合句	主句＋从句；从句＋主句	从句在前，主句在后，中间用逗号隔开
按功能分类	陈述句	肯定陈述句：主语＋谓语＋... 否定陈述句：主语＋助动词＋not＋...	
	疑问句	一般疑问句：助动词＋主语＋...？ 特殊疑问句：疑问词＋一般疑问句？ 选择疑问句： 一般疑问句(包括第一选项)＋or＋第二选项？ 特殊疑问句＋第一选项＋or＋第二选项？ 反义疑问句： 前肯定后否定：肯定的句子，助动词＋not＋主语？ 前否定后肯定：否定的句子，助动词＋主语？	否定的一般疑问句回答： Yes＋肯定陈述（不，……） No＋否定陈述（是的，……）
	感叹句	What＋a(n)＋形容词＋单数名词＋主语＋谓语！ What＋形容词＋复数名词＋主语＋谓语！ What＋形容词＋不可数名词＋主语＋谓语！ How＋形容词/副词＋主语＋谓语！ How＋形容词＋a(n)＋单数名词＋主语＋谓语！	
	祈使句	肯定的祈使句：以动词原形或 be 开头 否定的祈使句：以 don't，no 或 never 开头	祈使句并不是没有主语，而是省略掉了第二人称主语 you。

> 重点考查题型：选句填空、选词填空、短文改错、句子翻译

知识梳理

一、按结构分类

按句子结构可把句子可分为三类：简单句、并列句和复合句。

（一）简单句

简单句是指只包含一个主谓结构的句子。

I   love China ！   我爱中国！

主语   谓语

Today   is   a   fine   day.   今天真是好天气。

主语   谓语

简单句不包含从属子句，但可以有并列主语和并列谓语。

Lucy and Lily   are   twins.   露西和莉莉是双胞胎。

并列主语   谓语

The college   agreed and adopted   my   suggestion. 学校同意并采纳了我的意见。

     主语   并列谓语

Tom and Jerry   drink and eat   a lot every day. 汤姆和杰瑞每

并列主语   并列谓语

天都大吃大喝。

> **重点点拨**
>
> 简单句中的其他成分也可以有并列成分：
>
> We ate a lot of burgers and fries.（并列宾语）
>
> 我们吃了许多的汉堡和薯条。
>
> My mother is a hardworking and kind woman.（并列定语）
>
> 我的妈妈是一个勤劳和善良的女性。

（二）并列句

把两个或两个以上的简单句用并列连词连在一起构成的句子叫作并列句，其基本结构是"简单句＋并列连词＋简单句"。

英语并列句一般分为四类：联合并列句、选择并列句、因果并列句和转折并列句。

1. 联合并列句

联合并列句是指用 and，not only … but（also）…，neither … nor … 等连接词连接起来的具有同等关系的并列句。

My father is a lawyer and my mother is a teacher.

我的父亲是律师，而母亲是教师。

Not only the students but also their parents were invited.

不仅学生们被邀请，而且他们的父母也被邀请了。

Neither could Jenny help me nor could I help her at that time.

那时候珍妮帮不了我，我也帮不了她。

2. 选择并列句

选择并列句是指用 or，either … or … 等连接词连接起来的具有选择关系的并列句。如：

You can go home by yourself or you can ask your friend to go with you.

你可以一个人回家，也可以让朋友和你一起回去。

You can either go at once or wait till tonight.

你可以现在立刻就走，或者是等到晚上再走。

> **重点点拨**
>
> ★not only … but also … 使用时，前后两句话一般不能交换顺序，因为此句型重点在后半句。
>
> My father not only washed the car, but also polished it too. 我爸爸不仅冲洗了汽车，而且还给它抛了光。
>
> ★and使用时如不是表达同等关系，前后两句话不能交换顺序。
>
> She got up, and then she went to school. 她起床后，去了学校。

3. 因果并列句

因果并列句是指用 so，for，therefore 等连接词连接起来的具有因果关系的并列句。

You must be quick，for you are already late.

你必须快一点，因为你已经迟到了。

He studied hard so he got a job in Huawei.

他学习如此的努力，所以最后进入了华为工作。

He lost his pen；therefore he wrote with pencil.

他的钢笔丢了，所以他用铅笔写的。

4. 转折并列句

转折并列句是指用 but，yet，still，while，whereas 等连接词连接起来的具有转折关系的并列句。

It is raining but I must leave now.

现在正在下雨，但是我必须要走。

She wants to go，yet she feels obliged to stay.

她想走，但是她又觉得应该留下来。

This city is very comfortable；still I want to go back to my hometown.

这座城市很舒适，不过我还是想回到家乡。

While John's very good at study，his brother is good at singing.

约翰很擅长学习，而他的兄弟却擅长唱歌。

Some of the inspection results are positive，whereas others are not.

有一些检查结果还可以，有些则不太好。

> **重点点拨**
>
> ★while 和 whereas 使用时，前后两句话可以交换顺序。
>
> May prefers red while I prefer blue. 梅喜欢红色，而我喜欢蓝色。＝I prefer blue while May prefers red. 我喜欢蓝色，而梅喜欢红色。
>
> I live in Beijing whereas my sister lives in Shanghai. 我住在北京，我的妹妹却住在上海。＝My sister lives in Shanghai whereas I live in Beijing. 我的妹妹住在上海，而我却住在北京。

(三)复合句

复合句是指由一个主句和一个或一个以上的从句组成的句子。主句是复合句的主体，从句在复合句中充当某种成分，不能独立存在。复合句中的从句根据其在句子中的功能，可以分为：名词性从句、形容词性从句和副词性从句。

What you should do is to study hard instead of having daydream. （名词性从句）

你应该努力学习而不是白日做梦。

I can't find the pen which I bought yesterday. （形容词性从句）

我找不到昨天买的那支钢笔了。

He will not come to the party unless he is invited. （副词性从句）

除非他被邀请，否则他不会来参加派对。

二、按功能分类

(一)陈述句(Declarative Sentences)

陈述句用于陈述事实或表达说话人的看法，句末用句号。它可以分为肯定陈述句和否定陈述句，也就是肯定句和否定句。

1. 肯定陈述句（主语＋谓语）

I have been to Zhangjiajie twice.

我去过张家界两次。

The headmaster gave a speech to the freshmen yesterday.

昨天校长给新生们作了一次演讲。

2. 否定陈述句

(1)主语＋don't/doesn't/didn't＋实义动词/情态动词 have/has/had to.

I don't know where he is.

我不知道他在哪儿。

You don't have to work so late at night.

你没有必要晚上工作那么晚。

(2)主语＋be动词/助动词/其他情态动词＋not。

I am not good at dancing.

我不擅长跳舞。

She hasn't passed the final examination.

她没有通过期末考试。

(3)含有否定意义的词或短语，如：little，few，no，never，hardly，seldom，nothing，too … to …，not … at all，not any more/longer等。

These students have little interest in Maths.

这些学生对数学没什么兴趣。

Few people understand her choice.

很少有人理解她的选择。

She has never been abroad before.

她之前从没出过国。

We hardly know each other.

我们彼此还不太认识。

They seldom go to Grandma's house，because Grandma's house is in the suburbs.

他们很少去外婆家，因为外婆家在郊区。

> **重点点拨**
>
> ★there和here放在句首引导陈述句时，若主语是名词放在谓语动词之后。
>
> There are 50 students in my class. 我们班有50个学生。
>
> Here are some letters for you. 这里有一些信件给你。
>
> ★there和here放在句首引导陈述句时，若主语是代词放在谓语动词之前。
>
> Here he comes. 他来了。
>
> Here you are. 这些东西给你。

(二)疑问句(Interrogative Sentences)

疑问句是用来提问的句子，句末需要用问号。疑问句可分为：一般疑问句、特殊疑问句、选择疑问句和反义疑问句。

1. 一般疑问句(General Question)

一般疑问句是用来询问某人、某物或某事是否属实的问句，不带疑问词，通常可以用yes或no来回答，可分为肯定的一般疑问句和否定的一般疑问句。

(1)be动词＋主语＋表语(＋其他成分)?

—Is he in the classroom now? (肯定的一般疑问句)

—他现在在教室里吗？

—Yes，he is. / No，he isn't.

—是的，他在。/不，他不在。

(2)助动词/情态动词＋主语＋动词(＋其他成分)?

—Can you go home by yourself? (肯定的一般疑问句)

—你能自己回家吗？

—Yes，I can. /No，I can't.

—是的，我能。/不，我不能。

—Doesn't he work well? (否定的一般疑问句)

—他难道干得不好？

—Yes，he does. /No，he doesn't.

—不，他干得好。/是的，他干得不好。

> **重点点拨**
>
> ★肯定的一般疑问句回答方式：
>
> Yes＋肯定陈述(是的，……)
>
> No＋否定陈述(不，……)
>
> ★否定的一般疑问句回答方式：
>
> Yes＋肯定陈述(不，……)
>
> No＋否定陈述(是的，……)

2. 特殊疑问句（Special Question）

特殊疑问句是使用疑问词（what，which，who，whom，whose）或疑问副词（how，when，where，why）对句子中的某一部分进行提问。这种疑问句不能用 Yes 或 No 来回答，而应根据实际情况来进行回答。

(1)疑问词(作主语)＋动词＋其他成分？

—Which is my desk?

哪张是我的桌子？

—The one near the blackboard.

黑板旁边的那个。

(2)疑问词(作定语)＋主语＋动词＋其他成分？

—Whose desk is it?

这个书包是谁的？

—It's mine.

这个书包是我的。

(3)疑问词＋一般疑问句？

—When will you have your summer holiday?

你什么时候放暑假？

—Next month.

下个月。

3. 选择疑问句（Alternative Question）

选择疑问句是询问客观实事或主观意愿，并提出两种或两种以上的情况供选择，通常用连词 or 引出后一个选项。选择疑问句应根据实际情况进行选择并回答，不能用 Yes 或 No 回答。

(1)一般疑问句(包括第一选项)＋or＋第二选项？

—Is this woman your mother or your aunt?

这个女士是你妈妈还是你姨母？

—She is my mother.

她是我妈妈。

(2)特殊疑问句＋第一选项＋or＋第二选项？

—Which do you prefer, red or yellow?

你更喜欢红色还是黄色？

—I prefer red.

我更喜欢红色。

4. 反义疑问句（Disjunctive Question）

反义疑问句是在陈述句后面附加一个问句，对前述事实或观点提出质疑、强调或求证。

(1)前肯定后否定。

肯定的句子，助动词/be＋not＋主语？

You had your meal，didn't you?

你吃过饭了，不是吗？

Mr. Lee left home this morning，didn't he?

李先生今天早上离开家了，不是吗？

(2)前否定后肯定。

否定的句子，助动词/be＋主语？

He did not cry，did he?

他没有哭，是吗？

His teacher isn't angry with him, is he?

他的老师没有生他的气，是吗？

(三)感叹句

感叹句通常用来表示赞美、惊叹，有时候也可以表示喜悦和遗憾等比较强烈的情感，通常以 what 或 how 开头，句末用感叹号。

1. What 开头的感叹句

(1)What＋a(n)＋形容词＋单数名词＋主语＋谓语!

What a fashionable girl your sister is!

你的妹妹是个多么时髦的女孩子啊！

What an honest kid he is!

他真是个诚实的小孩儿！

(2)What＋形容词＋复数名词＋主语＋谓语!

What good students they are!

他们是多么好的学生啊！

(3)What＋形容词＋不可数名词＋主语＋谓语!

What good weather it is!

天气真好啊！

2. How 开头的感叹句

(1)How＋主语＋谓语!

How time flies!

时光飞逝！

(2)How＋形容词/副词＋主语＋谓语!

How well she plays the dulcimer!

她的扬琴弹得真好啊！

(3)How＋形容词＋a(n)＋单数名词＋主语＋谓语!

How interesting a person he is!

他真是个有趣的人！

(四)祈使句

祈使句通常用来表达请求、命令、建议、劝告、警告和叮嘱等，主要包括以动词原形开头的祈使句和以 let 开头的祈使句。

1. 肯定的祈使句

(1)以动词原形开头

Go out!

出去！

Clean your desk! 把你的课桌擦干净！

(2)以 be 开头

Be a man!

做个男人！

Be careful!

小心啊！

2. 否定的祈使句

(1)以 don't 开头

重点点拨

★前肯定后否定：

Yes＋肯定陈述（是的，……）

No＋否定陈述（不，……）

—You did finish your work, didn't you?

—Yes, I did. /No, I didn't.

—你完成了你的工作，不是吗？

—是的，我完成了。/不，我没有完成。

★前否定后肯定：

Yes＋肯定陈述（不，……）

No＋否定陈述（是的，……）

—You didn't finish your work, did you?

—Yes, I did. /No, I didn't.

—你没完成你的工作，是吗？

—不，我完成了。/是的，我没有完成。

重点点拨

★祈使句不是没有主语，而是省略掉了第二人称主语 you。

Go out! 出去！＝You go out! 你出去！

★真正没有主语的句子应该为 there be 句型。

There will be a press conference.

这里将有一场新闻发布会。

Don't go out!

别出去!

Don't cry!

别哭!

(2)以 no 开头

No smoking!

禁止吸烟!

No littering!

禁止乱扔废弃物!

(3)以 never 开头

Never be a liar!

永远不要说谎!

易错盘点

一、句子结构中的易混词

1. yet 和 but 的区别

yet 的转折更强烈,使用时前面通常加逗号,而 but 前的逗号可以省略。

He wants to leave, yet he feel obliged to stay.

He wants to leave but he feel obliged to stay.

2. for 和 because 的区别

Because 可以放在句首,前面不需要加逗号,同时 because 可以用于否定句;for 通常不能放在句首,而且它的前面要加逗号,同时 for 不能用于否定句。

(误)For I liked the color I bought them all.

→Because I liked the color, I bought them all.

因为我喜欢这个颜色,所以我把它们都买了。

→I bought them all, for I liked the color.

因为我喜欢这个颜色,所以我把它们都买了。

(误)For I liked the color I bought them all.

→I bought them all not because I liked the color.

我把它们都买了并不是因为我喜欢这个颜色。

3. so 和 therefore 的区别

therefore 的用于表示"为此、所以、因此",作副词而不是连词,引导结果、结局或结论;so 可以是副词(意为"如此、这样")、连词(意为"因此、所以")或代词和名词。

so 前面一般要用逗号,therefore 前面用分号;so 和 therefore 通常可以和 and 连用,并且用逗号把它们和前面的句子隔开。

therefore 比 so 更正式,侧重符合逻辑的结果,so 强调根据某种原因而得出的结果。

The apartment house was being rebuilt; therefore they had to rent a new one.

The apartment house was being rebuilt; and therefore they had to rent a new one.

公寓正在被重建,因此他们不得不租一个新的。

The conference starts at 8:00, so we can go there at 7:30.

The conference starts at 8:00, and so we can go there at 7:30.

会议 8 点开始,所以我们可以 7 点半到那里。

二、There be 句型

There be 句型是一种表示"存在"的特殊句型，属倒装结构。主要结构为"There ＋be 动词＋名词词组（＋修辞语）"。其中 there 是引导词，没有词义；主语是 be 后面的名词，be 是谓语动词。句型的否定句构成方式是将否定副词 not 放在 be 之后。

There is a sofa in my bedroom.

我的卧室里有一个沙发。

There aren't any exercise books on your desk.

你的课桌上没有任何作业本。

There be 句型的一般疑问句是将 be 放在主语 there 之前，回答时用 Yes 或 No，后接简单答语。

Is there a bunch of flowers in the vase?

花瓶里有一束花吗？

Yes，there is. / No，there isn't.

是，有。/ 不，没有。

Will there be a meeting tonight?

今晚有会吗？

Yes，there will. / No，there won't.

是的，有。/ 不，没有。

There be 句型的特殊疑问句主要有 how many 和 how much 做引导词两种情况。

How many students are there in your school?

你们学校有多少学生？

How much water is there in your kettle?

你的水壶里有多少水？

> **重点点拨**
>
> ★There be 句型中的 be 应和其后出现的补充语在单复数上保持一致，即"就近原则"。
>
> There are some oranges on the plate. 盘子里有一些橘子。
>
> There are five pens, two pencils and a ruler in the pencil-box. 文具盒里有五支钢笔，两支铅笔和一把尺子。
>
> ★如果主语是复数名词，表示一笔金额或一个总数或表达一个单个概念时，则仍用单数 be 形式。
>
> There is five hundred *yuan* to pay. 我们要付 500 元。
>
> There is still another 20 miles to go. 还有 20 英里要走。

小试牛刀

Combine each pair of sentences into one sentence using a proper conjunction.

1. Your nose is bleeding. You'd better lie down immediately.

2. Leo could not read. Leo could not write.

3. You can travel by car. You can travel by plane.

4. Time goes on. It's getting warmer and warmer.

5. He works as hard as others. He is in poor health.

6. The nurse could not decide what to do. She asked the doctor for advice.

7. The tourist lost his way. He had to ask the way.

8. You know the rules traffic. You will be able to pass the examination.

9. Get up quickly. You will be late for school.

10. The doctor went into the clinic. The doctor began to work.

学以致用

Ⅰ. **Choose the best answer from the four choices A, B, C and D.**

1. They didn't go to bed _____ the work was finished.

A. when　　　　　B. while　　　　　C. until　　　　　D. after

2. She was _____ delighted _____ she jumped up and down.

A. too; to　　　　B. enough; to　　　　C. as; as　　　　D. so; that

3. Our parents love you very much _____ they seldom say "I love you."

A. unless　　　　B. or　　　　　C. so　　　　　D. although

4. Life is like a mirror. _____ you smile at it, it will smile back.

A. Unless　　　　B. When　　　　C. Until　　　　D. Though

5. I don't know _____ he will come or not this afternoon.

A. if　　　　　B. when　　　　C. whether　　　　D. that

6. Angela didn't go to bed _____ her parents came home last night.

A. as soon as　　B. if　　　　　C. while　　　　D. until

7. WeChat Pay makes our life convenient. We can buy things _____ we only take a mobile phone with us.

A. unless　　　　B. because　　　　C. even if　　　　D. so that

8. I didn't accept other one's help _____ I believe I can do it by my own hands.

A. because　　　　B. though　　　　C. until　　　　D. unless

9. —What have you learned after five years' study in this school?

—I was taught _____ knowledge _____ good manners.

A. either; or　　　B. not only; but also　　C. neither; nor　　　D. not; but

10. We'll stay at home _____ it rains tomorrow.

A. and　　　　　B. if　　　　　C. but　　　　　D. so

11. —What was your brother doing at this time yesterday?

—He was watching TV _____ I was doing my homework.

A. as soon as　　B. after　　　　C. until　　　　D. while

12. The teacher asked me to run fast _____ I could keep up with the team.

A. so that　　　B. for　　　　C. because　　　　D. in order to

13. They spoke _____ quietly _____ I could hardly hear them.

A. such; that　　B. so; that　　　C. neither; nor　　　D. both; and

14. People in China were deeply hurt _____ seeing Giant pandas didn't live well in other countries.

A. when　　　　B. while　　　　C. before　　　　D. since

15. The little boy is _____ young _____ he can't go to school.

A. enough; to　　B. too; to　　　C. so; that　　　D. such; that

16. _____ many kids like fried chicken, I think they'd better try not to eat it too often.

A. Because　　　B. When　　　C. Although　　　D. If

17. Mary, put on your coat, _____ you'll catch a cold.

A. and　　　　　B. or　　　　　C. so　　　　　D. but

18. —How do you like the two pairs of shorts?

—They don't fit me well. They are _____ too long _____ too short.

A. not only; but also　　B. both; and　　　C. neither; nor　　　D. either; or

19. —I want to be a teacher when I grow up.

—Work hard, _____ your dream will come true.

A. or　　　　　B. but　　　　C. though　　　　D. and

20. —I hear Susan will go to Xinjiang alone.

   —That's true. _____ her father _____ her mother will go with her.

   A. Both；and   B. Either；or   C. Neither；nor   D. Not only；but also

Ⅱ. Please mark and correct the 10 mistakes in the following passage.

In our life，we often regret what we did and what we couldn't did. Actually，it doesn't benefit us at all. As for most of us，we missed much chances to earn more money，to get a high position and to realize our dreams. We often regret that we don't seize those opportunities，thus feeling upset. Although we do know regretting the past is of no benefit，so we still shouldn't help doing it. To avoid the problem above we need to pay more attention to who you are doing now，making us busier and having no time to recall the past. However，we'd better to set reasonable goals one by one. Only by doing so must we struggle for our future better.	1. _____ 2. _____ 3. _____ 4. _____ 5. _____ 6. _____ 7. _____ 8. _____ 9. _____ 10. _____

Ⅲ. Translate the following sentences into English.

1. 他不仅洗了衣服，而且还打扫了房间。

2. 我和他都不喜欢这首歌。

3. 她不是喝醉了就是疯了。

4. 我的房间很小，但是很舒服。

5. 他在学校工作还是在医院工作？

6. 我起得早，但我哥哥起得晚。

7. 坚持你的梦想，否则有一天你会后悔的。

8. 他大学毕业后不久就开始做这份工作。

9. 如果有人打电话，告诉他们我不在。

10. 我们使用计算机是为了节约时间。

模块二　重点语法梳理

第一章

时　态

重点知识概览

时态重点知识概览

时体	类别	谓语	备注
过去时	一般过去时	过去式	注意不规则动词的过去式形式。
	过去进行时	was/were + v.ing	重读闭音节结尾的动词后双写最后一个辅音字母,再加"ing"
	过去完成时	had + v.ed	"过去的过去"用过去完成时
	过去完成进行时	had been + v.ing	
现在时	一般现在时	动词原形或 v.+s/es	表示客观事实和普遍真理时,永远都用一般现在时。
	现在进行时	am/is/ are + v.ing	
	现在完成时	have/has+v.ed	注意区分"have been to …"和"have gone to …"
	现在完成进行时	have/has been+v.ing	
将来时	一般将来时	will / shall + v.	shall 用于第一人称
		be going to +v.	
		be to +v.	按计划要做的事,一般不更改
		be about to+v.	强调最近的将来
	过去将来时	would/ should + v. was/were going to +v.	
	一般将来进行时	shall / will　be + v.ing	
	将来完成时	shall/will+have + v.ed	常用时间状语"by+将来的时间"

📖 **知识梳理**

时态分类

英语时态是用来表示动作发生的时间和状态的语法形式。英语时态主要分为三大类：过去时、现在时和将来时。每一大类时态又可以细分为四种：一般时、进行时、完成时和完成进行时。

过去时：表示过去某个时间发生的动作或状态。

现在时：表示现在正在发生或常态发生的动作或状态。

将来时：表示将来某个时间将要发生的动作或状态。

还有一些衍生出来的时态。

过去将来时：表示过去某个时间将会发生的动作。

现在完成进行时：表示从过去某个时间开始，一直持续到现在，并且有可能继续持续下去的动作或状态。

过去完成进行时：表示过去某个时间一直在进行，直到另一个过去的时间点停止的动作。

一、过去时(Past Tense)

过去时用来表示过去某个时间发生的动作或存在的状态。根据动作的完成程度，过去时又可以分为一般过去时(Simple Past Tense)、过去进行时(Past Continuous Tense)、过去完成时(Past Perfect Tense)和过去完成进行时(Past Perfect Continuous Tense)。

1. 一般过去时(Simple Past tense)

一般过去时表示过去某个时间点发生的动作或状态，通常通过动词的过去式来体现。动词的过去式有规则和不规则之分，对于规则动词，通常在词尾加上 ed 来构成过去式(例如：walk → walked)；对于不规则动词，则需要记忆其特殊的过去式形式(例如：go → went，see → saw)。除 be 动词以外，其余动词没有人称和数的变化。

规则动词的过去式的变化规则如下(不规则动词的过去式则需要特殊记忆)：

· 直接＋ed：work → worked，start → started

· 以 e 结尾的动词，直接加 d：smile → smiled；skate → skated

· 以辅音字母＋元音字母再加辅音字母(除 r、y、x 外)结尾的重读闭音节，双写最后一个辅音字母再加 ed：stop → stopped；plan → planned

· 以 y 结尾的情况：

元音字母＋y 结尾的动词，直接加 ed：employ → employed；enjoy → enjoyed。

辅音字母＋y 结尾的动词，变 y 为 i，再加 ed：try → tried；study → studied。

一般过去时的用法归纳如下。

(1)一般过去时表示过去的动作或状态，常与表过去的时间状语连用，如 yesterday，last week/month，the day before yesterday，in 1999 等，或与 when，before，after 等连词引导的状语从句连用。

The museum was closed last night.

博物馆昨晚关闭了。

He was a teacher before he became a writer.

他成为作家之前是一名教师。

He lived in Beijing in 2018.

他 2018 年住在北京。

重点点拨

一般过去时表虚拟的动作。

表示与现在事实相反或表示对将来事态的主观设想。

例如：I wish you were healthy. (我希望你健康。)

例如：I'd rather you went right now. (我宁愿你现在就走。)

例如：If I were you, I would go with him. (如果我是你的话，我会和他一起去。)

---

(2)表示过去一段时间内经常或反复发生的动作。

My father often went fishing when he was a child.

我父亲小时候经常去钓鱼。

I visited my grandparents every other week last year.

去年我每隔一星期就去拜访我的祖父母。

(3)表示发生在过去的连续动作。

He got up at five, washed his face, brushed his teeth, and then had breakfast.

他5点起床，然后洗脸、刷牙，再吃早餐。

She tried all the chairs but chose the smallest one because it had the softest cushion.

她挑遍了所有的椅子，最后找了个最小的坐下，因为那上面有最柔软的垫子。

2. 过去进行时(Past Continuous Tense)

表示过去某一时刻或某一阶段正在进行或发生的动作。过去进行时通常由"was/were ＋ 动词的现在分词"构成。过去进行时的用法主要有以下几种。

(1)表示过去某一时刻正在进行或发生的动作。

We were playing volleyball at nine o'clock yesterday morning.

我们昨天上午9点在打网球。

I was washing my clothes at this time yesterday.

昨天这个时候我正在洗衣服。

(2)表示过去某阶段持续进行的动作。

I was staying at home last week.

我上周一直待在家。

(3)常与过去某一特定的时间状语连用，如 last night，at that time，at 7：00，yesterday，last month，at this time yesterday，from 8 to 10 last night 等。

> **重点点拨**
>
> 在含有 when/while 引导的时间状语从句的复合句中，若主要动作和背景动作是同时发生的，那么主从句都可用过去进行时。
>
> 例如：Jenny was reading while Danny was writing. (当杰妮在读书时，丹妮在写东西。)

有些句子中有时没有时间状语，要通过上下文的提示来确定用过去进行时。

The students all worked hard. Everyone knew what he was studying for.

学生们学习都非常努力，每个人都知道自己为什么而学。

(4)表示过去将来时间里的动作，通常仅限于趋向性动词。

He wanted to know when they were leaving for Shanghai.

他想知道他们什么时候去上海。

(5)过去进行时用来描述故事发生的背景。

It was late at night. The wind was blowing and rain was falling heavily. There was a little girl standing at the corner of the street.

夜深了。风刮得很大，雨下得很大。有　个小女孩站在街道拐角处。

3. 过去完成时(Past Perfect Tense)

过去完成时既可表示过去某个时间或动作之前所发生的事情(常用的时间状语有 already，before，ever，just，never，still，yet)，也可表示过去某个时间或动作之前所发生的动作一直持续到过去某个时间(常接时间状语：since ＋时间点，for ＋ 时间段，by the time ＋过去的时间)。

When he got to the railway station, the train had left.

当他到达火车站时，火车已经开走了。

We had learnt ten lessons by last week.

到上周为止，我们学完了10篇课文。

He had stayed here for three days before he left.

他走之前在这儿待了 3 天。

She said that she had lived there since she was five.

她说她 5 岁起就住在那儿了。

By the time they arrived，we had already left.

他们到达时，我们已经离开了。

(1)过去完成时的谓语结构

过去完成时由"had ＋ 动词的过去分词"构成。其中，规则动词的过去分词与之前过去式的变化规则相同，不规则动词的过去分词则需要特殊记忆。

(2)过去完成时的用法

与过去完成时连用的时间状语可以多种多样，使用它的主要依据是看其是否发生在"过去的过去"。

I had learnt some French before I came here.

在来这儿之前我学过一些法语。

He had written five stories by the end of last month.

到上月月底他已经写了 5 篇故事。

We had cleaned the house when he arrived there.

当他到那儿时，我们已经把房子弄干净了。

He went home after he had finished his work.

他把事做完之后，就回家了。

注意：当主句与由 before，after，as soon as 等所引导的时间状语从句的动作连接很紧密时，从句也可用一般过去时。

He went there after he read the letter.

他看了那封信后就去那儿了。

(3)过去完成时还经常用于主句是过去时的宾语从句中。

He said he had ever been a soldier.

他说他当过兵。

They said they had seen the film already.

他们说他们已经看过这部电影了。

(4)在 hardly / scarcely…when…，no sooner…than… 的结构中的主句通常要用过去完成时，并使用部分倒装。

Hardly had I told her the news when she began to cry out.

她一听到这一消息就大哭了起来。

Scarcely had he finished dinner when he went out.

他一吃完晚饭就出去了。

No sooner had the child fallen asleep than he lay down on the bed.

这个小孩一躺到床上就睡着了。

(5)过去完成时还经常用于条件状语从句或 I wish …，I'd rather…后的宾语从句，表示与事实不符的情况。

I wish I had gone with you to the theatre.

我希望我和你去了剧院的。

I wish you had done a favor.

重点点拨

动词 expect，hope，suppose，think，want，mean 等的过去完成时可用来表示未实现的计划、打算或希望。

例如：I had hoped to see you. 我本希望来看你的。

例如：He had wanted to buy a house in Hangzhou. 他本想在杭州买套房子。

我希望你做了件好事。

I'd rather you had told me the truth.

我宁愿你告诉了我事实。

If you had known that you were very busy, I would not have

called you.

如果我知道你很忙，我就不打电话给你了。

4. 过去完成进行时(Past Perfect Continuous Tense)

过去完成进行时是英语语法中的一种复合时态。它结合了过去完成时和进行时的形式，用来表示在过去某一时间点之前一直在进行的动作或状态。过去完成进行时的结构为：had been ＋ 动词的现在分词形式。下面是过去完成进行时的用法归纳。

(1)表示过去某一时刻之前一直持续的动作。

We had been waiting for over three hours when the concert finally began.

当音乐会终于开始时，我们已经等了3个多小时了。

(2)表示过去某一时刻之前一直存在的状态。

She had been living in London for five years before she moved

back to Shanghai.

她在回到上海之前已经在伦敦住了5年了。

(3)用于某些状语从句中，表示在过去某一时间点之前一直在进行的动作或状态。

I was tired because I had been climbing the mountain all morn-

ing.

我累了，因为我整个上午一直在爬山。

(4)用于强调过去某一时间点之前与之相比更晚或更长的动作或状态。

> **重点点拨**
>
> ★在使用过去完成进行时时，应注意以下两点。
>
> 1. 过去完成进行时的结构为：had been ＋ 现在分词形式。
>
> 2. 它表示的动作一定是发生在"过去的过去"。

He had been doing his homework for three hours when his mother told him it was time for bed.

他妈妈告诉他是睡觉时间时，他已经做了3个小时的作业了。

(5)用于与过去完成时形式相连的时间段，表示该时间段内一直持续的动作或状态。

By the time I arrived, he had been waiting for me for three hours.

当我到达时，他已经等我3个小时了。

总之，过去完成进行时是一种复合时态，它主要用来表示在过去某一时间点之前一直在进行的动作或状态。正确使用过去完成进行时可以让我们的英语表达更准确、更生动。

二、现在时(Present Tense)

现在时是英语中的一种基本时态，用来描述现在正在发生或存在的动作或状态。它也可以用来描述习惯性动作或普遍真理。现在时分为一般现在时(Simple Present Tense)、现在进行时(Present Continuous Tense)、现在完成时(Present Perfect Tense)和现在完成进行时(Present Perfect Continuous Tense)四种。

1. 一般现在时(Simple Present Tense)

一般现在时用来描述习惯性动作、经常发生的事情、普遍真理或状态等。它的谓语构成主要有两种形式：动词的原形或第三人称单数形式。动词的第三人称单数形式的构成规则如表2-1-1。

表 2-1-1　动词第三人称单数变化规则表

规则	原形	第三人称单数形式
1. 一般情况下直接在动词词尾＋s	wait enjoy	waits enjoys
2. 以 s，x，sh，ch，o 结尾的动词，在词尾＋es	guess fix wash watch go 和 do	guesses fixes washes watches goes 和 does
3. 以辅音字母＋y 结尾的动词，先变 y 为 i，再加 es	study try carry	studies tries carries
4. 不规则动词(特殊情况)	have be	has is

一般现在时主要有以下几种用法。

(1)表示经常性或习惯性的动作，常与 always，usually，regularly，every morning/night/evening/day/week，often，sometimes，occasionally，from time to time，twice a week，rarely，seldom，hardly ever，never 等表示频度的时间状语连用。

I leave home for school at 7 every morning.

我每天早上 7 点去上学。

He usually goes to work by subway.

他通常坐地铁上班。

(2)表示主语具备的性格、能力和特征。

My brother likes collecting stamps.

我哥哥喜欢集邮。

We are Chinese，and we love our great motherland very much.

我们都是中国人，我们非常热爱我们伟大的祖国。

(3)表示现在的状态。

I'm in the library now，and he is at home.

我现在在图书馆，他在家。

(4)表示客观事实和普遍真理。

The sun rises from the east.

太阳从东方升起。

Shanghai lies in the east of China.

上海位于中国的东部。

Two plus three makes/is five.

2 加 3 等于 5。

(5)在时间状语从句和条件状语从句中，常用一般现在时表将来的动作，而主句通常用将来时，即"主将从现"。

As soon as I see him，I'll tell him the good news.

我一见到他，就会把这个好消息告诉他。

If it doesn't rain tomorrow，we'll go to the countryside.

重点点拨

★一般现在时常用于格言或警句中。

例如：Pride goes before a fall. 骄者必败。

★注意：此用法如果出现在宾语从句中，即使主句是过去时，从句谓语也要用一般现在时。

例如：Columbus proved that the earth is round.（哥伦布证实了地球是圆的。）

如果明日不下雨，我们将去乡下。

(6)表示预先计划或安排好的行为。

We leave very soon.

我们很快就会离开。

The ship starts at 5 o'clock in the morning.

船在早上 5 点出发。

(7)一些表示状态和感觉的动词表示现在发生的具体行为时，只用一般现在时，而不用进行时态。

I feel a little tired now.

我现在感觉有点儿累。

2. 现在进行时(Present Continuous Tense)

现在进行时用来描述正在进行的动作或当前阶段的暂时性状态。它的谓语构成："am/is/are ＋ 动词的现在分词"。现在分词的构成规则如表 2-1-2。

表 2-1-2　现在分词的构成规则

规则	原形	现在分词形式
1. 一般情况直接在动词词尾加 ing	wait enjoy	waiting enjoying
2. 以不发音的字母 e 结尾的动词，先去 e，再加 ing	take ride come	taking riding coming
3. 以重读闭音节结尾的动词，中间只有一个元音字母，词尾只有一个辅音字母，应双写末尾的辅音字母，再加 ing	put begin stop	putting beginning stopping
4. 以 ie 结尾的动词，把 ie 变成 y 再加 ing	die tie lie	dying tying lying

现在进行时的基本用法如下。

(1)表示说话时正在进行的动作，常和 now 连用，有时用一个动词如 look(看)、listen(听)来表示 now(现在)这一时间概念。

Look! A train is coming.

看！火车来了。

Listen! He is playing the piano.

听！他在弹钢琴。

(2)表示现阶段正在进行的动作，但不一定是说话时正在进行的，常和 at present(目前)，this week(本星期)，these days(这几天)，constantly/ continually(不断地)等时间状语连用。

What lesson are you studying this week?

你们本星期学哪一课了？（说话时并不在学）

He is constantly complaining about the poor condition.

他不断地抱怨条件太差。

(3)现在进行时有时可用来表示最近按计划或安排要进行的动作，这时一般要与表示将来的时间状语连用，而且仅限于少量趋向性动词。例如：go，come，leave，start，arrive，return，sleep 等。

Are you going to Tianjin tomorrow?

你明天要去天津吗？

He is arriving at ten this evening.

他今晚 10 点到。

3. 现在完成时(Present Perfect Tense)

现在完成时用来描述过去发生的动作对现在造成的影响或结果,或者是由过去开始一直持续到现在的动作。它的谓语构成是"have/has ＋ 动词的过去分词"。其主要用法如下。

(1)表示动作发生在过去某个不确定的时间,对现在造成的某种影响和结果。常被 just,already(用于肯定句中),yet(用于否定句和疑问句中)before,up to now,so far,the past few years 等副词或时间状语连用。

—Have you had breakfast yet?

—Yes,I have. I've just had it.

——你吃过早饭了吗?——是的,我刚刚吃过。

This is one of the most interesting novels that he has ever written.

这是他写过的最有趣的小说之一。

(2)表示从过去某一时刻开始一直持续到现在的动作或状态。这个动作可能刚停止,也有可能仍然在进行,常带有 for 和 since 等表示一段时间的状语。

He has taught here since 1989.

他自 1989 年就在这儿教书。

I haven't seen her for several years.

我已经有几年没见过她了。

但是,像 come,arrive,buy 等终止性动词或短暂性动词不能与表示"一段时间"的状语连用,终止性动词/短暂性动词必须改为延续性动词来表述。现归纳总结一下由终止性动词/短暂性动词到延续性动词的转换。

arrive → be here/in	begin(start) → be on	die → be dead
come back → be back	leave → be away	begin to study → study
buy → have	get to know → know	go out → be out
finish → be over	put on → wear/be on	open → be open
borrow → keep	close → be closed	join → be in / be a member of…
catch a cold → have a cold	fall ill(sick, asleep) → be ill(sick, asleep)	

He has been a soldier for five years.

他当兵 5 年了。

His mother has been dead for two years.

他的母亲去世 2 年了。

The concert has been on for ten minutes.

音乐会开始 10 分钟了。

The play has been over for half an hour.

这部戏已经结束半小时了。

> **重点点拨**
> ★ 只有在时间状语是 since 和 for 的现在完成时的肯定句中,才考虑动词的延续性。如果是否定句,则无须转换。如:They haven't seen each other for years.(他们已经好几年没见过面了。)

(3)表示说话前发生过一次或多次的动作,现在成为一种经验,一般译为汉语"过",常与 twice,three times,ever,never 等时间状语连用。

I have been to the Great Wall twice.

我去过长城两次。

This is the first time he has come to China.

这是他第一次来中国。

(4)拓展延伸：have/has been(to)与 have/has gone(to)的区别如下。

have been(to)表"去过某地(现在已经回来了)"，可用于各种人称；通常可与表次数的词连用。

have gone(to)表"去某地了(说话时某人不在当地)"，常用于第三人称。

They have been to Beijing twice.

他们去过北京两次。

His father has gone to HK.

他父亲去香港了。(现在还在香港，未回)

4. 现在完成进行时(Present Perfect Continuous Tense)

现在完成进行时用来描述从过去开始一直持续到现在的动作，并且可能还要继续下去。它的谓语构成是"have/has been ＋ 动词的现在分词"。

现在完成进行时的基本句型：

肯定式	I/We have been working.
疑问式	Have you been working?
简略回答	Yes，I/we have. No，I/we haven't.
肯定式	He/She/It has been working.
疑问式	Has he/she/it been working?
简略回答	Yes，he/she/it has. No，he/she/it hasn't.

现在完成进行时的用法：

(1)强调动作还未结束，还要继续下去。

I've been reading this story for two days, but I haven't finished it.

这个故事我已读了两天了，但我还没读完。

How long have you been learning dancing?

你学跳舞多长时间了？

(2)强调长时间的延续的动作或表达某种感情色彩。

She has always been working like that.

她一贯是这样工作的。

(3)现在完成进行时也可表示现在以前一段时间内反复发生的事情。

The couple has been searching for their lost son for past three years.

这对夫妻在过去的 3 年里一直在寻找他们丢失的孩子。

> **重点点拨**
> ★有些不能用于现在进行时的动词如 be，have，know，see，love，hear 等，同样不能用于现在完成进行时，只能用现在完成时。
> 例如：He has been ill for a week. 他生病一星期了。
> I have loved you since I met you for the first time. 自从我第一次见到你我就爱上你了。

三、将来时(Future Tense)

表示将来某个时间将要发生的动作或状态。将来时主要分为一般将来时(Simple Future Tense)、过去将来时(Past Future Tense)、将来进行时(Future Continuous Tense)和将来完成时(Future Perfect Tense)。

1. 一般将来时(Simple Future Tense)

一般将来时用来表示将来某一时刻的动作或状态，或将来某一时间内经常发生的动作或状态。谓语结构是："will(各种人称) / shall(第一人称) ＋ 动词原形"。一般将来时的用法有如下几种。

(1)表示将来的动作或状态，常与表将来的时间状语连用，如 tomorrow，next week，in three days，in the future 等。

We shall have a lot of snow next month.

下个月将有大量降雪。

I guess he will pass the exam this time.

我想他这次考试会及格的。

(2)用"be going to do"表打算和预测。

I'm going to stay here for a week.

我准备在这里待一星期。（表打算）

I'm afraid he is going to lose the game this time.

恐怕他这次比赛会输。（表预测）

注意：be going to 后如果接动词 go 和 come 时，通常用现在进行时表将来。

Where are you going?

你打算到哪里去?

(3)用"be to do"表示按计划或安排即将要发生的动作；有时也表示命令、禁止或可能性。

We are to leave for Hangzhou tomorrow.

我们决定明天去杭州。

Tell her she is not to be back late.

告诉她不准晚归。

(4)用"be about to＋动词原形"表示即将要发生的事。

He is about to leave.

他马上要走了。

Be quiet，everyone. The film is about to start.

请安静，电影马上要开始了。

注意：此结构通常不与具体的时间状语连用。

He is about to leave soon.（正）

He is about to leave tomorrow.（误）

(5)用"be due to do"表示按计划或时间表将要发生某事。

The train is due to arrive at ten.

火车 10 点钟到站。

His book is due to be published in February.

他的书计划 2 月出版。

2. 过去将来时（Past Future Tense）

过去将来时与一般将来时的用法相同，只是过去将来时必须以"过去"为起点，而一般将来时以"现在"为起点。

(1)过去将来时常用于宾语从句中。

He said he was going to accompany her abroad.

他说他将陪她出国。

They wanted to know who would attend the important conference.

他们想知道谁将出席这次重要会议。

(2)过去将来时可用"would＋do""was/were going to do""was/were ＋ doing""was/were to do""was/were about to ＋do"等结构表示。

She didn't watch the movie, because she was playing the piano in the afternoon.

由于下午她要弹钢琴，她没去看电影。

3. 将来进行时（Future Continuous Tense）

将来进行时表示将来某一时刻或某一时段正在进行的动作或存在的状态。将来进行时由助动词 shall/will＋ be doing 构成。其用法如下。

> **重点点拨**
>
> ★在表示时间、条件等的状语从句以及某些名词性从句、定语从句等中，通常用一般现在时表示将来的意义。
>
> 例如：If I'm free tomorrow, I'll go to visit my teacher. 如果我明天有空，我会去拜访我的老师。
>
> 例如：As soon as he gets to the classroom tomorrow, he will return you the book. 明天他一到教室就会还你书。

(1)表示在将来某一时刻或某段时间正在进行的动作。

I shall be doing morning exercises at 7：00 tomorrow morning.

明天早上 7 点我会做早操。

(2)表示将来被客观情况所决定的动作或按照安排将要发生的动作。

I'll be having breakfast at seven o'clock in the morning.

早上 7 点我会在吃早饭。

She will be washing all evening.

整个晚上她都会在洗东西。

(3)表示对将来的预测。

You will be feeling hungry after all that exercise.

锻炼过后，你会感到饥饿。

I'll be seeing you in the evening.

我晚上来找你。

Will you be taking your vacation in Yunnan?

你会在云南休假吗?

4. 将来完成时(Future Perfect Tense)

将来完成时表示将来某个时间之前已经发生或完成的动作。将来完成时由 shall(第一人称)或 will (第二、三人称)＋ have done 组成。其用法如下。

By the time we call they'll have left already.

我们打电话时他们可能已经走了。

易错盘点

1. 一般过去时与现在完成时的用法区别

(1)误：I read the book, it's a good one.

　　正：I've read the book，it's a good one.

(强调读这个动作产生的结果是"它是一本好书"，故应使用现在完成时)

　　正：I read the book yesterday.

(一般过去时仅表示过去发生的动作，通常带有表过去的时间状语)

(2)误：He has gone to Beijing last month.

　　正：He has gone to Beijing since last month.

(现在完成时不能与表过去的时间状语连用，只能与 since＋过去的时间或 for＋时间段这样的时间状语连用)

2. 现在完成时与现在完成进行时的用法区别

(1)学生们为考试作了准备。

误：The students have been preparing for the exam.

(现在完成进行时表过去发生的动作一直持续到现在，并且有可能继续进行。故本句应译作"学生们一直在准备考试。")

　　正：The students have prepared for the exam. （已经结束）

(2)误：She has always spoken in that way.

　　正：She has always been speaking in that way.

她一贯这样说话。(现在完成进行时可以表示某种感情色彩，但现在完成时无法体现这种感情色彩)

小试牛刀

Choose the best answer from the four choices A、B、C and D.

1. — I guess Anny will win the first prize in the competition.

— I think so. She _____ for it for months.

A. is preparing   B. was preparing

C. had been preparing   D. has been preparing

2. By the time she realizes she _____ into a trap，it'll be too late for her to do anything about it.

A. walks   B. walked   C. has walked   D. had walked

3. So far this year every one _____ a fall in house prices by between 5 and 10 percent.

A. saw   B. see   C. had seen   D. has seen

4. Caddy is learning the grammatical rules in class at Sunny School，where she _____ Japanese for a year.

A. studies   B. studied   C. is studying   D. has been studying

5. Mr. Yang _____ English this term.

A. teaches our   B. teaches us   C. teaches we   D. teach our

6. — I have got a headache.

—No wonder. You _____ in front of that computer too long.

A. work   B. are working   C. have been working   D. worked

7. The unemployment rate in this district _____ from 9％ to 7％ in the past five years.

A. has fallen   B. had fallen   C. is falling   D. was falling

8. We have known that from geography the earth _____ round.

A. is   B. was   C. has been   D. has being

9. —_____ you _____ him around the museum yet?

—Yes. We had a great time there.

A. Have; shown   B. Do; show   C. Had; shown   D. Did; show

10. If we _____ Beijing next month，we'll call on you.

A. went to   B. had gone   C. have gone to   D. go to

学以致用

I. Choose the right words to fill in the blanks.

Robots have a long history. The first one was made by a Greek inventor. You may see robots in some movies. The robots in these movies are stronger，1. _____ and cleverer than people. In real life, most robots are 2. _____ in factories. They do many dangerous，3. _____ or boring jobs.

Some people cannot look after themselves and robots are used to help them. For example, some people can't see, so they use a dog 4. _____ themselves move around. This dog is called a guide dog. Scientists are 5. _____ a robot to help them. In the future, robots might take the place of these dogs.

Robots are 6. _____ used in hospital. In one hospital，a robot 7. _____ meals from kitchen to the sick people's rooms. It never 8. _____ its way because it has a map of the hospital in its computer systems.

In the future, robots 9. _____ in space. But robots will never take the place of human, they can, however, help 10. _____ in a lot of different bays.

A. will used	B. takes	C. faster	D. to help	E. difficult
F. also	G. us	H. loses	I. making	J. working

Ⅱ．Please mark and correct the 10 mistakes in the following passage.

When I was a very young children，my father created a regular practice I remember well years late. Every time he arrived home at end of the day，we'd greet him at the door. He would ask who we was and pretend not to know us. Then he and my mother would have had a drink while she prepared dinner and they would talking about his day and hers. While they chat，my father would lift my sister and me up to sit in the top of the fridge. It was both exciting and frightened to be up there! My sister and I thought he was so cool for put us there.

1. _____
2. _____
3. _____
4. _____
5. _____
6. _____
7. _____
8. _____
9. _____
10. _____

Ⅲ．Translation

1. Translate the following sentences into English.

1. 老人过去常常坐在宁静的公园里的一条长椅上，看着其他的人。

2. 他以前总是每星期看望一次他的母亲。

3. 他一星期以前去了纽约。

4. 你什么时候和他首次见面的？

5. 她告诉我她要来看我。

6. 从 1983 到 1998 年，他正在耶鲁大学教书。

7. 去年冬天他们正在造一座桥。

8. 如果我们不那样做，我们就会犯严重的错误。

9. 有人把窗户打破了。

10. 我们在这里住了很多年了。

11. 等你的答复我已等了一个星期了。

12. 我父亲一向骑车上班。

13. 汤姆发生了严重的车祸。

14. 汤姆发生过严重车祸。

15. 他现在是个工人，他曾在部队服过 5 年兵役。

2. Translate the following sentences into Chinese.

1. They visited the Great Wall last year.

2. I will travel to Japan next year.

3. He was watching TV when I called him.

4. I haven't finished my homework yet.

5. My father was making a phone call when I got home.

6. I'll go to Beijing by the end of this month.

7. When I was watching TV，she called me.

8. By the time we arrive，they'll have left already.

9. She will be studying the whole night.

10. The plane is due to take off at ten.

第二章

语 态

语态重点知识概览

类别	基本构成	常用时态	谓语结构	备注
被动语态	be +v.ed	一般现在时	am/is/are +v.ed	含情态动词的被动语态：can/may/must/should be +v.ed
		一般过去时	was/were+v.ed	
		一般将来时	will/shall be+ done	
		现在进行时	am/is/are being + v.ed	
		过去进行时	was/were being+v.ed	
		现在完成时	have/has been+ v.ed	
		过去完成时	had been+ v.ed	
		将来完成时	will/shall have been+ v.ed	
		过去将来时	would be+ v.ed	
		过去将来完成时	should/ would have been+ v.ed	

☕ **知识梳理**

一、语态的分类

主动语态：主语是动作的发出者。

被动语态：主语是动作的承受者。

She cleans the house every day.

她每天打扫屋子。

The house is cleaned（by her）every day.

屋子每天都由她打扫。

二、被动语态的基本构成

1. be ＋ done(过去分词)

The school was built in 2010.

这所学校建于 2010 年。

2. 谓语动词必须是及物动词，谓语动词的时态和语态要与主语保持一致

The trees in the park were cut down last night.

公园里的树昨晚被砍了。

Chinese is spoken /used by the largest number of people in the world.

汉语被全世界最大数量的人说/使用。

3. 常用的被动语态的结构

表 2-2-1　常用被动语表的结构

时态	被动语态构成	时态	被动语态构成
一般现在时	am/is/are ＋ done	现在完成时	have/has been＋ done
一般过去时	was/were＋ done	过去完成时	had been＋ done
一般将来时	will/shall be＋ done	将来完成时	will/shall have been＋ done
现在进行时	am/is/are being ＋ done	过去将来时	would be＋ done
过去进行时	was/were being＋ done	过去将来完成时	should/ would have been＋ done
情态动词	can/may/must/should be＋ done		

4. 主动表被动的情况

在英语中，主动表被动的情况时有发生，这些情况主要涉及特定的动词、短语以及语境。以下是几个典型的主动表被动的现象。

(1)感官动词

感官动词(如 see，hear，feel，smell，taste，notice，observe，watch 等)后接不带 to 的不定式作宾语补足语时，通常使用主动形式表达被动意义。这是因为这些感官动词描述的是主语的感受或观察，而不是主语执行的动作。

I saw the cat climb the tree.

我看见那只猫爬上了树。

在这个句子中，"climb"是主动形式，但它表达的是被动意义，即"那只猫被看见爬上了树"。

(2)某些特殊动词

如 sell，wash，cut，wear，read 等，当描述某物具有某特性时，常用主动形式表达被动意义。

This book sells well.

这本书销路好。

这里"sells"虽然是主动形式，但实际上表达的是"这本书被卖得很好"的被动意义。

(3)"need/want/require ＋ doing"结构

在这些结构中，通常使用主动形式的动名词表示被动意义，表示"需要/应该被……"，因此，need/want/require ＋ doing ＝ need/want/require to be done

The room needs cleaning.

这个房间需要打扫。

这里"cleaning"虽然是主动形式，但实际上表达的是"这个房间需要被打扫"的被动意义。

(4)某些类型的名词后接不定式

当某些名词(如 thing，job，task，duty，responsibility 等)后接不定式作定语时，不定式常用主动形式表示被动意义。

I have a lot of work to do.

我有许多工作要做。

在这个句子中，"to do"虽然是主动形式，但它表达的是"有许多工作需要被做"的被动意义。

(5) be worth doing… 值得被做……

The film is worth watching.

这部电影值得一看。

The museum is worth visiting.

这个博物馆值得参观。

易错盘点

(1)误：The book was given me by my English teacher.

正：The book was given to me by my English teacher.

这本书是英语老师送给我的。

解析：像 give，bring，hand，lend，offer，pass，sell，show，wave，tell 等接双宾语的动词，变被动语态时需要加上介词"to"。

(2)误：A cake was made to me by my mother.

正：A cake was made for me by my mother.

妈妈给我做了个蛋糕。

解析：像"buy，make，mend，cook 等接双宾语的动词，变被动语态时需要加上介词"for"。

(3)误：The workers are made work all day by the boss.

正：The workers are made to work all day by the boss.

老板让工人们工作一整天。

解析：通常感官动词和使役动词后不带 to 的不定式作宾补，变为被动语态时，需补充不定式符号 to。

口诀：感使动词真叫怪，to 来 to 去记心怀，主动语态 to 离去，被动语态 to 回来。

动词：make / let /have/ hear /see /watch / notice sb. do sth.

make sb. do sth. → sb. ＋ be ＋made ＋to do sth.

(4)误：The old should be taken care.

正：The old should be taken care of.

老年人应该得到照顾。

解析：以动词短语(如 take care of)作谓语的主动语态变被动语态时，不可丢掉后面的介词或副词。

重点点拨

★被动语态的特殊考点

1. 系动词无被动语态。

主语 ＋ feel，look，sound，smell，taste ＋ 形容词例如：It smells terrible. 它闻起来很臭。

2. 某些动词和短语无被动语态。

appear，die，happen，lie (躺着，位于)，remain，occur，last，benefit，join，become，suffer，own，possess，come true，take place，belong to，fall asleep，keep silent…

小试牛刀

Choose the best answer from the four choices A，B，C and D.

1. A lot of watermelons were rotten before reaching the market and _____ away.

    A. could be thrown   B. had to be thrown   C. could throw   D. had to throw

2. We believe that the environment in Sichuan _____ greatly through our hard work in the near future.

    A. will be improved   B. is improved   C. was improved   D. has been improved

3. These posters _____ on campus last week.

    A. was taken   B. were taken   C. has taken   D. have been taken

✎ 学以致用

Ⅰ. Choose the best answer from the four choices A, B, C and D.

1. The hall _____ next month to celebrate this year's Art Festival.

　　A. is decorated　　　B. will decorate　　　C. is decorating　　　D. will be decorated

2. — Mom，can I eat a hamburger?

　　—Sure，if your hands _____ .

　　A. washed　　　B. are washed　　　C. will wash　　　D. will be washed

3. Don't discuss the problem with your friends unless you _____ to.

　　A. ask　　　B. are asked　　　C. will ask　　　D. will be asked

4. In China，things like paper，glass and plastic _____ into different groups and then recycled.

　　A. separate　　　B. separated　　　C. are separated　　　D. is separated

5. —Can Mr. Shi spare some time for the charity show?

　　—If he _____ , he will try his best to make it.

　　A. will be invited　　　B. is invited　　　C. invites　　　D. invited

6. —Aunt Wang，who is the pretty girl in red in the picture?

　　—It's my daughter. The picture _____ 10 years ago.

　　A. took　　　B. is taken　　　C. has taken　　　D. was taken

7. The farmers expect that the road _____ before the rainy season comes.

　　A. is completed　　　B. was completed　　　C. will be completed　　　D. has been completed

8. — Mom，when will we go out for dinner?

　　— As soon as your homework _____ .

　　A. will finish　　　B. will be finished　　　C. is finished　　　D. finishes

9. Don't touch that machine _____ you _____ .

　　A. if；are allowed　　　　　　　　　　B. unless；are allowed

　　C. if；allow　　　　　　　　　　　　　D. unless；are allowed to

10. — Why have I never seen this kind of 5G mobile phone?

　　— Because it _____ by Huawei last week.

　　A. was produced　　　B. would produce　　　C. have produced　　　D. was producing

11. The worker _____ leave by his boss.

　　A. is made to　　　B. is made　　　C. was made to　　　D. was made

12. — Amy，do you know what will happen in Sichuan?

　　— The high-speed railway from Chengdu to Zigong _____ soon.

　　A. will be completed　　B. will complete　　　C. was completed　　　D. completed

13. The man _____ take the lady's handbag by the policeman at the station.

　　A. was noticed　　　B. is noticed to　　　C. was noticed to　　　D. is noticed

14. — Soccer ball first started in England in the 12th century，didn't it?

　　— Yes，but now it _____ all over the world.

　　A. plays　　　B. is played　　　C. is playing　　　D. has played

15. A display of music and fireworks _____ for the great success in our company on July 20，2018.

　　A. was held　　　B. were held　　　C. has held　　　D. will be held

16. Chinese _____ by more and more people in the world now.

A. speak   B. spoke   C. is spoken   D. was spoken

17. —I saw several boxes of books at the gate of our school just now.

   —They _____ to children in poor areas.

   A. were sent   B. are sent   C. will be sent   D. were being sent

18. —How do you like the novel?

   —It's a bit too long, but anyway, it _____ well.

   A. reads   B. is read   C. is reading   D. has read

19. Once fighting _____ between the two villages and many people were killed.

   A. broken   B. broke out   C. broke out   D. was broke out

20. —Hello, Jane!

   —Oh, Jack! What a surprise! I _____ you were still on business in Beijing.

   A. told   B. tell   C. will be told   D. was told

Ⅱ. Choose the right words to fill into the blanks.

John was six years old and he liked 1. _____ very much. But his mother never gave him 2. _____ they were bad for his teeth. John had a very nice 3. _____ . The old man loved his grandson very much, and sometimes he 4. _____ chocolates when he came to visit him, then his mother let him eat them because she wanted to 5. _____ the old man happy.

One evening, a few days 6. _____ John's 7th birthday, he was saying prayers(祈祷)in his room before he went to bed. "Please, God," in a 7. _____ voice, "make them give me a big box of chocolates for my birthday on Sunday.

His mother was in the kitchen, but she 8. _____ the small boy shouting and went into his bedroom quickly.

"Why are you shouting, John?" she asked her son. "God can hear you when you talk 9. _____ ."

"I know, " answered the clever boy, "10. _____ my grandfather is in the next room, and he can't."

A. chocolate	B. so	C. but	D. quietly	E. because	F. heard
G. grandfather	H. some	I. brought	J. loud	K. make	L. before

第三章

主谓一致

主谓一致重点知识概览

应用原则	句子主语	备注
谓语动词用单数	单数名词/代词以及不可数名词作主语	不可数名词有数量词修饰时,应根据数量词决定谓语的单复数
	度量名词	
	each, every, many a 等修饰名词作主语	
谓语动词用复数	both, both…and, some, few, many 等用作主语或修饰主语	后接人称代词或名词复数
	"the ＋形容词"作主语,在表示一类人或事物	
	a number of, a lot of, any of, most of, the rest of, some of, none of, all of 修饰复数名词	
使用就近原则	n.＋or＋n.	靠近谓语动词的主语确定谓语的单复数形式
	either… or…, neither…nor…, not only …but also…	
	There be 句型	
特殊情况	分数、百分数修饰名词时	名词是 population 时,谓语动词用复数
	the number of＋n.（复数）,谓语动词是单数,表"……的数量"。	注意：a number of ＋n. （复数）表"许多",谓语动词用复数
	one of the	名词复数	that /who 引导定语从句	从句谓语动词用单数

知识梳理

主谓一致(Subject-verb Concord)是指主语和谓语在语法形式上的协调关系，即主语和谓语在人称和数上保持一致的关系。

一、指导原则

处理主谓关系一般遵循三个原则，即语法一致原则(Principle of Grammatical Concord)、意义一致原则(Principle of Notional Concord)、就近原则(Principle of Proximity)。

1. 语法一致原则(Principle of Grammatical Concord)

主语和谓语直接的一致关系主要表现在"数"的形式上，即在语法上取得一致，主语中心词为单数，谓语动词用单数形式；主语中心词为复数，谓语动词用复数形式。这种一致关系叫"语法一致"。

Money is needed for the project.

这个工程需要钱。

They have arrived already.

他们已经到了。

2. 意义一致原则(Principle of Notional Concord)

有时，主语和谓语动词的一致关系并非取决于语法上的单复数形式，而是取决于主语的单复数意义。比如有时主语形式虽为单数，但意义上却为复数，谓语动词要用复数形式。反之，主语在语法形式上是复数，而在意义上却为单数，随后的谓语动词也用单数。这种一致关系叫作意义一致。

The group have been discussing this topic for two hours.

这一组已经针对这个问题讨论两个小时了。

group 虽然是单数形式，但这里指组里的所有成员，具有复数意义，因此谓语动词用复数的 have。

Ten miles seems like a long walk to me.

10 英里对我来说是很长的路了。

Ten miles 虽然是复数形式，但这里指长度单位，具有具体意义，因而谓语用单数形式.

3. 就近原则(Principle of Proximity)

有时，谓语动词的单复数形式取决于最靠近它的词语的单复数形式，这种关系所依据的原则叫就近原则。如：or, either…or…, neither…nor…, not only… but also 等连词连接的并列主语，谓语单复数使用遵循就近原则。

Neither you nor I am right.

你和我都不对。

(谓语动词靠近 I，故用 am)

二、具体应用

1. 谓语动词用单数

(1) 单数名词/代词以及不可数名词作主语，谓语动词用单数。

常见的不可数名词有：clothes，news，idea，poetry，baggage/ luggage，furniture，machinery，equipment，water，ice，knowledge，information 等。

His idea about the problem is very novel and practical.

他对这个问题的想法非常新颖、实用。

The furniture in his house is very luxurious.

他家的家具非常奢华。

Knowledge is power.

知识就是力量。

(2)度量名词(表时间、距离、金钱等)作主语，谓语动词用单数。

Five thousand dollars is a large number for him.

5 千美元对他来说是一笔巨款。

Ten years is like one day.

十年如一日。

There is a distance of 5,000 kilometers between him and me.

我和他之间隔着 5000 千米的距离。

(3)each，every 等修饰名词作主语，谓语动词用单数。

当 each，every，either of…，each of 等作主语或修饰主语时，谓语动词用单数。each，every，no 修饰两个主语时，也用单数。

Every student has an English dictionary.

每个学生都有一本英语词典。

Either of them likes sandwiches.

他们俩都喜欢三明治。

(4)主语被 many a(许多)，more than one(不止一个)修饰时，谓语动词用单数。

Many a girl likes dolls.

很多女孩都喜欢布娃娃。

More than one student in our class doesn't like running.

我们班上有不止一个学生不喜欢跑步。

(5)形式复数但意义单数的名词作主语，谓语动词用单数。

学科名词：physics 物理学　statistics 统计学　politics 政治学　economics 经济学　mathematics 数学

其他名词：news 消息　means 手段

It is widely known that politics is difficult.

众所周知，政治学很难。

No news is good news.

没有消息就是好消息。

(6)动名词短语、不定式短语、主语从句、疑问词+to do 作主语时，谓语动词用单数。

Saving is having.

省钱就是赚钱。

What she told me is true.

她告诉我的是真的。

Protecting the environment has profound significance.

保护环境具有深远的意义。

> **重点点拨**
> ★谓语动词用单数
> 1. 度量名词作主语，谓语动词用单数。
> 2. many a/more than one +n.（单数），谓语动词用单数。
> 3. 动名词短语、不定式短语、主语从句、疑问词+to do 作主语时，谓语动词用单数。
> 4. 学科名词(虽是复数形式)作主语，谓语动词用单数。

2. 谓语动词用复数

(1)both，both…and，some，few，many 等用作主语或修饰主语时，谓语动词用复数。

Both of my parents are over sixty years old.

我父母都 60 多岁了。

Many students in his class are creative and knowledgeable.

他班上很多学生都有创造性思维和广泛的知识。

(2)"the +形容词"作主语，在表示一类人或事物时，谓语动词用复数。

The aged are well taken care of by the government.

老年人得到了政府很好的照顾。

The poor are often looked down upon by the rich.

富人通常看不起穷人。

The young have respect for the old in China.

在中国，年轻人尊重老年人。

(3)a number of，a lot of，any of，most of，the rest of，some of，none of，all of 修饰复数名词时，谓语动词用复数。

Most of the teachers are responsible and knowledgeable.

大多数老师都很负责，且知识渊博。

A number of books have been published on the subject.

已经出版了许多关于这个主题的书籍。

None of the books attract me a lot.

没有一本书特别吸引我。

注意：the number of 表示"……的数量"，谓语动词用单数。

The number of books published on this subject is simply amazing.

关于这个主题出版的书籍数量简直令人惊叹。

The number of foreign visitors to China has been increasing over the last several years.

近年来，来中国的外国游客数量一直在增加。

(4)集合名词作主语时，当名词表示整体时，谓语动词用单数；当名词强调集体中的个体时，谓语动词用复数。

常见的集体名词有：family, class, people, police, clothes, cattle(牛，牲畜), audience(听众), goods(货物)等。

The family is the basic unit of society.

家庭是社会的基本单位。

The family have agreed among themselves to spend their vacation in Europe.

家庭成员之间达成一致，决定去欧洲度假。

Such clothes are usually very expensive.

那样的衣服通常很贵。

If goods are not well made you should complain to the manufacturer.

如果货物质量不好，你应该向制造商投诉。

> **重点点拨**
> ★ 谓语动词用复数的情况。
> 1. 可数名词复数形式作主语，谓语动词用复数。
> 2. "The+adj."表示一类人，作主语，谓语动词用复数。
> 3. 集合名词强调个体，作主语，谓语动词用复数。

3. 就近原则

就近原则指动词离哪个主语近，就根据这个主语确定谓语动词的单复数。常用就近原则的结构如下。

(1)名词＋or＋名词　或者……

You or Jack is to be sent to attend the conference.

你或者杰克会被派去开会。

(2)either…or…　或者……或者……；要么……，要么……

Either he or you are not telling the truth.

要么他要么你没说实话。

(3)neither…nor…　既不……也不……

Neither he nor his father likes going shopping.

他和他父亲都不喜欢购物。

(4)not only…but also…　不仅……而且……；not…but…　不是……而是……

Not only I but also Lucy and Tim are willing to do volunteer work.

不仅是我还有露西和提姆都愿意做志愿者工作。

Not I but he wants to go there.

不是我而是他想去那里。

(5)There be 句型

There is a pen, two books and several rulers in the box.

盒子里有一支钢笔、两本书和几把尺子。

4. 特殊情况

(1)表示数量的短语及分数、百分数修饰名词时，谓语动词取决于名词的单复数。

Three quarters of the students in our college are girls.

我们学校 3/4 的学生都是女孩子。

50% of the money was wasted.

50% 的钱都被浪费了。

(2)one of the＋ 名词复数＋ that /who 引导定语从句，从句的谓语动词用复数。

Lu Yao is one of the writers who were awarded a prize at that time.

路遥是当时获奖的作家之一。

注意：当 the only/the very/ the mere ＋ one of the＋ 名词复数＋ that /who 引导定语从句时，从句的谓语动词用单数。

Lu Yao is the only one of the writers who was awarded a prize at that time.

路遥是当时获奖的作家中唯一的一个。

(3)the number of ＋单数谓语，表"……的数量"。

The number of the participants is 200.

参加者的数量是 200 人。

注意：a number of ＋谓语动词的复数形式＝ many＋谓语动词的复数形式。

(4)集体名词强调集体用谓语动词的单数形式，强调成员用谓语动词的复数形式。

常见的集体名词有：family，team，class，audience，group，crowd，army 等。

All the class are ready to take the examinations.

全班同学都为考试作好了准备。

Our class is like a warm family filled with love.

我们班像一个充满爱的、温暖的大家庭。

(5)单复数同形的单词，谓语动词应与其表达的具体意义保持一致。

A deer is running along the bank of the river.

一只小鹿正沿着河边跑。

A herd of deer are running along the bank of the river.

一群小鹿正沿着河边跑。

(6) a quantity of ＋ 可数名词复数，谓语用复数形式；a quantity of ＋ 不可数名词，谓语用单数形式。但 quantities of ＋可数名词复数/不可数名词，谓语均用复数形式。

a quantity of food has been thrown away.

大量的食物被扔掉了。

Large quantities of trees have been cut down in the past 10 years in the area.

在过去的 10 年里，这个地区大量的树木被砍伐了。

(7)由 and 连接的两个名词作主语"a/the＋名词单数＋and＋名词单数"表示一个人（双重身份），谓语动词用单数。

The lawyer and poet often gives lectures around the city.

这位律师兼诗人经常在全市各地作讲座。

注意："a/the＋名词单数＋and＋a/the＋名词单数"表示两个人，谓语动词用复数形式。

The lawyer and the poet have just arrived.

律师和诗人刚刚到达。

(8)"every＋名词单数＋and＋every＋名词单数"表示每一个人，谓语动词用单数形式。

Every boy and every girl has the right to receive education in our country.

在我国每一个男孩和女孩都有权利受教育。

(9)通常由两个部件组成的物品，如：a knife and fork（一副刀叉）等作主语时，谓语动词用单数形式。

Bread and butter is his favorite breakfast.

面包加黄油是他最喜欢的早餐。

(10)不可数名词表示类别时，有复数形式，谓语动词用复数形式。如：fruit，hair，fish，etc.

There are many fruits on sale in the market.

市场上有许多种水果卖。

易错盘点

(1)误：Physics are an important subject in middle schools.

　　正：Physics is an important subject in middle schools.

　　　　物理是中学里一门很重要的学科。

解析：像 physics 这类以 -ics 结尾的学科名词，虽然看似一个复数名词，但其意义是单数含义，通常用作单数，故 be 单词用 is。这类学科名词还有：mathematics 数学、politics 政治学、economics 经济学、linguistics 语言学、athletics 体育学等。

(2)误：Susan's new trousers is colorful.

　　正：Susan's new trousers are colorful.

　　　　苏珊的新裤子是彩色的。

解析：英语中，有一些由两部分组成的物体名称通常是以 -s 结尾，如 scissors 剪刀、pincers 钳子、glasses 眼镜、shorts 短裤、trousers 裤子、suspenders 吊带裤等。这类名词，如果不和数量词连用，通常用作复数。

(3)误：The only means to achieve success have been tried out，but failed.

　　正：The only means to achieve success has been tried out，but failed.

　　　　唯一取得成功的方法都试过了，但还是失败了。

解析：means 指"方式，方法"，并非复数名词，且由 the only 修饰，故用作单数。

(4)误：Mr. Green，together with his wife and children，are going to the party this weekend.

　　正：Mr. Green，together with his wife and children，is going to the party this weekend.

　　　　本周末格林先生将和他的妻子和孩子们一起去参加聚会。

解析：英语中有些词跟在主语后作伴随状语，其后的谓语应根据主语的单复数决定。这样的词有：with，together with，along with，as well as，but，including，except 等。本句中的主语是 Mr. Green，"together with his wife and children"用作状语，并非主语，故谓语的 be 动词用 is。

小试牛刀

Choose the best answer from the four choices A，B，C and D.

1. Either you or the president _____ the prizes to these gifted winners at the meeting.

　　A. is handing out 　　　　　　　　　　B. are to hand out

　　C. are handing out 　　　　　　　　　　D. is to hand out

2. He，who _____ your dear friend，will try his best to help you out of trouble.

　　A. is 　　　　　B. am 　　　　　C. are 　　　　　D. be

3. The Olympic Games in the year 2008 _____ in Beijing of China，which _____ known to us all.

    A．is to hold；is   B．is to be held；was

    C．were to hold；was   D．were to be held；was

4. There _____ a lot of paper on the floor so I asked May to sweep _____ up.

    A．were；it   B．are；them

    C．was；it   D．is；them

5. Three million tons of coal _____ every year in the city.

    A．is exploited   B．are exploited

    C．had exploited   D．have exploited

6. *Stories of the Long March* _____ popular with the young age now.

    A．is   B．was   C．are   D．were

7. Mathematics _____ the language of science.

    A．are   B．are going to be   C．is   D．is to be

8. Both rice and wheat _____ grown in our country.

    A．is   B．are   C．was   D．were

9. _____ either of your parents come to see you recently?

    A．Have   B．Had   C．Has   D．Is

10. What the children in the mountain village need _____ good books.

    A．is   B．are   C．have   D．has

学以致用

Ⅰ. Fill in the blanks with the right forms of the words.

1. Neither he nor I _____ (be) for the plan.

2. My family as well as I _____ (be) glad to see you.

3. My father，together with some of his old friends，_____ (have) been there already.

4. There are two roads and either _____ (lead) to the station.

5. Nine plus three _____ (make) twelve.

6. Twenty miles _____ (be) a long way to cover.

7. Very few _____ (know) his address in the town.

8. When and where this took place _____ (be) still unknown.

9. I know that all _____ (be) getting on well with her.

10. The rest of the novel _____ (be) very interesting.

Ⅱ. **Please mark and correct the 10 mistakes in the following passage.**

When I was a child，I hoped to live in the city. I think I would be happy there. Now I am living in a city，but I misses my home in countryside. There the air is clean and the mountains are green. Unfortunately，on the development of industrialization，the environment has been polluted. Lots of studies have been shown that global warming has already become a very seriously problem. The airs we breathe in is getting dirtier and dirtier. And much rare animals are dying out. It's necessary that we must found ways to protect the environment. So，let's do something to make the environment much beautiful.	1. _____ 2. _____ 3. _____ 4. _____ 5. _____ 6. _____ 7. _____ 8. _____ 9. _____ 10. _____

Ⅲ. **Translate the following sentences into English.**

1. 多亏了同事们的帮助，他迅速适应了新环境。

2. 女子网球队赢得世界冠军的消息传来了。

3. 尽管我也很忙，但我会尽力相助的。

4. 这个区的图书馆遗失的书籍数量很大。

5. 戴口罩是避免疾病传染的有效方法之一。

6. 所有这些事实证明，你和我一样能胜任主管一职。

7. 他是这次英语演讲中我们学校唯一一个获得一等奖的新生。

8. 近年来，这种关于"真人秀"的节目很受观众喜爱。

9. 他的儿子尽管平时调皮，却知道客人到访时该怎么做。

10. 随着科学的发展，我们以后将会住在和现在大不相同的城市里。

第四章

非谓语动词

非谓语动词重点知识概览

类别	功能	备注
to do 不定式	可作主语、宾语、表语、定语、状语或补语。	作主语常用句型:It is +*adj.* + to do 作补语时:感官动词和使役动词后省略 "to"。
动词的-ing 形式	表动名词特征时,可作主语、表语、宾语。	当动词-ing 形式作主语时,谓语动词应用单数形式。
	表现在分词特征时,可作表语、定语、状语。	
动词的-ed 形式	可作表语、定语、状语、还可与其他单词构成谓语。	动词-ed 分词作表语时,其主语是人。

☕ **知识梳理**

　　非谓语动词是指在句子中不作谓语的动词,主要包括动词不定式、动词的-ing 形式和动词的-ed 形式三种。非谓语动词在句子中可以充当除谓语以外的其他句子成分,如主语、宾语、定语、状语或补语等。

一、不定式(Infinitives)

1. 动词不定式的结构与功能

　　动词不定式的结构为"to＋动词原形",如 to read, to write,表示一种目的或未发生的动作,可以在句子中作主语、宾语、表语、定语、状语或补语。

　　To see is to believe.
　　眼见为实。(作主语)

　　I want *to learn* how to play the erhu.
　　我想学习如何演奏二胡。(作宾语)

　　My job is *to protect* the giant panda.
　　我的工作是保护大熊猫。(作表语)

> **重点点拨**
>
> 　　1. 不定式作为主语时,可以直接出现在句首,也可以在某些特殊句型中作为真实主语。
>
> 　　2. 不定式作为表语时,常用在 be 动词或其他系动词后面,描述主语的状态或特征。
>
> 　　3. 不定式还可以用于构成某些固定句型,如"It is＋形容词＋for sb. to do sth."表示"做某事对某人来说是……的"。

I have a lot of work *to do*.

我有很多工作要做。(作定语)

He was too tired *to walk* any further.

他太累了走不动了。(作状语)

The teacher asked me *to clean* the classroom.

老师叫我打扫教室。(作补语)

2. 动词不定式有四种时态(一般式、进行式、完成式和完成进行式)、两种语态(主动语态和被动语态)见表2-4-1。

表 2-4-1 动词不定式的时态和语态

时态	主动语态	被动语态
一般式	to do	to be done
进行式	to be doing	—
完成式	to have done	to have been done
完成进行式	to have been doing	—

(1)不定式的一般式:to+动词原形,表示不定式动作与谓语动词的动作几乎同时发生或在其后发生。

I plan *to visit* my grandparents next week.

我打算下星期去看望我的祖父母。

(2)不定式的进行式:to be+现在分词,表示不定式动作正在进行中,且与谓语动词的动作同时发生。

I am happy *to be helping* you with your study.

我很高兴能在学习上帮助你。

(3)不定式的完成式:to have+过去分词,表示不定式动作发生在谓语动词的动作之前。

I am sorry *to have missed* your party.

很抱歉我错过了你们的聚会。

(4)不定式的完成进行式:to have been+现在分词,表示不定式动作从过去某一时间开始,一直持续到谓语动词发生的时间并且仍在进行。

I am glad *to have been working* with such a great team.

我很高兴能和这样一个伟大的团队一起工作。

(5)不定式的被动语态:当不定式的逻辑主语是不定式所表示的动作的承受者时,用不定式的被动形式,即 to be done 或 to have been done。

The book is said *to be published* next month.

据说这本书下个月出版。

I am honored *to have been given* the opportunity to speak at this conference.

我很荣幸有机会在这次会议上发言。

二、动词的-ing形式(-ING Participle)

1. 动词-ing形式的时态与语态

动词的-ing形式包含动名词和现在分词两种特征,主要表达正在进行的或习惯性、反复性的动作。它有两种时态(一般式和完成式),两种语态(主动语态和被动语态)。

	主动语态	被动语态
一般式	doing	being done
完成式	having done	having been done

2. 动词的-ing 形式的规则变化见表 2-4-2。

表 2-4-2　动词的-ing 形式的规则变化

变化规则	动词原形	动词-ing
一般情况直接加 ing	call answer cry	calling answering crying
以不发音的字母 e 结尾的单词，去 e 加 ing	move close like	moving closing liking
以辅元辅结尾且是重读闭音节的单词，双写最后一个字母，再加 ing	stop swim run travel	stopping swimming running traveling 或 travelling
以 ie 结尾的单词，变 ie 为 y，再加 ing	die lie tie	dying lying tying

重点点拨

当动词-ing 形式作主语时，谓语动词应该用单数形式，例如：

Reading books are my favorite pastime. （×）

Reading books is my favorite pastime. （√）

动词的-ing 形式的规则变化，可简要总结为"直、去、双、变"四个字，以便记忆。

3. 动词的-ing 形式在句子中作名词使用时，为动名词，可以作主语、表语或宾语

Reading can broaden one's horizon.

读书能开阔人的视野。（作主语）

My hobby is *reading*.

我的爱好是读书。（作表语）

I like *reading books* in my spare time.

我喜欢在业余时间读书。（作动词宾语）

We save energy by *carpooling*.

我们通过拼车来节省能源。（作介词宾语）

4. 动词的-ing 形式不起名词作用的时候，则为现在分词，可以与助动词 be 构成进行时态，可以作表语、定语、状语

She *is reading* a book in the library.

她正在图书馆看书。（构成进行时态）

His interview speech was *amazing*.

他的面试演讲太棒了。（作表语）

The *smiling* child received a gift from his mother.

微笑的孩子从他母亲那里得到了一个礼物。（作定语）

Speaking loudly, he made sure everyone could hear him.

他大声说话，确保每个人都能听到。（作状语）

三、动词的-ed 形式(-ED Participle)

1. 动词-ed 形式的功能

动词的-ed 形式一般指动词的过去分词，主要表达被动或完成的动作，强调对主语的影响或结果，在句子中可以作表语、定语、状语，还可以与其他单词构成谓语。

You are *mistaken*.

你错了。（作表语）

Everything *bought* must be registered.

所有购买的东西都必须登记。（作定语）

Filled with anticipation，she stepped onto the university campus.

她满怀期待地走进了大学校园。（作状语）

All the sweat will *be rewarded*.

所有汗水都会得到回报。（构成被动语态）

The Great Wall is the most spectacular sight I *have* ever *seen*.

长城是我所见过的最壮观的景象。（构成完成时态）

2. 动词的-ed 形式的规则变化，见表 2-4-3。

表 2-4-3　动词的-ed 形式的规则变化

变化规则	动词原形	动词-ed
一般情况直接加 ed	finish answer look	finished answered looked
以不发音的字母 e 结尾的单词，直接加 d	live hope change	lived hoped changed
以辅元辅结尾且是重读闭音节的单词，双写最后一个字母，再加 ed	stop plan prefer	stopped planned preferred
以辅音字母加 y 结尾的单词，变 y 为 i，再加 ed	study carry cry	studied carried cried

重点点拨

动词-ed 形式的不规则变化也有规律可循。

1. AAA 形式，即原形、过去式和过去分词三者的词形和读音都相同，如 cut，cost，let，put 等。

2. ABA 形式，即过去分词和原形相同，而过去式不同，如 become，run，come 等。

动词的-ed 形式的规则变化，仍可总结为"直、去、双、变"四个字来记忆，但要注意，不规则变化的过去分词数量较多，需要平时多加积累。

易错盘点

一、不定式 to 和介词 to 的辨析

不定式"to"后面接动词原形，构成不定式，表示目的、意愿、结果或可能性等，可以作主语、宾语、表语、定语、状语或补足语等。如句子 I want to go school. 中"to go school"就是一个动词不定式，表示目的。

介词"to"后面可接名词、代词或动名词，构成介词短语，主要用于表示方向、位置、对象或关系等。如句子 She went to school. 中的"to school"就是一个介词短语，表示方向或位置。

还有一些看似是不定式但实为介词的结构，如"look forward to"，"pay attention to"等，这些结构后面跟的是动词的-ing 形式作宾语，而不是原形。解决这一问题的方法是熟记一些常用的介词 to 短语，例如：get used to，make a contribute to，be addicted to，object to，stick to，respond to，等等。

二、不定式 to 的省略

1. 不定式用于 let，make，have 等使役动词和 feel，hear，notice，observe，see，watch，look at，listen to，sense 等感官动词后作宾语补足语时一般省略 to。例如：

What he said *made me feel* embarrassed.

他说的话使我感到尴尬。

2. 动词 help 后面用作宾语或宾语补足语的不定式可以不带 to。例如：

She often *helps her mother do* the housework.
她经常帮妈妈做家务。

3. 在主语部分有 to do，系动词为 is 或 was 时，作表语的不定式通常省去 to。 例如：

All he wants（to do）is（to）finish his homework on time.
他所要做的就是按时完成作业。

4. 当两个或多个不定式并列时，其后的不定式符号可以省略，但有对比关系时不可省略。 例如：

I want *to meet you and discuss* this plan again.（并列关系，第二个 to 可省略）
我想再和你见面讨论一下这个计划。

To be or not to be，this is a question.（对比关系，第二个 to 不可省略）
生存还是毁灭，这是一个问题。

5. 在 would rather…than… 等结构中，不定式符号通常要省略。 例如：

I would rather *stay at home than go* to see a film.
我宁愿待在家里也不愿去看电影。

三、动名词作后置主语与其复合结构

有时动名词(真实主语)作主语可以后置，用 it 作为形式主语放在句首，但 important，necessary，essential 等形容词不适用于该用法。例如：

It's nice *meeting* you again.
再次见到你真好。

注意：如果动名词有自己的逻辑主语，则可以在其前面加上一个名词或代词的所有格，构成动名词的复合结构。例如：

Mary's speaking at the conference was very impressive.
玛丽在会议上的发言令人印象深刻。

四、现在分词作定语与动名词的合成词辨析

有时候，同一个动词的现在分词作定语，与其作为动名词构成合成词时的用法存在区别，现在分词表示所修饰名词的动作或状态，而动名词则表示名词的目的、功能或者用途等。见表 2-4-4。

表 2-4-4　现在分词作定语和动名词构成的合成词

现在分词作定语的短语	动名词构成的合成词
dancing couple 跳舞的情侣	dancing floor 舞池
swimming child 游泳的孩子	swimming pool 游泳池
singing birds 唱歌的鸟儿	singing competition 歌唱比赛
cooking woman 做饭的女人	cooking recipe 烹饪食谱

五、动词-ed 形式作状语

动词的-ed 形式作状语时，可以表示动作发生的时间、原因、条件、让步、方式或伴随等情况。

Having finished her work，she went home.
完成工作之后，她回家了。（时间状语）

Bitten by a snake，the boy was taken to the hospital immediately.
被蛇咬后，这个男孩立即被送往医院。（原因状语）

Given more time，I could have done it better.
如果给予更多的时间，我本可以做得更好。（条件状语）

Although *broken*，the vase was still beautiful.
尽管破了，这个花瓶仍然很漂亮。（让步状语）

Guided by the teacher，the students completed the experiment successfully.
在老师的指导下，学生们成功地完成了实验。（方式状语）

The boy sat there，*lost* in thought.

那男孩坐在那里，陷入了沉思。（伴随状语）

小试牛刀

Please fill in the blanks with the appropriate forms of the following verbs.

A. interest	B. solve	C. break	D. learn	E. teach
F. surprise	G. see	H. finish	I. satisfy	J. improve

1. I'm planning _____ a new skill this summer.

2. After _____ the window，he apologized to the owner.

3. She is always _____ in reading books，especially historical novels.

4. We are all looking forward to _____ the new movie tonight.

5. He found it difficult _____ the math problem.

6. The teacher asked us _____ our homework before the weekend.

7. My English has _____ a lot since I changed learning methods.

8. The teacher's _____ method really helped me understand the subject better.

9. We were all _____ by the news that our team won the championship.

10. I'm _____ with my current job and am looking for something more challenging.

学以致用

Ⅰ. Choose the best answer from the four choices A，B，C and D.

1. _____ the book，he found it very interesting.

    A. Reading   B. To read   C. Read   D. Having read

2. The child was seen _____ by the window.

    A. to sit   B. sitting   C. sit   D. sat

3. She suggested _____ a walk after dinner.

    A. to take   B. taking   C. taken   D. take

4. I remember _____ to the Great Wall when I was young.

    A. going   B. to go   C. go   D. gone

5. It's important for us _____ English well.

    A. learning   B. to learn   C. learned   D. learn

6. I am very happy _____ your letter.

    A. receiving   B. to receive   C. received   D. receive

7. The problem _____ at the meeting was very important.

    A. discussing   B. to discuss   C. discussed   D. discuss

8. _____ the news，he couldn't help crying.

    A. Hearing   B. Heard   C. To hear   D. Hear

9. _____ the window，you can see the beautiful scenery.

    A. Look out of   B. Looking out of   C. To look out of   D. Looked out of

10. The teacher advised the students _____ more time on their studies.

    A. to spend   B. spending   C. spend   D. spent

Ⅱ. Please mark and correct the 10 mistakes in the following passage.

We should to value our time and use it wisely. Time is a precious resource that cannot be replacing or recovered. Therefore, it is important to making every minute count.	1. _____
	2. _____
	3. _____
Firstly, we should sets clear goals. Without a goal, our time can easily be wasting on unimportant tasks. By setting goals, we can ensure that we are used our time effectively.	4. _____
	5. _____
	6. _____
Secondly, we should avoid distractions. Distractions, such as social media and TV, can take up a lot of our time. To been productive, we need to focus on our tasks and avoid getting distracting.	7. _____
	8. _____
Lastly, we should take breaks. Work continuously without breaks can lead to fatigue and reduced efficiency. By take regular breaks, we can refresh our minds and be more productive when we return to work.	9. _____
	10. _____

Ⅲ. Translate the following sentences into English.

1. 看到他如此努力，我深受鼓舞。

2. 我喜欢晚饭后散步。

3. 完成所有任务后，他放松地坐下来。

4. 我喜欢被大自然环绕的感觉。

5. 这个问题已经得到了妥善的处理。

6. 为了保持健康，他每天坚持锻炼。

7. 为了达成目标，我们需要制订一个详细的计划。

8. 完成所有准备工作后，会议开始了。

9. 站在山顶，我们可以看到整个城市的美景。

10. 这座由著名建筑师设计的建筑充满了中国风。

第五章
从　句

第一节　名词性从句

🔍 重点知识概览

名词性从句重点知识概览

类别	结构	备注
主语从句	连接词＋主语从句＋V＋其他成分	谓语动词一般用单数。
宾语从句	S＋V＋连接词＋宾语从句	当主句谓语动词是 think，believe，suppose，expect 等词，宾语从句常把否定转移至主句表示。
表语从句	S＋link v. ＋连接词＋表语从句	当 where，how，why 引导表语从句时，分别译为：这就是……的地方，这就是……的原因，这就是……的方法，而非疑问含义。
同位语从句	名词 ＋ 连接词 ＋ 同位语从句	连接词不在从句中充当成分，且不能省略。

☕ 知识梳理

　　名词性从句是在句子中起名词作用的句子，其功能相当于名词词组，通常能在复合句中担任主语、宾语(介词宾语)、表语、同位语。

　　一、主语从句(Subject Clause)

　　主语从句是在复合句中充当主语的从句，通常放在主句谓语动词之前，或由形式主语 it 代替，而本身放在句子末尾。主语从句使用陈述语序，其通常结构为"连接词＋主语从句＋谓语＋其他成分"。

　　主语从句的引导词有从属连词(如 that，whether)，其中 that 在从句中不作成分，也无意义，不能省略，whether 在从句中不作成分，仅表示"是否"的含义，不能省略；连接代词(如 who，whoever， whom，whose，what，whatever，which，whichever），它们在从句中可以作主语、宾语、表语和定语；连接副词（如 when，where，how，why，whenever，wherever，however），在从句中作状语。

Who will meet him is not decided.

谁将去见他还没决定。（who 在从句中作主语）

How we will go there is a question.

我们怎么去那儿是个问题。（how 在从句中作状语）

What you told me just now was really a surprise.

你刚才告诉我的真是一个惊喜。（what 在从句中作宾语）

When he will go abroad is being discussed.

他什么时候出国正在讨论中。（when 在从句中作状语）

Why he is crying is not clear.

他为什么哭还不清楚。（why 在从句中作状语）

That the earth is round is a widely accepted fact.

地球是圆的是一个被广泛接受的事实。（that 在从句中不作成分）

Whether he can get the plane ticket doesn't matter much.

他是否能买到机票并不重要。（whether 在从句中不作成分，表"是否"含义）

Which class will win the football game is not clear so far.

到目前为止，哪个班将赢得这场足球赛还不清楚。（which 在从句中作定语）

> **重点点拨**
>
> 主语从句的主句谓语动词一般用单数。由 what 引导的主语从句，其谓语动词需要根据表语来决定。
>
> What you left at school are two old books.（表语 two old book 是复数，谓语动词用 are）
>
> What you said to him is of great importance.（表语 of great importance 不可数，谓语动词用 is）

二、宾语从句（Object Clause）

宾语从句是在复合句中充当宾语的从句，位于及物动词、介词或复合谓语之后，其基本结构一般为"动词/介词/形容词 ＋ 连接词 ＋ 宾语从句"。

宾语从句的引导词有从属连词：that(可省略)，if 和 whether(不可省略，且 whether 后可紧跟 or not)。that 引导表示陈述句的宾语从句，而 if 和 whether 引导表示"是否"的宾语从句；连接代词主要有：who，whom，whose，what，whoever，whomever，whosever，whatever，whichever 等，在从句中可充当主语、宾语或定语；连接副词主要有：when，where，how，why 等，用于引导时间、地点、方式、原因等状语从句。

I know (*that*) he is a good teacher.

我知道他是一个好老师。（that 在从句中不作成分，无意义，可省略）

She asked me *what* I wanted for my birthday.

她问我想要什么生日礼物。（what 在从句中作宾语）

He didn't tell me *who/whom* he was talking to.

他没有告诉我他在和谁说话。（who/ whom 在从句中作宾语）

Can you tell me *whose* book this is?

你能告诉我这本书是谁的吗？（whose 在从句中作定语）

I'm not sure *which* movie we should watch.

我不确定我们应该看哪部电影。（which 在从句中作定语）

He asked me *when* I would arrive.

他问我什么时候到。（when 在从句中作状语）

Do you know *where* the nearest bank is?

你知道最近的银行在哪里吗？（where 在从句中作状语）

I don't understand *why* he is angry.

我不明白他为什么生气。（why 在从句中作状语）

She wants to know *how* to use this machine.

她想知道如何使用这台机器。（how 在从句中作状语）

I don't know *if/whether* he will come tomorrow.

我不知道他明天是否会来。（if/ whether 在从句中不作成分，表"是否"的意义）

三、表语从句（Predicative Clause）

表语从句是在复合句中充当表语的从句，用于说明主语是什么或怎么样，其基本结构一般为"主语＋系动词＋连接词＋表语从句"。表语从句的引导词有从属连词：that，whether；连接代词：what，who，which；连接副词：when，where，why，how。此外，表语从句还可以由 as if，as though，because 引导。

The fact is *that* he doesn't really try.

事实是他没有做真正的努力。（that 在从句中不作成分，无意义，不可省略）

The question is *whether* the film is worth seeing.

问题是这部电影是否值得看。（whether 在从句中不作成分，表"是否"的意义）

The problem is *who* will lead the project.

问题是谁来领导这个项目。（who 在从句中作主语）

The most important thing is *what* you believe in.

最重要的事情是你所信仰的。（what 在从句中作宾语）

The question is *which* car is yours.

问题是哪辆车是你的。（which 在从句中作定语）

The question is *where* we should hold the meeting.

问题是我们应该在哪里举行会议。（where 在从句中作状语）

The reason is *why* he didn't come.

原因是他为什么没有来。（why 在从句中作状语）

The issue is *how* we can solve the problem.

问题是我们如何解决这个问题。（how 在从句中作状语）

The problem is *when* we can start the project.

问题是我们什么时候可以开始这个项目。（when 在从句中作状语）

That's *because* he didn't understand me.

那是因为他不理解我。

四、同位语从句（Appositive Clause）

同位语从句是在复合句中充当同位语的从句，一般在某些抽象名词之后，用于说明解释前面的名词的具体内容。常跟的抽象名词有：idea，fact，problem，order，news，reason，truth，promise 等，其基本结构一般为"名词＋连接词＋同位语从句"。同位语从句的引导词有从属连词：that，whether；连接代词：who，what，which；连接副词：when，where，why，how。

The idea *that* honesty is the best policy is deeply rooted in Chinese culture.

诚实为上的观念在中国传统文化中根深蒂固。

The problem *whether* we should continue to do the experiment has been solved.

我们是否应该继续做这个实验的问题已经解决了。

I have no doubt *who* the winner of the competition will be.

重点点拨

★宾语从句否定的转移

当主句谓语动词是 think，believe，suppose，expect 等词，而宾语从句的意思是否定时，常把否定转移至主句表示。

I don't think it is right for him to treat you like that. 我认为他那样对待你是不对的。

重点点拨

当 where，how，why 引导表语从句时，分别译为：这就是……的地方，这就是……的原因，这就是……的方法。例如：

This is where Lu Xun once lived. 这就是鲁迅曾经住过的地方。

That was how they won the match. 他们就是这样赢得这场比赛的。

This is why she got up so early this morning. 这就是她为什么今天早上起得这么早的原因。

我毫不怀疑谁会是比赛的赢家。

The question is *what* we should do next.

问题是接下来我们应该做什么。

I have no idea *which* book is the best.

我不知道哪一本书是最好的。

I have no idea *when* he was born.

我不知道他何时出生的。

The teacher had no idea *why* Jack was absent.

老师不知道杰克为什么缺席。

It's a question *how* he did it.

问题是他是怎么做的。

We haven't yet settled the question *where* we are going to spend our summer vacation.

我们还没有决定到什么地方去度暑假。

> **重点点拨**
> ★同位语从句和定语从句的区别
> 同位语从句是对前面名词作进一步解释说明，that 不作成分，不能省略；
> 定语从句是修饰限定前面的先行词，that 在句中充当主语或宾语，有实际意义，作宾语时可以省略。例句：
> The news that our team has won the game was true. 我们队赢了那场比赛的消息是真的。（同位语从句）
> The news that he told me yesterday was true. 昨天他告诉我的那个消息是真的。（定语从句）

易错盘点

一、主语从句中，it 作形式主语

在主语从句中，当主语从句较长或结构复杂时，为了避免句子头重脚轻，我们通常会使用"it"作为形式主语，将真正的主语从句置于句尾。一般采用"It ＋ be(is/was) ＋ 名词/形容词/动词的过去分词 ＋ that 从句"的句型结构。这里的"it"是形式主语，真正的主语是"that"引导的从句。此时，我们可以将 it 去掉，把 that 引导的主语从句放在句首，还原成常规的主语从句。

It ＋ be ＋ 名词 ＋ that 从句：

It is a fact that he is innocent. ＝That he is innocent is a fact. 事实上，他是无辜的。

It ＋ be ＋ 形容词 ＋ that 从句：

It is important that you attend the meeting. ＝That you attend the meeting is important. 你参加会议很重要。

It ＋ be ＋ 动词的过去分词 ＋ that 从句：

It is said that he has resigned. ＝That he has resigned is said. 据说他已经辞职了。

二、宾语从句中，it 作形式宾语

当宾语从句后跟有宾语补足语时，通常在宾语从句处使用形式宾语 it，而将真正的宾语从句移至句末。

They believe *it* necessary *that everyone should wear a mask in public places.*

他们认为每个人在公共场所都应该戴口罩是必要的。

（it 是形式宾语，"that everyone should wear a mask in public places"是宾语从句）

They think *it* important *that everyone attends the training.*

他们认为每个人参加培训是很重要的。

I feel *it* unfair *that he was not given a chance to explain.*

我觉得他没有得到解释的机会是不公平的。

三、if 和 whether 引导宾语从句

一般情况下 if 和 whether 可以互换，但出现以下情况，只能用 whether 引导宾语从句。

1. 直接与 or not 连用时。例如：

I wonder whether he will come to the party or not.

我想知道他是否会来参加聚会。

2. 介词之后。例如：

It depends on whether you are ready or not.

这取决于你是否准备好了。

3. 不定式前。例如：

I haven't decided whether to accept the job offer or not.

我还没有决定是否接受这个工作邀请。

4. 位于句首。例如：

Whether she likes it or not，she has to finish the assignment before Friday.

无论她是否喜欢，她必须在星期五之前完成作业。

四、宾语从句的时态呼应

宾语从句的主句和从句谓语动词的时态呼应需要遵循以下原则。

1. 如果主句的谓语动词是一般现在时，宾语从句的谓语动词可用任意时态。例如：

She says that she loves reading books.

她说她喜欢读书。（从句为一般现在时）

I know that he will arrive tomorrow.

我知道他明天会到。（从句为一般将来时）

He mentions that he had visited Paris last year.

他提到他去年去过巴黎。（从句为过去完成时）

2. 如果主句的谓语动词是过去时，宾语从句的谓语动词只能选用一般过去时、过去进行时、过去将来时或过去完成时中的其中一种形式。例如：

She told me that she visited Paris last summer.

她告诉我她去年夏天去了巴黎。（从句为一般过去时）

He said that he was studying for his exams when I called.

他说当我打电话给他时他正在为考试而学习。（从句为过去进行时）

The teacher explained that they would have a test next week.

老师解释说他们下星期有考试。（从句为过去将来时）

I remembered that I had finished my homework before going to bed.

我记得我在睡觉前已经完成了作业。（从句为过去完成时）

3. 如果宾语从句所表示的是客观事实、普遍真理、自然现象或习惯性动作等，都用一般现在时，不受主句谓语动词时态的影响。例如：

The teacher said that the earth goes around the sun.

老师说地球绕着太阳转。

She explained that water boils at 100 degrees Celsius.

她解释说水在 100 摄氏度时沸腾。

He mentioned that the sun rises in the east.

他提到太阳从东方升起。

五、如何选择名词性从句的引导词

(1)如果原句是一个陈述句，则引导词用 that。

(2)如果原句是一个一般疑问句，引导词为 if/ whether。但要注意有些情况不能用 if，只能用 whether。

(3)如果原句是一个特殊疑问句，引导词为 wh-特殊疑问词。

六、名词性从句中的虚拟语气

1. 在主语从句中，下面的几种情况谓语动词通常用"should ＋动词原形"，should 可以省略。

①"It is/was＋形容词＋that …"句型。常见的形容词有 important，necessary，natural，strange，surprising 等。

It is important that we uphold socialist core values in our daily lives.

在我们的日常生活中坚持社会主义核心价值观是很重要的。

It was natural that the Chinese people cherished traditional virtues such as honesty and kindness.

中国人民珍视诚实和善良等传统美德是很自然的。

②"It is/was＋名词＋that …"句型。常见的名词有 pity，shame，advice，suggestion，proposal，requirement，request，desire，order 等。

It is a shame that some people forget the traditional Chinese festivals and their cultural significance.

有些人忘记中国传统节日及其文化意义是可耻的。

It was a wise proposal that we combine modern technology with traditional Chinese art forms.

将现代科技与中国传统艺术形式相结合是一个明智的提议。

③"It is/was＋动词的过去分词＋that …"句型。常见的动词有 advise，order，propose，request，suggest，demand，require 等。

It is suggested that we promote the spirit of patriotism and collectivism through education.

建议我们通过教育来弘扬爱国主义和集体主义精神。

It was required that students learn about the history and culture of China as part of their curriculum.

要求学生将学习中国的历史和文化作为课程的一部分是必需的。

2. 在下列动词后的宾语从句中，谓语动词用"should＋动词原形"，should 可以省略。

这类动词有：insist(坚持)，urge(力劝)，order(命令)，command(命令) request(请求，要求)，demand(要求)，require(要求，需要)，suggest(建议)，advise(建议)，propose(建议)，recommend(建议，推荐) 等。

The teacher ordered that we (should) read classic Chinese literature as part of our homework.

老师命令我们应该把阅读中国古典文学作为家庭作业的一部分。

The guide recommended that we (should) visit the Forbidden City to learn about Chinese history.

导游建议我们应该去参观故宫以了解中国历史。

3. 在含有 advice, order, demand, proposal, requirement, suggestion 等名词的表语从句和同位语从句中，谓语动词用"should＋动词原形"，should 可以省略。

His advice is that we (should) respect and promote the traditional virtues of China.

他的建议是，我们应该尊重并弘扬中国的传统美德。

His proposal that we (should) study more about the history of Chinese civilization is well received.

他提出的我们应该更多地学习中国文明史的建议受到了广泛欢迎。

4. 在 wish 后的宾语从句中。

①表示将来的愿望实现的可能性非常小时，宾语从句的谓语动词用情态动词 should/could/would/might＋动词原形。

They wish they could travel to the moon in the future.

他们希望他们将来能去月球旅行。

②表示与现在事实相反的愿望时，宾语从句的谓语动词用一般过去时(be 动词用 were)。

She wishes she could speak Chinese fluently.

她希望她能说一口流利的中文。

③表示与过去事实相反的愿望时，宾语从句的谓语动词用过去完成时。

How he wished he hadn't wasted too much time on playing computer games while at school.

他多么希望上学时没有浪费太多时间玩计算机游戏。

5. 在 would rather 后的宾语从句中，从句谓语常用一般过去时表示与现在或将来事实相反的愿望，用过去完成时表示与过去事实相反的愿望。

She would rather the young generation preserved and passed down the essence of Chinese traditional culture.

她宁愿年轻一代能够保存并传承中国传统文化的精髓。

They would rather the society had valued traditional Chinese festivals and customs more in the past.

他们宁愿过去社会更加重视中国传统节日和习俗。

6. as if/ as though 引导表语从句时的虚拟语气。

当 as if / as though 引导的表语从句时，如果描述的情况与事实相反，需要用虚拟语气。

①当表示与现在事实相反的情况时，从句使用一般过去时（be 动词用 were）；

He acts as if he knew everything.

他表现得好像他什么都知道似的。（实际上他可能不知道）

②当表示与过去事实相反的情况时，从句使用过去完成时（had done）；

He talked as though he had met the president before.

他说话的样子好像以前见过总统似的。（实际上他以前没见过）

③当表示与将来事实相反的情况时，从句使用 would＋动词原形。

It seems as though the meeting would never end.

会议似乎永远开不完。（实际上总会结束的）

✎ 小试牛刀

Indicate the types of the following clauses.

1. What he said made me angry.

2. I don't know where he lives.

3. The problem is who will lead the project.

4. The fact that he has won the prize is known to everyone.

5. I heard that he told her what had happened.

6. What the teacher said yesterday is that we should study hard.

7. The reason why he was late is that he missed the bus.

8. The news that he has been promoted to manager came as a surprise.

9. Can you tell me why you are late?

10. It is clear that he is not suitable for this job.

✎ 学以致用

Ⅰ. Choose the best answer from the four choices A, B, C and D.

1. _____ is known to all is that the earth goes round the sun.

    A. It   B. What   C. As   D. Which

2. She asked _____ I would go with her to the concert or not.

    A. whether   B. if   C. that   D. what

3. The problem is _____ we lack experienced teachers.

    A. that   B. what   C. how   D. why

4. The news _____ he was promoted came as a surprise to us all.
    A. which　　　　B. that　　　　C. when　　　　D. where

5. _____ you would have succeeded if you had tried harder.
    A. I suggest　　B. I regret　　C. I demand　　D. I doubt

6. It is essential that _____ the task as soon as possible.
    A. he finished　B. he finish　C. he finishes　D. he would finish

7. I wish _____ you could stay with me for a few more days.
    A. that　　　　B. how　　　　C. which　　　　D. what

8. _____ she said was right.
    A. That　　　　B. What　　　　C. How　　　　D. Why

9. I insisted that _____ my homework.
    A. he finished　B. he had finished　C. he finish　D. he would finish

10. My suggestion is _____ we should hold a meeting to discuss the problem.
    A. if　　　　　B. that　　　　C. what　　　　D. which

Ⅱ. Please mark and correct the 10 mistakes in the following passage.

More and more young people are choosing to pursue further education overseas. Study abroad has many benefits. It is believed where studying abroad can broaden our horizons.	1. _____ 2. _____
Firstly, we can learn a new language and understand the culture that the country we go to. Secondly, we have the opportunity to make friends with people from all over the world, who help us understand different perspectives. Also, it is important what we learn to be independent and manage our own lives. Some people think why studying abroad is expensive and risky. They are afraid of face challenges and difficulties.	3. _____ 4. _____ 5. _____ 6. _____ 7. _____
In my opinion, whether studying abroad has its challenges, the benefits far outweigh the disadvantages. It is clear to studying abroad is a valuable experience and a important step towards personal growth.	8. _____ 9. _____ 10. _____

Ⅲ. Translate the following sentences into English.

1. 保护环境是我们每个人的责任。

2. 我听说旅游可以开阔视野，丰富人生经历。

3. 最大的问题是什么导致全球变暖。

4. 她看起来就好像已经准备好面对任何挑战。

5. 什么时候举行运动会还没决定。

6. 我们得到了一个令人兴奋的消息，即我们的队伍赢得了比赛。

7. 我坚信，乐观的心态能带来幸福和成功。

8. 我们是否该接受这个提议需要进一步讨论。

9. 老师的建议，即我们应该每天阅读，对我们的英语学习很有帮助。

10. 这本书的主要观点是我们应该珍惜并保护我们的地球。

第二节　形容词性从句

🔍 重点知识概览

形容词性从句重点知识概览

基本结构	先行词类别	关系代词				关系副词		备注
先行词＋关系词＋从句	人	that	who	whom	whose	/		限制性定语从句通常紧跟先行词，与先行词之间不加逗号，对先行词起限定作用；非限制性定语从句与先行词之间以逗号分隔，对先行词进行补充说明。
		主语或宾语	主语	宾语	定语			
	物	that	which		whose			
		主语或宾语	主语或宾语		定语			
	表地点的名词	/				where=介词+which	地点状语	
	表时间的名词					When=介词+which	时间状语	
	表原因的名词（reason）					why=for which	原因状语	

☕ 知识梳理

形容词性从句(也称定语从句或关系从句)，是一类由关系词引导的从句，在复合句中起形容词作用，其功能相当于形容词词组，充当定语。

在复合句中，形容词性从句通常位于它所修饰的词或词组后面，被它修饰的词或词组叫作先行词，引导形容词性从句的词叫关系词，关系词指代先行词，并在形容词性从句中充当一定成分。形容词性从句的基本结构是先行词＋关系词＋形容词性从句，例如：

The book *which* I bought yesterday is very interesting.

我昨天买的那本书非常有趣。

在这个句子中"which I bought yesterday"是形容词性从句，修饰先行词 book，关系词 which 指代先行词 book，并在从句中充当宾语，这句话可以拆分为两个句子来理解，即：

The book is very interesting. 和 I bought the book yesterday.

一、关系词(Relative Word)

引导形容词性从句的关系词分两种，关系代词和关系副词。

1. 关系代词

在形容词性从句中，关系代词有 that，which，who，whom，whose，as，在从句中可作主语、宾语、定语等。

	that	which	who	whom	whose
先行词类别	人或物	物	人	人	人或物
在从句中的成分	主语或宾语	主语或宾语	主语	宾语	定语

（1）that 在定语从句中作主语时不可以省略，作宾语时可以省略，一般不引导非限制性定语从句，其前面也不加介词。

The person *that* you are looking for is in the office.

你找的人在办公室。

（2）which 在定语从句中作主语时不可以省略，作宾语时可以省略；既可引导限制性定语从句，也可引导非限制性定语从句。引导非限制性定语从句时不能省略，前面可以有介词。which 有时可以指代前面句子的全部或部分意思，意为"这一点……"，此时，which 引导的定语从句通常位于主句的后面。

The car *which* is parked outside is mine.

停在外面的那辆车是我的。

（3）whom 在定语从句中可以省略，但其前若有介词时，则不能省略。

The teacher *who* taught us math last year has retired.

去年教我们数学的老师退休了。

The man *whom* I met at the airport is my English teacher.

我在机场遇到的那个人是我的英语老师。

（4）whose 后必须接名词，相当于"the＋名词＋of which/whom"，前可以有介词。

This is the house *whose* windows are broken.

这是窗户坏了的房子。

（5）as 常与 such 和 the same 连用。

I don't like *such* books *as* you read.

我不喜欢你读的那种书。

This is *the same* cellphone *as* I bought yesterday.

这手机和我昨天买的一样。

重点点拨

关系词 as 引导定语从句，意为"正如……，正像……"，一般用于非限定性定语从句中：

He was late for the meeting, as was expected. 他开会迟到了，正如大家所预料的。

2. 关系副词

在形容词性从句中，关系副词有 where，when，why，在从句中可作地点、时间、原因状语，见表 2-5-1。

表 2-5-1　关系副词的用法

	where	when	why
先行词类别	表地点的名词	表时间的名词	表原因的名词（reason）
在从句中的成分	地点状语	时间状语	原因状语

（1）where 在定语从句中作地点状语，相当于"介词＋which"。如果表示地点的名词在后面的定语从句中作主语或宾语，用 that/which 引导定语从句，而不用 where。当 position，stage，situation，case，activity 等在后面的定语从句中作地点状语时，用 where 引导定语从句。

The school *where* he studied is very famous.

他上学的学校很有名。

（2）when 在定语从句中作时间状语，相当于"介词＋which"。如果表示时间的名词在后面的定语从句中作主语或宾语，用 that/which 引导定语从句，而不用 when。

I remember the day *when* we first met.

我记得我们第一次见面的那天。

(3)why 在定语从句中作原因状语，相当于 for which。如果先行词 reason 在后面的定语从句中作主语或宾语，用 that/which 引导定语从句，而不用 why。

The reason *why* he was late is unknown.

他迟到的原因未知。

二、限制性定语从句与非限制性定语从句(Defining / Non-defining Attributive Clause)

1. 限制性定语从句

限制性定语从句通常紧跟先行词，与先行词之间不加逗号，对先行词起限定作用，指出先行词的具体特征，与先行词的关系比较密切，如果去掉，整个句子意思会不完整或不通顺。

The man *who* stole my wallet was arrested by the police.

偷我钱包的那个人被警察逮捕了。

2. 非限制性定语从句

非限制性定语从句为先行词提供附加的、非必要的信息，对所修饰的先行词或句子进行补充说明，与先行词之间以逗号分隔，与主句之间关系不太密切，去掉从句，对句子的基本意义没有直接影响，主语的意思依然完整。

The house, *which* was built in the 19th century, is now a museum.

那座房子，建于 19 世纪，现在是一座博物馆。

3. 限制性定语从句与非限制性定语从句的区别

(1)大部分关系词既可以引导限制性定语从句，也可以引导非限制性定语从句，但是 that 和 why 通常不用来引导非限制性定语从句。

(2)关系代词 which/who/whom 在所引导的限制性定语从句中作宾语时可以省略，但在非限制性定语从句中不省去。

(3)它们在表达的意思上也有区别，试比较以下例句。

限制性定语从句：The students who study hard will pass the exam.

非限制性定语从句：The students, who study hard, will pass the exam.

第一个句子中的限制性定语从句指出了哪些学生会通过考试，即限定了"students"的范围。而第二个句子中的非限制性定语从句提供了关于先行词"students"的额外信息，即他们努力学习，但这个信息并不限定"students"的范围，去掉这个从句，句子的基本意义仍然是"学生将通过考试"。

在使用定语从句时，需要根据句子的具体内容和所要表达的意义来决定使用限制性定语从句还是非限制性定语从句。

> **重点点拨**
>
> 1. 非限制性定语从句通常译成一个并列句(相当于 and…)，有时还可以译作表原因、目的等的状语从句。
>
> 2. 限制性定语从句通常译在被修饰词前，可译作"……的"。如例句：
>
> My sister who lives in Beijing is a taxi driver. 我那位在北京的姐姐是出租车司机。
>
> My sister, who lives in Beijing, is a taxi driver. 我的姐姐在北京，她是一位出租车司机。

易错盘点

一、介词＋关系词的用法

1. 关系代词中 whom 和 which 的前面可以加介词，构成"介词＋whom/which"。例如：

The man with whom I spoke is my teacher.

和我说话的那个人是我的老师。

在这个句子中，whom 是介词 with 的宾语，形成了"介词＋whom"的结构，并在定语从句 I spoke with 中修饰先行词 the man。例如：

The old man from which I borrowed the money is very tall.

借给我钱的那位老人个子很高。

在这个句子中，which 是介词 from 的宾语，形成了"介词＋which"的结构，并在定语从句 I borrowed the money from 中修饰先行词 the old man。

2. 关系代词 whose 前可以加介词，构成"介词＋whose＋名词"。例如：

The building from whose roof we saw the sunrise was magnificent.

我们从其屋顶看到日出的那座大楼非常壮观。

在这个句子中，"from whose roof"具体指出了观看日出的位置。

3. 关系副词 where/when 前可以加介词，构成 from where 或 since when。例如：

The small village is a beautiful place，from where you can see the entire valley.

这个小村庄是一个美丽的地方，从那里你可以看到整个山谷。

I still remember the day when we first met，since when we have been close friends.

我仍然记得我们第一次见面的那一天，从那以后我们就成了亲密的朋友。

4. "数词/代词＋of which/whom"常用于非限制性定语从句中。例如：

The company has ten employees，two of which are native English speakers.

这个公司有 10 个员工，其中两个是英语母语者。

The students in our class，many of whom are very talented，are working hard for the final exams.

我们班的学生，其中很多人都非常有才华，正在为期末考试努力学习。

5. 当 way 作先行词时，定语从句用 that/in which 引导或省略关系词。例如：

(1)She showed me the way *that* leads to the station.

她向我指出了通往车站的路。

(2)Can you think of a better way *in which* we can do this？

你能想到一个我们可以更好地完成这件事的方法吗？

(3)I don't like the way he talks to me. ＝ I don't like the way in which he talks to me. 我不喜欢他跟我说话的方式。

(4)She did it in the way I had suggested. ＝ She did it in the way that/in which I had suggested. 她按照我建议的方式做了。

二、形容词性从句中的主谓一致

1. 形容词性从句中的谓语动词由先行词决定。例如：

I，who am your good friend，will try my best to help you.

作为你的好朋友，我将尽力帮助你。

The book which contains many useful information is very helpful.

包含许多有用信息的书非常有帮助。

2. 当"one of＋复数名词"后接定语从句时，从句中的谓语动词用复数；而"the only one of＋复数名词"后接定语从句时，从句中的谓语动词用单数。例如：

China is one of the countries that have a rich history of cultural and artistic achievements.

中国是拥有丰富的文化史和艺术成就的国家之一。

China is the only one of the countries that has a rich history of cultural and artistic achievements.

中国是世界上唯一一个具有丰富的文化史和艺术成就的国家。

三、通常只用 that，不用 which，who 或 whom 的情况

1. 当先行词为 all，everything，nothing，anything，little，few，much，none 等不定代词时。例如：

All *that* glitters is not gold.

发光的不都是金子。

Everything *that* he told me was a lie.

他告诉我的一切都是谎言。

Nothing *that* you said makes sense.

你说的话都没有道理。

Is there anything *that* you need help with？

你有什么需要帮助的吗？

I have little *that* I can offer you.

我几乎没什么能给你的。

He ate few *that* were left on the table.

他吃了桌上剩下的不多的几个。

I'll do much *that* I can for you.

我会尽我所能为你做些事情。

None *that* you see here are genuine.

你在这里看到的都不是真的。

2. 当先行词被 any, few, little, some, no, all, every 等词修饰时。例如：

Any book *that* you recommend will be on my reading list.

你推荐的任何一本书都会在我的阅读清单上。

Few people *that* I know are interested in politics.

我认识的人中很少有对政治感兴趣的。

There is little money *that* he has left.

他剩下的钱不多了。

Some people *that* I met at the party were quite interesting.

我在聚会上遇到的一些人很有趣。

No problem *that* we encounter can defeat us.

我们遇到的任何问题都不能打败我们。

All the books *that* you see on the shelf are mine.

书架上你看到的所有书都是我的。

Every person *that* I spoke to was very friendly.

我和每一个人交谈时，他们都很友好。

3. 当先行词被 the only, the very 修饰时，这强调了先行词的唯一性或特指性。例如：

She is the only girl *that* won the first prize in the competition.

她是比赛中唯一获得一等奖的女孩。

The very person *that* helped me yesterday is my neighbor.

昨天帮我的那个人正是我的邻居。

4. 当先行词本身是形容词最高级或被形容词最高级修饰时，这强调了先行词的极端性或最高程度。

例如：

The most important thing *that* I learned in school is to be kind to others.

我在学校学到的最重要的事情是对他人友善。

5. 当先行词本身是序数词或被序数词修饰时。例如：

The first person *that* arrived at the party was the host.

第一个到达聚会的人是主持人。

6. 当先行词既有人又有物时。例如：

He described the teachers and books *that* he had encountered in his first year of college.

他描述了在大学第一年遇到的老师和书籍。

小试牛刀

Please fill in the correct relative words.

1. The book _____ I bought last week is very interesting.

2. He is the man _____ helped me find my lost dog.

3. The city _____ we visited last year has changed a lot.

4. I will never forget the day _____ I first met her.

5. This is the factory _____ produces toys for children.

6. The hotel _____ we stayed last summer was very comfortable.

7. She is the only person _____ knows the truth.

8. The room _____ window is broken needs to be repaired.

9. Do you know the reason _____ he was late for school?

10. The teacher _____ class we are having is very strict.

学以致用

I. Choose the best answer from the four choices A, B, C and D.

1. The book _____ I borrowed from the library is very interesting.
   A. which   B. what   C. where   D. who

2. The man _____ talked to me yesterday is my uncle.
   A. who   B. whom   C. whose   D. which

3. She lives in a house _____ windows are very large.
   A. which   B. that   C. whose   D. who

4. I don't like the way _____ you speak to me.
   A. that   B. what   C. in that   D. /

5. Is this the factory _____ you visited last week?
   A. where   B. that   C. in which   D. the one

6. The reason _____ he was late was that he missed the bus.
   A. why   B. for which   C. that   D. which

7. The place _____ we visited last year is very beautiful.
   A. what   B. which   C. where   D. who

8. The woman _____ is standing at the door is our teacher.
   A. which   B. who   C. whom   D. whose

9. The school _____ I studied at is very famous.
   A. where   B. which   C. that   D. /

10. The student _____ I talked to just now is very friendly.
    A. who   B. whom   C. which   D. that

II. Please mark and correct the 10 mistakes in the following passage.

The Internet has become a essential part of our lives. It's a place that we can get all sorts of information. The websites，which we visit regularly，is often full of useful articles and videos. However，there are also some websites who provide misleading information. This kind of websites should be avoiding. They can confuse people or even cause trouble. Another problem with the Internet is a amount of time people spend on it. Many people which are addicted to the Internet often forget of their responsibilities and relationships. We should encourage people to use the Internet responsibly，for which can be a valuable tool for learning and communication.	1. _____ 2. _____ 3. _____ 4. _____ 5. _____ 6. _____ 7. _____ 8. _____ 9. _____ 10. _____

III. Translate the following sentences into English.

1. 这是一本介绍中国文化的书。

2. 我梦想中的学校是一个充满爱和欢乐的地方，每个人都互相帮助和尊重。

3. 她是我见过的最聪明的学生。

4．昨天我遇到了一位教了我很多英语知识的老师。

5．这是一部讲述了一个关于爱和勇气的故事的电影。

6．这是我见过的最美丽的花园。

7．我父母送给我的那个礼物是我最喜欢的。

8．你给我的那个建议非常有用。

9．我们学校有一个大操场，我们可以在那里做运动。

10．我喜欢这个老师，她的课总是很有趣。

第三节　副词性从句

🔍 重点知识概览

副词性从句重点知识概览

类别	从属连词	备注
时间状语从句	when，as(当……时)，while(在……期间)，before，after，since(自从……以来)，not…until(直到……才)，until/till(直到……时)，(不久，立即)，as soon as(一……就……)，no sooner…than(一……就……)，hardly…when(刚一……就……)，scarcely…when(刚……就……/一……就……)等。	1.动词时态通常遵循"主将从现"的原则 2．"the minute/ the moment/ the second/every time/the day/the instant(瞬间,顷刻)/ immediately/ directly ＋ 从句"表示"一……就……"
地点状语从句	where，wherever，everywhere，anywhere。	
原因状语从句	because，since，as,for,now that（既然），considering/ given that（考虑到,既然），seeing that,in that	because 表示直接的原因或理由,语气最强。 since 引导的从句放在句首,译为"既然……"。
目的状语从句	such that(以便)，so that(以便)，in order that(为了;以便)，lest(免得;唯恐)，for fear that(生怕;以免)，in case(以防;以免)	lest 的从句一般要用虚拟语气(should＋v.);
结果状语从句	so that,so…that 和 such…that	so that 在目的状语从句中,表示"以便";在结果状语从句中,表示"因此导致"。
方式状语从句	as(正如;按照)，as if/as though(好像)，the way	
让步状语从句	though, although, as, even if (though)，however, whatever, whoever, whenever, no matter ＋ wh一词	"as,however"引导的从句部分倒装。
条件状语从句	if,unless, in case, as long as, only if, on condition that, supposing that, provided that	动词时态通常遵循"主将从现"的原则。
比较状语从句	as…as(和一样)， not as/so…as(与……不一样)，than(比)，the more…，the more…(越……越……)	"than"后面的代词可用宾格和主格。

知识梳理

在英语语法中，副词性从句也被称为状语从句，在复合句中起副词的作用，为句子提供额外的信息，如时间、地点、原因、条件、方式、结果、目的或让步等。这些从句通常包含一个从属连词，该连词连接从句与主句，并表明从句与主句之间的逻辑关系。

副词性从句一般可分为时间、地点、原因、目的、结果、方式、让步、条件、比较九种。

When the sun rises，I wake up.

当太阳升起时，我醒来。（时间状语从句）

Wherever you go，I will be there with you.

无论你走到哪里，我都会和你在一起。（地点状语从句）

Because she was sick，she didn't come to school.

因为她生病了，所以她没来上学。（原因状语从句）

She saved money in order that she could buy a new book.

她存钱以便能买一本新书。（目的状语从句）

He worked so hard that he passed the exam with excellent grades.

他如此努力地学习，以至于他以优异的成绩通过了考试。（结果状语从句）

As she spoke，she waved her hand.

她说话时，挥动着手。（方式状语从句）

Although it was raining，they still went for a walk.

尽管下着雨，他们还是出去散步了。（让步状语从句）

If you finish your homework，you can watch TV.

如果你完成了作业，你可以看电视。（条件状语从句）

She sings better than I do.

她唱得比我好。（比较状语从句）

一、时间状语从句(Adverbial Clause of Time)

时间状语从句用于表达主句动作发生的时间背景或时间顺序。

时间状语从句的从属连词有：when，as(当……时)，while(在……期间)，before，after，since(自从……以来)，not…until(直到……才)，until/till(直到……时)，the minute，the moment，the second，every time，the day，the instant(瞬间，顷刻)，immediately，directly(不久，立即)，as soon as(一……就……)，no sooner … than(一……就……)，hardly … when(刚一……就……)，scarcely … when(刚……就……/一……就……)等。

I'll call you *when* I arrive.

我到达时会给你打电话。

As he spoke, she nodded in agreement.

当他说话时，她点头表示同意。

While I was cooking, the phone rang.

当我在做饭时，电话响了。

He finished his homework *before* dinner.

他在晚饭前完成了作业。

After the concert，we went for a drink.

音乐会后，我们去喝了杯饮料。

I've been learning English *since* I was a child.

我从小就开始学英语了。

I *didn't* realize the problem *until* it was too late.

当我意识到这个问题时已经太迟了。

Wait here *until* I come back.

等我回来再离开。

The moment I saw her，I knew she was the one.

我一看到她，我就知道是她了。

Every time I see him，he's always smiling.

我每次看到他，他总是面带微笑。

The day he arrived，we had a big party.

他到的那天，我们举行了一个大派对。

The instant I heard the news，I knew it was true.

我一听到这个消息，就知道它是真的。

As soon as I finish my work，I'll call you.

我一完成工作就给你打电话。

No sooner had he arrived *than* he started working.

他一到就开始工作了。

Hardly had I sat down *when* the phone rang.

我刚坐下电话就响了。

二、地点状语从句(Adverbial Clause of Place)

地点状语从句在句子中用于描述动作发生的地点、方向或距离。

引导地点状语从句的从属连词有：where，wherever，everywhere，anywhere。

We must camp *where* we can get water.

我们必须在能找到水的地方露营。

You can go *where* you want to go.

你可以去你想去的地方。

You can find traces of history *everywhere* you look.

到处都能找到历史的痕迹。

I can't find my keys *anywhere* I look.

我到处都找不到我的钥匙。

三、原因状语从句(Adverbial Clause of Reason)

原因状语从句是用于解释主句动作或状态发生原因的从句，通常它的从属连词，如 because，since，as，for，now that（既然），considering/ given that(考虑到，既然)，seeing that，in that 等引导。

I didn't go to the party *because* I was tired.

我没去参加聚会，因为我累了。

Since you're hungry，let's have lunch.

既然你饿了，那我们就吃午饭吧。

As it was raining，we decided to stay indoors.

因为下雨了，我们决定待在室内。

It must have rained，*for* the ground is wet.

一定下过雨了，因为地面是湿的。

Now that you're here，let's get started.

重点点拨

从属连词 when 引导时间状语从句和宾语从句时，从句的谓语动词时态有所不同。试比较以下两个例句：

1. I don't know when she will come tomorrow.

2. When she comes, please tell me.

第一个例句是宾语从句，句意是"我不知道她明天什么时候来。"从句谓语动词用一般将来时 will come。

第二个例句是时间状语从句。句意是"当她来时，请告诉我。"从句谓语动词用一般现在时表将来。

重点点拨

★当 where 引导地点状语从句和定语从句时的区别。

作状语的是状语从句；作定语修饰名词的是定语从句。例如：

1. Go back to the village where you came. 回到你来的那个村子里去。（where 引导定语从句，修饰 village）

2. Go back where you came from. 回到你来的地方去。（where 引导地点状语从句）

既然你来了，那我们就开始吧。

We decided to postpone the meeting, *considering that* many people were unavailable.

我们决定推迟会议，鉴于很多人都无法参加。

Given that we have a limited budget，we have to be very careful with our spending.

既然我们的预算有限，我们必须非常小心我们的开支。

Seeing that it's raining, we should probably cancel the outdoor event.

既然在下雨，我们可能应该取消户外活动。

In that he has the necessary skills, I believe he is the right person for the job.

既然他具备必要的技能，我相信他是这份工作的合适人选。

四、目的状语从句(Adverbial Clause of Purpose)

目的状语从句用于说明主句谓语动词发生的目的，通常置于主句之后，并通过特定的引导词来连接主句和从句，如 that(以便)、so that(以便)、in order that(为了；以便)、lest(免得；唯恐)、for fear that(生怕；以免)、in case(以防；以免)等。

Let's take the front seats *that* we may see more clearly.

我们坐前排，以便看得清楚一点。

She left early *so that* she could avoid the rush hour traffic.

她早早地离开了以便避开高峰时段的交通。

He left a note *in order that* they would know where he went.

他留下了一张便条以便他们知道他去了哪里。

He spoke quietly *lest* he should disturb the other students.

他轻声说话以免影响其他同学。

He didn't tell her the truth *for fear that* she would be upset.

他没有告诉她真相，生怕她会难过。

Take an umbrella with you *in case* it rains.

带一把伞，以防下雨。

五、结果状语从句(Adverbial Clause of Result)

结果状语用于描述某个动作或状态所引发的结果，一般由 so that，so…that 和 such…that 引导。

He worked hard *so that* he passed the exam.

他学习很努力，结果通过了考试。

The wind was *so* strong *that* he could hardly move forward.

风刮得太猛了，他几乎走不动。

He is *such* a kind man *that* everyone likes him.

他是如此善良的人，以至于每个人都喜欢他。

六、方式状语从句(Adverbial Clause of Manner)

方式状语从句主要用于描述某人的行为或做某事的方式。通常由 as(正如；按照)，as if/as though(好像)，the way 等引导。

重点点拨

because，since，as 和 for 引导原因状语从句用法辨析。

1. because 表示直接的原因或理由，语气最强。

2. since 但语气较 because 弱，侧重已知的事实或理由。

3. as，语气比 because 弱，更侧重于补充性的解释或理由。

4. for 引导的原因状语从句是对主句的推断和解释，不是直接原因，通常放在句尾，前面用逗号隔开。

He must be ill, for he looks very pale. 他一定是病了，因为他看起来脸色很苍白。

重点点拨

1. lest 的从句一般要用虚拟语气，形式是"should＋动词原形"或省掉 should。

2. for fear that 和 in case 从句一般用虚拟语气，但有时也可以用陈述语气。

重点点拨

so that 引导目的状语从句与结果状语从句时的区别。

1. 在目的状语从句中，表示"以便"。

2. 在结果状语从句中，表示"因此导致"。

1. as 和 just as 引导方式状语从句

意为"如……，犹如……，正如……"。just as 比 as 的强调性更强。

Just as the water is the most important of liquids，air is the most important gases.

正如水是液体中最重要的一种一样，空气是气体中最重要的一种。

You must do everything as I do.

你们要照我这样去做。

2. as if 和 as though 引导方式状语从句

as if 和 as though 意为"好像、仿佛"，可以用虚拟语气表示不符合事实或与事实相反的情况；也可以用陈述语气表示描述的情况是事实或者实现的可能性较大。

He walked slowly as if he had hurt his leg.

他慢慢地走，好像腿受伤的样子。

He spoke as if he knew the question very well.

他说得好像对这个问题知道得很清楚。

3. the way 引导方式状语从句

the way 引导方式状语从句的时候意思相当于 as，例如：

He did it the way I had shown him.

他按照我给他展示的方式做了。

判断 the way 后面是方式状语从句还是定语从句的方法如下：

一是如果 the way 可以换成 as 就是方式状语从句，比如上一个例句可以改为：He did it as I had shown him.

二是看 the way 是否是前面动词的宾语，若是，就是定语从句，例如：

I like the way she smiles.

我喜欢她微笑的样子。

七、让步状语从句(Adverbial Clause of Concession)

让步状语从句主要用来表示与主句的说法相反、矛盾或不符的情况，但不影响主句陈述的基本事实。引导让步状语从句的从属连词有 though，although，as，even if（though），however，whatever，whoever，whenever，no matter ＋wh 词等。

1. even if，even though，although，though 引导的让步状语从句

它们都表示"虽然、即使、尽管"的含义。even if 和 even though 带有较强的意味，语气比 although 和 though 强。though 比 although 通俗，但不如 although 正式，都不能和 but 连用，但可以和 yet，still 或 nevertheless 连用。可放在主句前面也可放在主句后面。even if，even though 连接的从句常用虚拟语气。例如：

We wouldn't give up even if we should fail ten times.

即使是我们失败 10 次，我们也不会放弃。

He might have given you more help，even though he was very busy.

尽管他很忙，他可能给了你更多的帮助。

2. as 或 though 引导让步状语从句

as 和 though 前面可用形容词、副词、动词、名词或者分词，

后接主语和谓语。

（1）由 as 或 though 引导让步状语从句用倒装语序，例如：

重点点拨

★用法与位置

1. as，(just) as…so…引导的方式状语从句通常位于主句后，但在(just) as…so…结构中，位于句首。

2. as if，as though 引导的从句可以位于主句前或后，从句中的时态和语气取决于说话者的意图。

Proud as these nobles are, they are afraid to see me.

这些贵族尽管很傲慢，他们却害怕见到我。

(2)如果表语为单数可数名词，这个名词不带冠词，例如：

12-year-old girl as she is, she has had a good command of English.

她虽然只是个 12 岁的女孩，但是英语已经掌握得很好了。

Child as he is, he knows a lot.

虽然他还是个孩子，却懂得很多。

(3)如果句中谓语包含情态动词或助动词，则将实意动词放在 as 之前。例如：

Try as I might, I couldn't lift the stone.

我使多大劲儿也搬不动这块石头。

Praised as he was, he remained modest.

他虽然受到表扬，但仍然保持着谦虚。

(4)如果句中谓语仅有实意动词，则将实意动词(原形)放在 as 之前，并在主语后面加助动词 do, does, did 或 will。例如：

Torture her as they did, the enemy got nothing out of her.

虽然敌人拷打她，却没有能从她嘴里得到什么。

Fail as he did, he would never give up.

尽管他失败了，但他决不会放弃。

3. 由 no matter＋wh-词和由疑问词＋ever 引导让步状语从句

由 no matter 引导，表示"不管；无论"；由疑问词＋ever 引导，表示"不管，不论"。这类词有：whatever, whichever, whoever, however, whenever, wherever 等，他们相当于 no matter＋what(which, who, how, when, where)，都不能与 but, so, and 等并列连词同时使用。例如：

We'll have to finish the job, however (no matter how) long it takes.

不管需要多长时间，我们都一定完成这项工作。

No matter what (whatever) you do, don't tell him that I told you this.

无论你做什么，别告诉他我对你说过这件事。

4. 由 whether…or 引导让步状语从句

由 whether…or 引导让步状语从句表示"不论……还是"，提供两种对比的情况。例如：

I shall go, whether you come with me or stay at home.

不论你来还是留在家中，我都要去。

Whether we like a particular piece of news or not, all we have to do is sit in front of the TV and "let it happen".

不管我们喜欢不喜欢 条消息，我们所能做的只是坐在电视机前，"让它过去"。

八、条件状语从句(Adverbial Clause of Condition)

条件状语从句用于描述某个条件成立时，主句中的动作或状态将会如何，通常由 if、unless、in case、as long as、only if、let's say、on condition that、supposing、provided 等引导。

1. if 常用作条件状语从句的引导词，表示在某种条件下某事很可能发生。例如：

If you ask him, he will help you.

如果你请他帮忙，他会帮你的。

2. unless 表示除非某种条件成立，否则主句动作或状态不会发生。例如：

You will fail to arrive there in time unless you start earlier.

重点点拨

如果 as 引导让步状语从句时，谓语有副词修饰，则将副词放在 as 之前。

Again and again as he failed, he didn't lose heart. 他虽然多次失败，但仍不灰心丧气。

Much as I admire his courage, I don't think he acted wisely. 我虽然佩服他的勇气，但是我认为他这样做是不明智的。

如果你不早点动身，你就不能及时赶到那儿。

3. on condition that 表示在某种条件下，主句动作或状态才会发生。例如：

I can tell you the truth on condition that you promise to keep a secret.

我可以告诉你真相，条件是你答应保密。

4. supposing/provided 也用于表示假设条件。例如：

Supposing it rains, shall we continue the sports meeting?

倘若下雨，我们的运动会还要继续举行吗？

He will sign the contract provided we offer more favorable terms.

如果我们提出更优惠的条件，他就会在合同上签字。

> **重点点拨**
>
> 在条件状语从句中，主句和从句的时态通常遵循"主将从现"原则，即主句用将来时，从句用一般现在时。
>
> 但也有例外情况，如表示虚拟条件时，从句可能用一般过去时或过去完成时。

九、比较状语从句(Adverbial Clause of Comparison)

比较状语从句通过比较两个或多个事物，来描述它们之间的相似性或差异性。比较状语从句一般由 as…as(和……一样)，not as/so…as(与……不一样)，than(比)，the more…，the more…(越……越……)引导。例如：

The director gave me a better offer than he gave Dick.

导师给我的提议比给狄克的好。

John plays football as well as, if not better than, David.

如果说约翰的足球踢得不比大卫好，至少和他踢得一样好。

I can't run as/so fast as he can.

我不能跑得像他那样快。

In recent years travel companies have succeeded in selling us the idea that the further we go, the better our holiday will be.

近几年旅游公司已成功地对我们公众宣传了去得越远，假日越好的观点。

> **重点点拨**
>
> "than"后面的代词在不影响句子意思歧义的时候，口语中常用宾格，较正式的文体中用主格。但有时用宾格或主格，句子意思会有不同。例如：
>
> Tom likes Mary more than I. 汤姆比我更喜欢玛丽。
>
> Tom likes Mary more than me. 汤姆喜欢玛丽胜过喜欢我。

📔 易错盘点

一、时间状语从句中 when，while，as 的用法区别

1. 当 when 引导的时间状语从句，从句的谓语动词可以用短暂性动词，也可用延续性动词，可以指一个时间点，也可以指一段时间，从句和主句的动作可以同时发生，也可以先于主句的动作发生。例如：

It was raining when we arrived.

我们到达时，正下着雨。(动作同时发生，指时间点)

When you read the poem a second time, the meaning will become clearer to you.

当你再读一遍这首诗，你就更清楚它的含义。(动作有先后，指时间点，不能用 while)

2. 当 while 引导时间状语从句时，从句的谓语动词必须是延续性动词，强调主句和从句的动作同时发生。例如：

Don't talk so loudly while others are working.

别人工作时，请勿大声说话。

3. 当 as 引导时间状语从句时，表示"一边……一边"，从句的谓语动词一般是延续性的，用于主句和从句动作同时发生。例如：

As time went on，his theory proved to be correct.

随着时间的推移，他的理论被证明是正确的。

二、时间状语从句中 since 和 before 的用法比较

since 表示"自从……以来"，所在主、从句的谓语动词的时态关系是：It is/has been sometime since sb. did sth.

而 before 的含义是"（过了多久）才……"，主、从句的时态关系是：It was/had been some time before sb. did sth. 例如：

It is 30 years since he joined the revolution.

他参加革命已经 30 年了。

It was three days before he came back.

他 3 天后才回来。

三、时间状语从句的省略现象

在时间状语从句中，如果从句的主语和主句的主语相同，且从句的谓语动词包含 be 动词，那么从句的主语和 be 动词可以省略。例如：

When（he was）young，he was interested in music.

他年轻时对音乐很感兴趣。

四、so that 引导目的状语从句和结果状语从句时的用法区别

1. 当 so that 表示"为了""以便"时，引导的是目的状语从句；当表示"以至于""因此"含义时，引导的是结果状语从句。例如：

If you do know，answer in a loud enough voice so that all the class may hear.（目的状语从句）

如果你的确知道，应大声回答，以便让全班同学都可以听见。

It rained hard the day before yesterday，so that she had to stay at home.（结果状语从句）

前天雨下得很大，因此她只好待在家里。

2. 当从句的谓语动词有情态动词 can，could，may，might 等时，so that 引导的是目的状语从句；当从句里没有情态动词，且谓语动词是一般现在时（过去时）、现在完成时等时态时，引导的是结果状语从句。例如：

We stopped at Salt Lake City so that we could（might）visit the monument to seagulls.（目的状语从句）

我们在盐湖城逗留，以便可以参观为海鸥修的纪念碑。

They have walked a long way，so that we are all tired.（结果状语从句）

他们走了很长的路，所以都很累。

3. 如果 so that 可被 in order that 代替时，是目的状语从句；如不能被代替，则是结果状语从句。例如：

We now study hard so that we may work well in the future. ＝We now study hard in order that we may work well in the future.（目的状语从句）

我们现在努力学习是为了将来更好地工作。

4. 如果 so that 之前有逗号，是结果状语从句；没有逗号则是目的状语从句。例如：

The story is very interesting，so that I like it very much.（结果状语从句）

这部小说很有趣，因而我非常喜欢。

五、结果状语从句中 so…that 与 such…that 的用法区别

so 是副词，后接形容词或副词；such 是形容词，后接名词。

1. 在 so…that 与 such…that 中间出现的是单数名词，且该名词前有形容词修饰时，这两种结构可互换，但要注意它们的词序不同：such＋a/an＋形容词＋名词＝so＋形容词＋a/an＋名词。例如：

She is such a good teacher that all of us love her. ＝ She is so good a teacher that all of us love her.
她是一位很好的老师，我们都敬爱她。

2. 如果被修饰的是不可数名词或复数可数名词时，一般须用 such…that。例如：

He made such rapid progress that before long he began to write articles in English.（不可数名词）
他进步很快，不久就开始用英语写文章。

They are such interesting books that we all want to read them.（可数名词复数）
这些书是那么有趣以致我们都想读一读。

3. 如果不可数名词或复数可数名词前有 many，much，little，few 修饰时，则用 so…that。例如：

I've had so many falls that I'm black and blue all over.（可数名词复数）
我摔了好多次跤，周身青一块紫一块的。

George had so little money that he had to get a job.（不可数名词）
乔治没有钱，所以他不得不找工作干。

They are such little children that they can't do anything.
他们是小孩，什么事情都干不了。

六、条件状语从句与时间状语从句中的时态照应

在条件状语和时间状语从句中，如果主句用一般将来时，从句则用一般现在时。有以下三种情况：

1. 如果主句是一般将来时，那么从句常常用一般现在时。例如：

Unless you apologize，I won't forgive you.
除非你道歉，否则我不会原谅你。

2. 如果主句是祈使句，那么从句通常要用一般现在时。例如：

Don't laugh at others when they make mistakes.
当别人犯错时，不要嘲笑他们。

3. 如果主句是含有情态动词的一般现在时，从句可以根据需要，常用一般现在时。例如：

When you are in a public place，you should speak quietly.
当你在公共场所时，应当小声说话。

小试牛刀

Indicate the types of the following clauses.

1. I remember the whole thing as if it happened yesterday.

2. Since you are going，I will go with you.

3. As long as you are happy，it doesn't matter what you do.

4. They risk their lives in order that we may live more safely.

5. I haven't heard from her since she went abroad.

6. It was so dark that he couldn't see the faces of his companions.

7. She was now happier than she had ever been.

8. Although it was raining，we still went for a walk.

9. I'll take you anywhere you like.

10. She was so tired that she fell asleep immediately.

学以致用

Ⅰ. Choose the best answer from the four choices A，B，C and D.

1. He will call you _____ he arrives in Beijing.

A. before B. after C. when D. until

2. I'll meet you at the station _____ the train arrives.

A. as soon as B. because C. although D. before

3. The park is so beautiful that I want to visit it _____ I am free.

A. whenever B. wherever C. whatever D. whoever

4. She will help you _____ you need help.

A. before B. unless C. until D. if

5. He is always late for school _____ he gets up late.

A. because B. so C. although D. but

6. _____ you don't study hard, you won't pass the exam.

A. If B. Unless C. Since D. While

7. She was late _____ she didn't catch the train.

A. so that B. such that C. enough to D. in order that

8. _____ you have seen the film, you can tell us about it.

A. Although B. Unless C. Since D. Before

9. _____ he is young, he knows a lot about science.

A. Because B. Although C. As D. If

10. _____ he is the last one to leave, he will turn off the lights.

A. As long as B. As soon as C. Even if D. As though

Ⅱ. Please mark and correct the 10 mistakes in the following passage.

Although many people enjoy the convenience of technology, some still resist it. They believe technology is making our lives too dependent in machines. If we rely too much on technology, we may lose some basic skills. When technology fail, people who depend on it may feel helpless. Unless we don't learn to use technology in balance, we could face problems. Because technology is advancing rapidly, it's crucial we adapt. Even though technology has its drawbacks, its benefits are undeniable. So we enjoy the fruits of technology, we must also are aware of its potential risks. Provided that we use technology wisely, our future will be bright.	1. _____ 2. _____ 3. _____ 4. _____ 5. _____ 6. _____ 7. _____ 8. _____ 9. _____ 10. _____

Ⅲ. Translate the following sentences into English.

1. 尽管他很累，但他还是继续工作。

2. 无论我走到哪里，我都会记得我的家乡。

3. 由于他生病了，他没有来参加会议。

4. 如果你不努力工作，你就不会成功。

5. 我带了雨伞，以防下雨。

6. 他跑得如此快，以至于没人能追上他。

7. 尽管下雨，比赛还是按计划进行了。

8. 正如你所建议的，我们采取了新的策略。

9. 随着时间的推移，她变得越来越独立。

10. 因为他很诚实，所以我们信任他。

第六章

虚拟语气

🔍 重点知识概览

虚拟语气重点知识概览

类别	虚拟情况	从句谓语	主句谓语	备注
If 引导的条件句	与现在事实相反	一般过去时	would（could, should, might）+ v.	Be 动词用 were。 若省略 if，从句部分倒装。
	与过去事实相反	had+ v. ed	would（could, should, might）+ have + v. ed	
	与将来事实相反	should ＋v. / were to ＋v.	would（could, should, might）+ v.	
名词性从句	表示愿望、命令、请求（要求）、建议、打算、督促等	(should)+ v.	一般现在时或一般过去时	主语从句中表示惊讶、失望等情感色彩时，也用虚拟语气。
Wish 引导的宾语从句	与现在事实相反	一般过去时或过去进行时	一般现在时或一般过去时	
	与过去事实相反	had+ v. ed/ would + have + v. ed		
	与将来事实相反	were to + v. /would (could)+ v.		
其他状语从句	表示以免、万一	(should) + v.	一般现在时或一般过去时	用 for fear that, lest, in case 引导
句型 " It is high/about time that ..."	表示"该做......的时候了"	一般过去时	一般现在时	
If only	表示"要是......就好了"	would（could）+ v. （现在或将来不能实现的愿望） Had + v. ed(过去未能实现的愿望)		

☕ **知识梳理**

语气(Mood)是英语中的一种动词形式,用来表示说话者的意图和态度。英语中的语气分为陈述语气、祈使语气、虚拟语气、疑问语气和感叹语气五类。

虚拟语气(Subjunctive Mood)是说话者用来表示假设或难以实现的情况,而非客观存在的事实,所陈述的是一个条件,不一定是事实,甚至完全与事实相反。此外如需表达主观愿望或某种强烈的感情时,也可用虚拟语气。虚拟语气通过谓语动词的特殊形式来表示。

一、虚拟语气的特点和功能(Characteristics and Functions of Subjunctive Mood)

1. 表明非真实情况,即某种与事实相反或者难以实现的情况,或者表达说话人的主观愿望。例如:

If there were no air or water, there would be no living things on the earth.

要是没有水和空气,地球上就不会有生物。

I would rather that she had not gone to the party.

我宁愿她没去参加那个派对。

2. 强制性虚拟语气,表示建议、命令、劝告等意义。例如:

He insisted that the old man(should)be sent to the hospital.

他坚持认为应该把老人送去医院。

It was required that the crops should be harvested at once.

要求立刻收割农作物。

> **重点点拨**
> 1. 虚拟语气表示与事实相反的情况。
> 2. 虚拟语气表示建议、命令、劝告、愿望。
> 3. 虚拟语气主句和从句时态不同。

3. 虚拟语气的表达形式是通过动词的形式变化实现的,特点是主从句时态往往不一致。例如:

I wish I could meet you tomorrow at the party.

我希望我明天在晚会上能遇见你。

If you had taken my advice, you wouldn't be in trouble now.

你要是听我的意见,现在就不会遇到麻烦了。

二、简单句中的虚拟语气(Subjunctive Mood in Simple Sentences)

1. 情态动词"will, can"的过去式"would, could"用于现在时态时,表示说话人的谦虚、客气、有礼貌,或委婉的语气,常用于日常会话中。例如:

Would you be kind enough to show me the way to the post office?

请你告诉我去邮局的路好吗?

It would be better for you not to stay up too late.

你最好别熬夜到很晚。

Could you help me?

你能帮助我吗?

Could you tell me what happened.

你能告诉我发生什么事了吗?

> **重点点拨**
> 1. "would, could＋动词原形"用于虚拟语气表示说话人的谦虚、客气、有礼貌,或委婉的语气。
> 2. "May＋sb.＋动词原形/名词"表示祝愿。

2. 表祝愿。

(1)常用"may＋动词原形"表示祝愿,但愿,may须置于句首(多用于正式文体中)。例如:

May you succeed!

祝你成功!

May you be happy!

祝你快乐!

May you have a good time.

祝愿你玩得痛快。

May the friendship between us last long.

祝愿我们的友情天长地久。

(2)用动词原形。例如:

Long live the people!

人民万岁!

注意:本句型属于部分倒装句型,主语后用动词原形。

3. 表示强烈愿望。谓语动词用动词原形。例如:

Heaven save these poor children.

老天爷救救这些可怜的孩子吧。

4. 在一些习惯表达中。例如:

You'd better set off now.

你最好现在就出发。

I'd rather not tell you the secret.

我情愿不告诉你这个秘密。

三、If 条件句中的虚拟语气(Subjunctive Mood in If-Clause)

1. 用于非真实条件状语从句中

英语中的条件句一般有两种:真实条件句和非真实条件句,虚拟语气用在非真实条件句中。真实条件句所表示的假设是有可能发生的,而非真实条件句则通常表示一种假想,与事实相反或不大可能会发生。例如:

If it is fine tomorrow, we will have a picnic by the river.

如果明天天气好,我们就去湖边野餐。(陈述语气)

If I were you, I would go with them.

假若我是你,我就同他们去。(虚拟语气)

(1)表示与现在事实相反。若与现在事实相反,从句用一般过去时,主句谓语用"should(would, could, might)+动词原形"。例如:

If I were you, I wouldn't talk like that.

我要是你,就不会那样说话。

I wouldn't work for them even if they paid me a million dollars.

即使他们给我 100 万美元,我也不会为他们工作。

(2)与过去事实相反:若与过去事实相反,条件从句的谓语用过去完成时(had+过去分词),主句谓语用"should(would, could, might)+have+过去分词"。

If I had left a little earlier, I would have caught the train.

如果我早一点离开的话,我就会赶上火车了。

If it hadn't rained so heavily I would surely have come to your meeting on Friday afternoon.

倘若不是天下大雨,我肯定会来出席你们星期五下午召开的会议。

(3)与将来事实相反:若与将来事实相反,条件从句的谓语用"should+动词原形;were to+动词原形"(be 通常用 were),主句谓语用"should(would, could, might)+动词原形"。例如:

If this were to happen again, you would be punished.

如果这样的事情再次发生,你会受到惩罚的。

> **重点点拨**
>
> 1. "If"引导的非真实条件句的三种情况。
>
> 2. 省略"if"的非真实条件句,"were, had, should"放在句首,句子部分倒装,如有否定词"not","not"放在主语后。
>
> 3. "but for, without, otherwise"等引导的无条件句的虚拟语气。

If they should dare to invade our country，we would wipe them out completely.

如果他们胆敢侵略我们国家，我们会将他们全部消灭掉。

2. 用于错综时间条件句

虚拟语气的错综条件句子，也就是常说的混合条件句，即虚拟条件从句和主句动作发生的时间不一致，因此，主句和从句的谓语动词应根据所指的时间选用适当的虚拟语气形式。例如：

If I were you，I wouldn't have missed the film last night.

如果我是你，我就不会错过昨天晚上的那部电影。（从句与现在事实相反，主句与过去事实相反。）

If I had followed your advice，I wouldn't be so busy now.

我要是听了你的建议，现在就不会这么忙了。（从句与过去事实相反，主句与现在事实相反。）

3. 用于省略 If 的虚拟条件句

虚拟条件句中如果有 were，had 或 should 等词时，可以省略 if，但要把 were，had，should 放在主语之前构成倒装的虚拟条件句。例如：

Were I rich（＝if I were rich），I would give you some money.

如果我富有的话，我会给你一些钱的。

Had he learnt about computers，we would have hired him to work here.

如果他懂计算机的话，我们已经聘用他来这里工作了。

Should you agree to go，we would send you there.

要是你答应去的话，我们就派你去那里。

4. 用于无条件的虚拟语气中

这里的所谓无"条件"，指的是句子表层没有通常使用的 if 或 I wish 等引起的表示条件的句子，但其深层结构或是上下文中还是有条件的。这种条件可以用介词、形容词、动词、分词、不定式、定语从句或上下文等表示出来，只不过是为了行文的简洁，用跳层的方法把条件省掉罢了。表示无"条件"的词有 with，without，but for，or，but，otherwise，even，in case of，what if(如果……将如何)等。这种句子往往是有主句而无从句。

(1)用 but for，under，with，without 等介词或介词短语引导虚拟条件句，例如：

But for air and water，no living thing could exist.

没有空气和水，任何生物都不能生存。

Without your help，we couldn't make such great progress.

没有你的帮助，我们不会取得如此大的进步。

(2)由 but，otherwise，or 等引导虚拟条件句，例如：

Who but a fool would believe that?

除了傻瓜，谁会相信这个?

I was ill that day，otherwise I would have come to see you.

我那天生病了，否则我就来见你了。

(3)由分词短语或不定式短语引导虚拟条件句，例如：

Given more time，they would do it better.

再给些时间，他们会做得更好。

It would be wrong not to take this into consideration.

不把这个考虑进去将是错误的。

(4)通过上下文或其他形式表现虚拟语气，例如：

An honest man would not say this.

诚实的人不会那样说!

I would do so in your position.

假如我处于你的位置，我会那样做的。

Such mistakes could have been avoided.

这样的错误本来是能够避免的。

四、虚拟语气用于宾语从句(Subjunctive Mood in Object Clause)

有几类动词后面的宾语从句用虚拟语气，其后的虚拟语气仅有一种形式"should＋动词原形"，其中，should 在美式英语中，可以省略掉。

1. 表示"要求、请求"后的宾语从句，这样的动词有 ask，demand，require，request，insist 等。例如：

He insisted that he (should) stay.

他坚持要求留下来。

The teacher asked that all the students (should) be on time.

老师要求学生们准时到校。

2. 表示"命令、指示"后的宾语从句，这样的动词有：order，command，direct 等。例如：

The boss ordered that the work (should) be finished on time.

老板吩咐这项工作必须按时完成。

The commission commanded that work on the building (should) cease.

委员会命令那栋大楼必须停建。

3. 表示"建议、敦促"后的宾语从句，这样的动词有 advise，suggest，propose，recommend，urge 等。例如：

I suggested that you (should) leave early.

我建议你们早点动身。

This report urged that all children (should) be taught to swim.

这份报告敦促教授所有儿童游泳。

4. 表示"希望、打算"后的宾语从句，这样的动词有 desire，intend 等。例如：

I desires that he (should) do it.

我希望他做此事。

The factory intended that production (should) start next month.

工厂计划下个月开始生产。

5. 表示"安排、提议、投票"后的宾语从句，这样的动词有 arrange，move，vote 等。例如：

I move that we (should) accept the proposal.

我提议通过这项提案。

The company arranged that I (should) go abroad to study.

公司安排我去国外学习。

注意：1. wish 引导的宾语从句中用虚拟语气表示与事实相反或不大可能实现的愿望。

(1)若要表示与现在事实相反的愿望，从句谓语用一般过去时或过去进行时。例如：

I wish I were a bird.

但愿我是只鸟儿。

I wish I knew what was going on.

我要是知道正在发生什么就好了。

(2)若表示与过去相反的愿望，从句谓语用过去完成时或"would／could＋have ＋过去分词"。

> **重点点拨**
>
> 1. 在表示"命令、指示、建议、敦促、要求、请求、愿望、打算、安排"等动词后的宾语从句用虚拟语气，其动词形式为：(should)＋动词原形。
>
> 2. 在动词"wish"后的宾语从句谓语动词有三种形式：一般过去时、过去完成时(或 would／could＋have ＋过去分词)、would (could)＋动词原形。
>
> 3. "would rather，would sooner，would as soon"后的从句用虚拟语气，其谓语动词形式为：一般过去时或过去完成时。

例如：

I wish I had learned painting.

我要是学过画画就好了。

I wish I had gone with you yesterday.

我多希望我昨天和你一起去了。

(3)若表示将来没有把握或不太可能实现的愿望，用"were to ＋ 动词原形"或"would (could)＋动词原形"。例如：

I wish I could help you.

但愿我能帮你。

I wish I could speak several languages.

但愿我会说好几种语言。

注意 2. 表示"愿望"的"would rather(宁愿)，would sooner(宁可)，would as soon (宁愿)"后面的宾语从句要用虚拟语气，表示过去的情况用过去完成时，表示现在与将来的情况用一般过去时。例如：

I'd rather you didn't tell me the truth.

我宁愿你不告诉我实情。

I'd as soon you had returned the book yesterday.

我宁愿你昨天还了书。

I'd rather you painted the wall green next time.

我宁愿你下次把墙涂成绿色。

五、虚拟语气用于主语从句 (Subjunctive Mood in Subject Clause)

在主语从句中可用虚拟语气表示建议、命令、愿望、要求或惊讶、失望等感情色彩。从句谓语用"should ＋动词原形"结构，其中 should 可以省略。以下句型常用虚拟语气。

1. It's important that…类型

这类句型中常见的形容词有：necessary, important, strange, natural, advisable, anxious, compulsory, crucial, desirable, eager, essential, fitting, imperative（绝对必要）, impossible, improper, obligatory, possible, preferable, probable, urgent, vital, amazing, odd, ridiculous, surprising, unthinkable, natural, astonishing, etc. 例如：

It's important that you（should）return the book to the library before they are due.

你应当在到期之前把书还给图书馆，这是很重要的。

It is surprising that he（should）finish the work without any help.

他没有借助任何帮助就完成了工作，这真让人吃惊。

2. It's a pity that…类型

这类句型中常见的词语有：pity, desire, must, order, proposal, recommendation, request, requirement, shame, suggestion, wonder, demand, etc. 例如：

It's a pity that he（should）talk to his friends like that.

真遗憾，他竟然会那样跟朋友说话。

It is their demand that their wages（should）be increased.

他们要求涨工资。

> **重点点拨**
>
> ★主语从句用虚拟语气的三种句型：
>
> 1. It is/was＋形容词＋主语从句
>
> 2. It is/was＋名词＋主语从句
>
> 3. It is/was＋过去分词＋主语从句
>
> 从句谓语动词用"should＋动词原形"，"should"可以省略掉。

3. It's desired…类型

这类句型中常见的词语有：desired，advised，arranged，decided，ordered，proposed，requested，required，recommended，suggested，settled，insisted，etc. 例如：

It was suggested that the meeting(should) be held at once.

建议马上举行会议。

It is desired that every student（should）pass the exam.

要求每位学生都得通过考试。

4. It worries me that…类型

这类句型中常见的词语有：worry，surprise，amaze，astonish，etc. 例如：

It worries me that we（should）be blamed for that.

我们竟要因此受责备真让人烦恼。

六、虚拟语气用于表语从句和同位语从句(Subjunctive Mood in Predicative Clause & Appositive Clause)

1. 在 advice，decision，demand，desire，idea，insistence，instruction，motion，necessity，order，plan，preference，pray，proposal，recommendation，request，requirement，resolution，suggestion，understanding 等名词后的表语从句、同位语从句中要用虚拟语气，其后的虚拟语气用"should＋动词原形"的结构。例如：

My suggestion is that he（should）take part in the game.

我建议让他参加比赛。

What do you think of my proposal that we（should）go to watch the game next Sunday?

我建议下星期日去看比赛，你们认为如何？

2. **"as if, as though"**意为"好像，似乎"，引导的表语从句可以用虚拟语气。

表示对现在情况的假设时，从句谓语动词用过去式(be 动词用 were)；表示对过去情况的假设时，从句谓语动词应用"had＋过去分词"的形式；表示对将来情况的假设时，从句谓语动词应用"would/could/might＋加动词原形"的形式。例如：

She looks as if she were ten years older.

她看起来似乎老了 10 岁。

It felt as though he had run a marathon.

感觉他好像跑了一场马拉松似的。

七、虚拟语气用于状语从句(Subjunctive Mood in Adverbial Clause)

1. 在 as if, as though 引导的状语从句中，可用虚拟语气来表达所述事情与实际不符，从句谓语形式与"wish＋宾语从句"的用法类似。例如：

I can remember our wedding as if it were yesterday.

我们的婚礼我记忆犹新，就好像昨天一样。

He behaved as though nothing had happened.

他表现得若无其事。

2. 在 for fear that, in case(以防)，lest(以免)引导的目的状语从句中，谓语多用"should＋动词原形"来表示虚拟，"should"可以省略掉。例如：

They spoke in whispers lest they（should）be heard.

他们低声耳语唯恐被听见。

重点点拨

1. 表示"命令、建议、请求、要求、愿望、打算"等意义的名词后的从句用虚拟语气，其谓语动词形式为"should＋动词原形"。

2. "as if, as though"引导的表语从句用法同"wish"引导的宾语从句。从句谓语动词用"would＋动词原形"。

He burned all the important documents for fear that they (should) fall into the enemy's hands.

他把所有的重要文件都烧毁了，怕它们会落在敌人手中。

3. 在 even if, even though 所引导的让步状语从句中，有时可用虚拟语气，主句、从句的结构与 if 所引导的条件从句结构相同。例如：

Nobody could save him even though Hua Tuo should come here.

即使华佗再世也救不了他。

Even if she were here herself, she should not know what to do.

即使她亲自来也不知该怎么办.

> **重点点拨**
>
> 1. "for fear that, in case, leat"引导的从句，其虚拟语气形式为"should ＋ 动词原形"。
>
> 2. "as if, as though"引导的从句，其虚拟语气同"wish"引导的宾语从句。

4. 以"be＋angry, annoyed, amazed, astonished, surprised, frightened, happy, pleased, proud, sorry, disappointed, upset"等后面的原因状语从句中常用虚拟语气，其虚拟语气的结构为：

（1）should ＋ 原形动词(指现在或将来)，例如：

The old man was angry that the young man should call him by name.

老人很生气，那位年轻人竟然对他直呼其名。

I was surprised that he should not answer such an easy question.

我很惊讶他竟答不出如此简单的问题。

（2）should ＋ have＋v. ed(指过去)，例如：

I'm very sorry that you should have failed the exam.

我很遗憾，你这次考试竟然失败了。

I was very astonished that he should have finished such difficult task by himself.

我很惊讶，他竟独自完成了如此困难的任务。

八、用于其他句型的虚拟语气(Subjunctive Mood in other sentence structures)

1. 用于 if only 句型中，意为"但愿，要是……就好了"；谓语动词用过去时或"would/could＋动词原形"表示现在或未来不能实现的愿望；用过去完成时表示过去没有实现的愿望。例如：

If only I could speak several foreign languages.

我要是能讲几种外语就好了!

If only I had passed the CET6!

我要是通过了大学英语六级考试就好了!

2. 用于 "It is(high/about)time that"之后的从句中，谓语动词用一般过去时表示虚拟语气。例如：

It is high time that you made the final decision.

你该做最后的决定了。

It's time that you went to school.

你该上学去了。

3. 句型"had hoped/thought /＋宾语从句"，表示"过去未实现的愿望或想法"，有"本来希望，本来以为"之意，从句谓语要用"would＋动词原形"的形式。例如：

I had hoped that she would answer my letter.

我本来以为她会回我的信的。

I had thought you would come.

我本来以为你会来的。

易错盘点

1. **表示强烈愿望。谓语动词用动词原形，该类型虚拟语气谓语仅用动词原形，第三人称单数也不加"s"。**

Long last friendship！友谊长存！（部分倒装，主语是 friendship）

2. **在虚拟条件句中，对于与将来事实相反的情形，请注意以下几点。**

(1)条件从句表示的内容与将来事实相反，实为对将来情况的推测，用过去时表示虚拟。例如：

If I were to do it，I would do it in a different way.

如果我做这件事，我会用不同的方法。

(2)条件从句谓语除用过去式外，有时也用"should＋动词原形（表示可能性极小，常译为"万一"）"。例如：

If you should have any question about our product，you could make a phone call to us.

万一对我们的产品有任何问题，您可以打电话给我们。

(3)条件从句使用"should＋动词原形"这样的谓语形式时，主句谓语除可用"should（would，could，might）＋动词原形"这样的虚拟语气形式外，也可用直陈语气或祈使语气。例如：

If it should rain tomorrow，don't expect me.

万一明天下雨，就不要等我了。（祈使语气）

If I should see him，I'll tell him.

万一我见到他，我就告诉他。（直陈语气）

3. **虚拟语气主句中 should（表第一人称），would（表结果），could（表能力、许可或可能性）和 might（表可能性）。试比较：**

If you tried again，you would succeed.

要是你再试一试，你就会成功的。（would 表结果）

If you tried again，you might succeed.

要是你再试一试，你可能会成功的。（might 表可能）

If you tried again，you could succeed.

要是你再试一试，你就能成功了。（could 表能力）

4. **当条件从句的主语为第三人称单数时，谓语动词若是系动词 be 时，可用 were 代替 was，特别是在倒装虚拟结构及 if I were you，as it were 中，只能用 were。例如：**

If he were here，he might be able to help.

如果他在这里，他或许会帮忙的。

Were I you，I would try to grasp the chance.

要是我是你的话，我要尽力抓住这次机会。

5. **wish 引导的从句中，从句的时态只与从句所指的时间有关，而与 wish 的时态无关。比较：**

I wish I were rich.

要是我现在有钱就好了。

I wish I had been rich.

要是那时我有钱就好了。

I wished I were rich.

当时我希望我有钱。（当时我后悔自己没有钱。）

I wished I had been rich.

当时我希望我自己曾经有钱。（当时我后悔自己曾经没有钱。）

6. 动词 **insist** 后接宾语从句时，除可用虚拟语气外，也可用陈述语气，两者的区别是：若谓语动词所表示的动作尚未发生，或尚未成为事实，意思是"坚持要求"，则用虚拟语气；若谓语动词所表示的动作已经发生，或已经成为事实，意思是"坚持认为"，则要用陈述语气。比较：

He insisted that I had stolen his book.

他坚持说我偷了他的书。

He insisted that I should read his letter.

他坚持要我看他的信。

小试牛刀

Fill in blanks with correct forms of the words in brackets.

1. If there _____（be）a heavy wind, many huts would be blown away.

2. If the teacher speaks louder, the students _____（hear）better.

3. If I _____（be）to pass the examination, my father would buy me a bicycle.

4. If the pilot _____（not be）so careless, that accident would have been avoided.

5. I'm sure if you _____（know）more about the matter, you will not feel so annoyed.

6. If he should finish his homework before lunch, please _____（let）me know.

7. Mother _____（feel）anxious if I came home late.

8. Those people will never work whole-heartedly if there _____（be）no sense of belonging.

9. If it _____（rain）in the past few weeks, the crops would be growing still better.

10. If she hadn't worked hard at English in the past two years, she _____（not get）on so well with her studies.

学以致用

Ⅰ. Choose the right answer to fill in the blank.

I have been wishing I were as free as a bird flying in the clean sky. However, the earth is in a little danger now! People suffer more from the natural disasters, pollution, global warming and so on. If only we 1. _____ in the clean and fresh air!

What do you suggest that we 2. _____ to save our earth? When everything is out of order, it looks as the world 3. _____. 4. _____ is about time that some effective measures 5. _____ to stop the damage to the earth, otherwise, the earth 6. _____ by human beings.

It is clear that it is the efforts people make that make 7. _____ possible for the environment to become clean. If actions 8. _____ as quickly as possible, the environmental problems 9. _____ (improve). I do wish that one day the earth 10. _____ as beautiful as the one before.

1. A. could walk   B. can walk   C. can walking   D. could be walking

2. A. will do   B. would do   C. do   D. can do

3. A. ends   B. ended   C. will end   D. should end

4. A. It   B. That   C. This   D. Which

5. A. should take   B. takes   C. taken   D. took

6. A. is destroyed   B. would be destroyed   C. was destroyed   D. will be destroyed

7. A. this   B. that   C. it   D. what

8. A. are taken   B. is taking   C. will be taken   D. has been taken

9. A. would improve   B. will improve   C. improves   D. should improve

10. A. would become   B. become   C. became   D. will become

II. Choose the best answer from the four choices A, B, C and D.

1. If only I _____ the answer, I would have told you.
   A. knew   B. have known   C. would know   D. had known

2. _____, I would take an umbrella with me.
   A. Had I been you   B. I were you   C. Were I you   D. I had been you

3. We recommend that work _____ at once.
   A. start   B. starts   C. will start   D. started

4. We had hoped that Mary _____ well again.
   A. will soon be   B. had soon been   C. is soon   D. would soon be

5. It is necessary that the course in general science _____ taken before the chemistry course.
   A. is   B. be   C. to be   D. will be

6. We hung out a lantern lest he _____ lost in the mist.
   A. gets   B. get   C. will get   D. got

7. The picture exhibition bored me to death. I wish I _____ to it.
   A. had not gone   B. have not gone
   C. did not go   D. can not have gone

8. Without air, we _____ forced to seek shelter from the sun, as there _____ no atmosphere to protect us from the sun's deadly rays.
   A. will; be   B. may be; may be
   C. would be; would be   D. are; is

9. The manager _____ that the new employers go through professional training before they started working.
   A. persisted   B. insisted   C. resisted   D. assisted

10. The professor gave orders that the test _____ before 5：30.
   A. be finished   B. will finish   C. will be finished   D. shall finish

III. Translate the following sentences into English.

1. 你愿意帮我一把吗？

2. 友谊万岁！

3. 我宁愿你没告诉我这件事。

4. 如果明天下雨，会议就推迟。

5. 万一我忘了，请明天再提醒我一下。

6. 我们很惊讶他们竟然得出这么一个结论。

7. 老师的要求是我们要在 3 小时内做完练习。

8. 如果我们过去几年没有努力工作，事情就不会进行得如此顺利。

9. 要不是有你的帮助，我就不会取得成功。

10. 我建议你马上开始你的工作。

第七章

特殊句型

第一节 感叹句和祈使句

🔍 重点知识概览

感叹句和祈使句重点知识概览

类别	形式	结构	备注
感叹句	What 开头	What a(an)＋*adj.*＋*n.*（单数)＋主语＋谓语	不可数名词和复数名词前无"a(an)"
		What ＋*adj.*＋*n.*＋主语＋谓语	
	How 开头	How ＋*adj.*/*adv.*＋主语＋谓语	
祈使句	肯定形式	Be＋*adj.*	
		Do＋其他	Do 表示动词原形
		Let's＋*v.*／Let us ＋*v.*	
	否定形式	Don't＋*v.*	
		No＋*v.* ing	

☕ 知识梳理

感叹句(Exclamatory Sentence)是用来表示说话人喜怒哀乐、惊讶、赞美等强烈感情的句子。

祈使句(Imperative Sentence)是表达说话人给对方的劝告、叮嘱、请求或命令的句式。

一、感叹句(Exclamatory Sentence)

句首多用 How 和 What。除 What 句型、How 句型外，还可以用陈述句、疑问句等句式；也可以用一个词组，甚至一个词来表达自己的感情，句尾通常用感叹号。

1. What 引导的感叹句句型。

What＋(a/an)＋*adj.*＋*n.*（单数)＋主语＋谓语！

What＋*adj.*＋*n.*（不可数）＋主语＋谓语！

What＋*adj.*＋*n.*（复数）＋主语＋谓语！例如：

What a nice day it is!

多么美好的一天！

What good children they are!

他们是多么好的孩子呀！

What delicious food it is!

多么美味的食物啊！

2. How 引导的感叹句句型。

How＋*adj.*（*adv.*）＋主语＋谓语！例如：

How beautiful they are!

他们多么漂亮啊！

How fluently she speaks English!

她英语说得多么流利呀！

How hard they are working now!

他们干得多么起劲呀！

3. 在表示同一意义时，既可用"what"引导，也可用"how"引导。例如：

What bright sunshine it is! ＝How bright the sunshine is!

多么明亮的阳光呀！

What a tall building it is! ＝ How tall the building is!

多么高的一幢建筑啊！

4. 感叹句在表示激动强烈的感情时，口语中常常采用省略句，其后面的主语和谓语往往略去不讲。 例如：

What an honest boy!

多么诚实的孩子呀！

How beautiful!

漂亮极了！

5. 感叹句有时可以用单词或短语表达。例如：

Wonderful!

真棒！

Good heavens!

天哪！

Fire!

着火啦！

Look!

看！

二、祈使句（Imperative Sentence）

祈使句说话的对象通常是第二人称 you，习惯上常省略。祈使句的肯定句谓语动词用原形，否定句一般用 don't，never 开始。

1. 肯定祈使句

(1)Be 型（Be＋*adj.*），例如：

Be careful!

当心！

Be quiet!

安静!

(2)Do 型（Do 代表动词原形，句首或句尾可加上"please"），例如：

Turn off the lights!

把灯关了!

Please open the window!

请把窗户关了!

(3)Let's 或 Let us 型(Let's ＋ 动词原形；Let＋第一人称或第三人称＋动词原形)，例如：

Let's go.

咱们走吧。

Let me help you.

让我来帮你。

Let him go.

让他走吧。

2. 否定祈使句(一般在句首加 Don't)

(1)Be 型和 Do 型前直接加 Don't，例如：

Don't be careless!

别粗心大意!

Don't open the door!

别开门!

(2)No＋动名词，多用在标语禁令中，例如：

No smoking!

不准吸烟!

No parking!

不准停车!

> **重点点拨**
>
> ★祈使句肯定形式：
>
> 1. Be 或动词原形开头
>
> 2. Let's ＋ 动词原型
>
> 3. let ＋ 第一、第三人称＋动词原形
>
> ★祈使句否定形式：
>
> Don't ＋ 动词原形

📋 **易错盘点**

1. 感叹句

(1)What 在感叹句中作定语，用于修饰名词，名词前可有形容词或冠词；How 在感叹句中作状语，用于修饰形容词、副词、动词或句子。

What a clever boy he is! ＝ How clever a boy he is!

他是多么聪明的孩子啊!

(2)感叹句中的主语、谓语通常可以省略。

What a nice girl (she is)!

她是多么好的姑娘啊!

How handsome (he is)!

他多么帅气啊!

(3)What 感叹句中可数名词单数前一般为不定冠词 a/an，而不用 the。转换成 how 感叹句时，该名词前一般用定冠词 the，以表示特指。

What a big fish it is! ＝ How big the fish is!

多么大的一条鱼呀!

2. 祈使句

(1)Let 型的否定式有两种："Don't＋let＋宾语＋动词原形＋其他成分"和"Let＋宾语＋not＋动词原形＋其他成分"。例如：

Don't let him go.

Let him not go.

别让他走。

(2)有时，为了加强语气，可以在动词之前加 do。例如：

Do sit down.

务必请坐。

Do study hard.

一定要努力学习。

(3)用客气的语气表示祈使句时，可在句首或句尾加上 please，但如果在句尾加 please，那在 please 之前一定要加一个逗号","。例如：

Please come in.

请进。

Go this way，please.

请这边走。

(4)祈使句中如果有称呼语，一定要用逗号","隔开，放在句首或句尾。例如：

Li Ming，come here.

李明，过来。

Come here，Li Ming.

过来，李明。

(5)Let's 型祈使句的反义疑问句用"shall we?"，Let us 型的反义疑问句用"will you?"

Let's have a rest，shall we?

咱们休息一会儿，好吗？

Let me go，will you?

让我走好吗？

小试牛刀

Fill in blanks with"What（a/an），How".

1. _____ wonderfully they dance!

2. _____ interesting lesson the students are having!

3. _____ brave the Chinese people are!

4. _____ beautiful clothes these are!

5. _____ very interesting story he told us!

6. _____ good news it is!

7. _____ the time flies!

8. _____ quickly the boy is running!

9. _____ I miss my hometown!

10. _____ bad weather!

✎ 学以致用

Ⅰ. Choose the best answer from the four choices A, B, C and D.

1. _____ excellent basketball player Yao Ming is! I really love this talented guy.
   A. How   B. What   C. How a   D. What an

2. _____ good advice the teacher gave me!
   A. How   B. What   C. What a   D. How a

3. Woo! _____ beautiful Chengdu is!
   A. How   B. What   C. What a   D. How a

4. _____ nice the ice cream looks! I can't wait to taste it.
   A. How a   B. How   C. What a   D. What

5. _____ children Simon and Jim are! They help Mrs. Li clean the house every day.
   A. How nice   B. How hardworking   C. What nice   D. What hardworking

6. _____ more, and you'll improve your spoken English.
   A. Speak   B. Speaks   C. Speaking   D. To speak

7. Boys and girls, _____ up your hands if you want to take part in the summer camp(夏令营).
   A. putting   B. to put   C. put   D. puts

8. Ssh! _____ talk loudly. The baby is sleeping right now.
   A. Do   B. Does   C. Don't   D. Doesn't

9. _____ me go. It is very important for me.
   A. Do let   B. Let do   C. Doing let   D. To do let

10. If you want to stay, let me know, _____?
    A. will you   B. shall we   C. do you   D. do we

Ⅱ. Please mark and correct the mistake in each sentence.

1. How exciting news it is!   _____

2. What a expensive sweater it is!   _____

3. How well the young man played the piano is!   _____

4. What wonderful the party was!   _____

5. How beautiful music it is!   _____

6. "Taking exercise every day, my child. It's good for your health," said Father.   _____

7. "To be here on time next time, or you'll be punished." said the director.   _____

8. Not play in the street. It's dangerous.   _____

9. Please lend me some money, shall we?   _____

10. Got up early tomorrow, or you can't catch the train.   _____

Ⅲ. Translate the following sentences into English.

1. 请照看好您的行李。

2. 咱们去图书馆看书吧。

3. 这个城市晚上看起来多么漂亮啊！

4. 她钢琴弹得多么好啊！

5. 请节约用水。

6. 多么激动人心的消息呀！

7. 请不要再迟到了，好吗？

8. 这是一场多么精彩的足球赛啊！

9. 他不诚实，所以不要相信他。

10. 同学们，如果想去参加夏令营请举手。

第二节　反义疑问句

重点知识概览

反义疑问句重点知识概览

类别	陈述句中谓语	疑问形式	备注
简单句	有助动词	助动词(not)＋人称代词	
	实义动词	do/does/did(not)＋人称代词	
	有情态动词 must	must/mustn't ＋人称代词	must 表示禁止、必须
		needn't(有必要)＋人称代词	must 表示有必要
		助动词（must 后的动词来确定）＋人称代词	must 表示推测
祈使句		will/ can(can't)/would you?	
感叹句		Isn't/aren't ＋人称代词	
并列句		助动词(not)＋人称代词	对后一分句进行反问
复合句	主从复合句	助动词(not)＋人称代词	与主句谓语动词和人称保持一致
	主语从句	助动词(not)＋ it	

知识梳理

反义疑问句(Tag Questions)又叫附加疑问句，是指当提问的人对前面所叙述的事实不敢肯定，而需要向对方加以证实时所提出的问句。其结构为：前一部分是一个陈述句，后一部分是一个简单的问句。

反义疑问句要根据前面陈述句的动词时态和人称来选择适当的助动词进行提问，前后两部分的人称和动词时态要保持一致。如果前一部分用肯定式，后一部分一般用否定式；反之，前一部分为否定式，后一部分要用肯定式，即"前肯定后否定，前否定后肯定"。

一、简单句结构中的反义疑问句(Tag Questions in Simple Sentences)

1. 当陈述句部分的主语是名词时，反义疑问句的主语必须用人称代词来代替。例如：

Your brother has gone to the library, hasn't he?

你弟弟去图书馆了，是吗？

Mary hasn't lived in the countryside, has she?

玛丽已经没有住在乡下了，是吗？

Sichuan dishes are very hot, aren't they?

川菜很辣，是吗？

Jack came across an old friend in the street yesterday, didn't he?

杰克昨天在街上遇到了一位老朋友，是吗？

Many foreigners like Chinese culture，don't they?

许多外国人喜欢中国文化，是吗？

2. 当陈述句的主语是指示代词 **this，that** 时，反义疑问句的主语用 **it** 代替；指示代词是 **these，those** 时，反义疑问句的主语用 **they** 代替。例如：

That isn't a useful book，is it?

那不是一本有用的书，是吗？

This is your last chance to learn from the beginning，isn't it?

这是你最后一次从头开始学习的机会，是吗？

These are important reading materials，aren't they?

这些都是重要的阅读材料，是吗？

Those are rare flowers，aren't they?

那些是珍稀花卉，是吗？

3. 当陈述句部分是 **I am…** 时，反义疑问句部分通常要用 **aren't I**；如陈述句部分的主语是 **I am not** 时，反义疑问句部分通常要用 **am I**。例如：

I'm late for the meeting，aren't I?

我开会迟到了，是吗？

I'm not doing well，am I?

我干得不好，是吗？

4. 当陈述部分是 **everyone / everybody, someone / somebody, no one / nobody, none** 等表示人的不定代词时，反义疑问句部分的主语多用 **they**，但也可用 **he**；当陈述部分的主语是 **everything, anything, something, nothing** 等表示物的不定代词时，反义疑问句部分的主语用 **it**。例如：

Nobody finish the task on time，did they?

没人按时完成这项任务，是吗？

Everybody is here，isn't he?

大家都在这，是吗？

Everything has been ready，hasn't it?

一切都准备好了，是吗？

Nothing is worth missing，is it?

没什么值得想念的，是吗？

5. 当陈述部分是"**there be ＋ 主语 ＋ 其他**"结构时，反义疑问部分要用"**be（not）＋ there**"结构。例如：

There are some grapes in the basket，aren't there?

篮子里有些葡萄，是吗？

There is nobody in the classroom，is there?

教室里没有人，是吗？

There is a big tree in front of the house，isn't there?

房前有一棵大树，是吗？

There aren't any animals on the hill，are there?

重点点拨

★反义疑问句结构形式：

结构一：前肯定，＋ 后否定

结构二：前否定，＋ 后肯定

★反义疑问句步骤：

1. 判定（判断该用肯定还是否定）。

2. 找动词（找句子的助动词：be 用 be；动原 do，三单 does，过去 did；完成 have）。

3. 换代词（将主语换为代词）。

★情态动词（can，will，should）的反义疑问句。

★祈使句反义疑问句。

★陈述句含有否定的词语，反义疑问句用肯定形式。

★陈述句含有实意动词 have 时，要依据意思而定。

★陈述句部分是"I think（believe，suppose，imagine，expect 等）＋ 宾语从句"，反义疑问句部分应与宾语从句的主谓保持一致，并要注意否定转移。

这座小山上没有动物，是吗？

6. 陈述部分是祈使句。

祈使句后一般加上 will you 或 won't you 构成反义疑问句，用 will you 多表示"请求"，用 won't you 多表示提醒对方注意。

(1)Let 引导的祈使句有两种情况：

①Let's…，后的反义疑问句用 shall we。例如：

Let's go home, shall we?

咱们回家，好吗？

②Let us/me…后的反义疑问句用 will you。例如：

Let me have a try, will you?

让我来试试，好吗？

(2)祈使句都可以用 will you。例如：

Keep quiet，will you?

保持安静，好吗？

Turn off the lights，will you?

把灯关了，好吗？

(3)否定祈使句，用 will you，can you。例如：

Don't make a noise, will / can you?

别发出噪声，好/ 可以吗？

Don't open the window，will/ can you?

别开窗户，好/ 可以吗？

(4)表示邀请，请求的祈使句，用 will you，won't you，would you。例如：

Come here, will you?

来这儿，好吗？（请求）

Please give me a cup of tea，would you?

请给我来一杯茶，好吗？（请求）

Come to have dinner with us this evening，won't you?

今晚跟我们一起来吃饭，好吗？（邀请）

注意：表示"请求"时，通常用 will you，would you；表示"邀请、劝说"时，用 won't you。

(5)表示告诉别人做某事的祈使句，用 will you，can you，would you，can't you，won't you。

Stop talking, can you?

禁止交谈，可以吗？

Write down the new words, will you / won't you?

写下这些新单词，好吗？

Finish the homework within an hour，can't you?

请 1 小时内完成家庭作业，可以吗？

7. 陈述部分的谓语动词是 have 时。

(1)have 作"有"解时，反义疑问句部分可用 have(not)或 do(not)的相应形式。例如：

She has two brothers, doesn't she / hasn't she?

她有两个哥哥，是吗？

They haven't a lot of time，have they?

他们没有多少时间，是吗？

(2)have 用作实义动词时，反义疑问句部分只可用 do(not)的相应形式。例如：

They all have a good time，don't they?

他们都玩得很开心，是吗?

She had the medicine before meal，didn't she?

她在饭前吃了药，是吗?

(3)陈述部分有 have to，反义疑问句用 do(not)的相应形式。例如：

We have to start early，don't we?

我们必须早点出发，是吗?

We have to get up early every day，don't we?

我们每天都得早起，是吗?

(4)陈述部分有 have got to，反义疑问句用 have(not)的相应形式。例如：

We have got to answer all the questions，haven't we?

我们不得不回答所有的问题，是吗?

8. 当陈述部分有情态动词时。

(1)陈述部分有 had better 时，反义疑问句用 should 或 had。例如：

We'd better go right now，shouldn't we / hadn't we?

我们最好现在就去，是吗?

You'd better go to school at once，hadn't you/shouldn't you?

你现在最好马上去上学，好吗?

You'd better not eat anything in class，had you/should you?

你最好不要在课堂上吃东西，是吗?

(2)陈述部分有 may 时，反义疑问句用"may ＋ 主语 ＋ not"。例如：

They may be here next week，may they not?

他们下星期或许在这里，是吗?

She may be from England，may she not?

她或许来自英格兰，是吗?

(3)陈述部分有 must(必须，禁止)时，反义疑问句用 must (mustn't)；当 must 表示"有必要"，反义疑问句用 needn't；当 must 用来表示对现在的情况进行"推测"时，反义疑问部分要根据 must 后面的动词采用相应的形式。例如：

You must do it today，needn't you?

你今天一定要做它，是吗?

I must study hard，mustn't I?

我必须努力学习，是吗?

He must be good at maths，isn't he?

他数学一定学得很好，是吗?

You mustn't talk like that，must you?

你禁止像他那样说话，知道吗?

(4)陈述部分有 need 和 dare 时，若 need 和 dare 为实义动词，反义疑问句用 do (not)的相应形式；若 need 和 dare 为情态动词，则用 need (must)或 dare。例如：

He needs help，doesn't he?

他需要帮助，是吗?

You dare to catch a snake，don't you?

你敢抓蛇，是吗?

They need to take one our to finish the work，don't they?

他们需要花 1 个小时来完成这项工作，是吗？

He dare not say so，dare he？

他不敢这样说，是吗？

He needn't do that，must he？

他不必做那件事，是吗？

（5）陈述部分有"ought to ＋ 动词原形"，反义疑问句部分要用 ought ／ should（oughtn't ／ shouldn't）。例如：

Such things ought not to be allowed，ought they？

这种事是不允许的，是吗？

You ought to take good care of your baby，oughtn't/ shouldn't you？

你应该照看好你的孩子，不是吗？

（6）陈述部分有 should，反义疑问句用 should（not）。例如：

Everyone should obey the laws，shouldn't they？

每个人都应该遵守法律，不是吗？

You should be late for class again，should you？

你不应该上课再次迟到，是吗？

（7）陈述部分有 will，反义疑问句用 will（not）。例如：

All of your friends will come to your birthday party，won't they？

你的所有朋友都愿意来参加你的生日派对，是吗？

He won't come，will he？

他不会来，是吗？

9. 陈述部分有" would rather ＋ 动词原形"或"would like to ＋ 动词原形"，用 wouldn't。例如：

You'd like to have some bananas，wouldn't you？

你想吃些香蕉，对吗？

He'd rather go to play basketball，wouldn't he？

他宁愿去打篮球，是吗？

10. 陈述部分有"used to ＋动词原形"，反义疑问句用 didn't 或 usedn't 。例如：

He used to live in the countryside，usedn't he / didn't he？

他过去住在乡下，是吗？

You used to be interested in travelling，usedn't you / didn't you？

你过去对旅行感兴趣，是吗？

11. 当陈述部分的谓语动词是表示愿望的 wish 时，反意疑问部分要用 may，而且前后两个部分均用肯定式。例如：

I wish to go to the moon by spaceship some day，may I？

我希望将来有一天乘坐宇宙飞船去月球，会吗？

He wishes to have a one-month holiday，may he？

他希望有一个月的假期，可以吗？

12. 陈述部分的主语是不定代词 one 时，反义疑问句的主语可以用 one，也可用 you。例如：

One should be ready to help others，shouldn't one？

一个人应该做好帮助他人的准备，是吗？

One should know dos and don'ts，shouldn't you？

一个人应该知道什么能做和什么不能做，不是吗？

13. 陈述部分是感叹句，反义疑问句用 isn't it/aren't…？例如：

What fine weather, isn't it?

多么晴朗的天气啊，不是吗？

How hard they are working, aren't they?

他们工作得多么努力啊，不是吗？

二、并列句结构中的反义疑问句(Tag Questions in Compound Sentences)

当陈述句是由并列连接词 and，but，or，for，so 等连接的两个并列分句组成时，反义疑问句部分一般与最接近的分句保持一致，也就是说，对后一分句进行反问。例如：

He was a hard working child, and he got good grades, didn't he?

他是努力的孩子，且考试取得了好成绩，是吗？

I love her, but she doesn't love me, does she?

我爱她，但她不爱我，是吗？

三、复合句结构中的反义疑问句(Tag Questions in Complex Sentences)

1. 一般情况下，陈述句部分是主从复合句时，反义疑问句部分的代词和助动词应与主句中的主语和动词保持一致。例如：

This is the second time that he has been to France, isn't it?

这是他第二次去法国，是吗？

You never told me why you were late for class, did you?

你从来没有告过我你为什么上课迟到，是吗？

He saw a former classmate whom lived in the same dorm in the middle school, didn't he?

他看到了一位中学里住同一个寝室的老同学，是吗？

2. 在宾语从句中，如果陈述句部分是"I think (believe, suppose, imagine, expect 等) ＋ 宾语从句"，反义疑问句部分应与宾语从句的主谓保持一致，并要注意否定转移。例如：

I don't think you have heard of him before, have you?

我认为你以前没有听说过他，是吗？

I suppose he is very serious, isn't he?

我认为他很严肃，是吗？

注意：当 think 等这些动词的主语不是第一人称，或主语是第一人称，而动词时态不是一般现在时或一般过去时，这时，反义疑问句的助动词和人称代词要与主句保持一致。例如：

Mary thinks you will come to the party, doesn't she?

玛丽认为你将来参加晚会，是吗？

3. 当陈述句部分为主语从句时，反义疑问句的主语用 it。例如：

That he didn't pass the entrance exam made his parents very angry, didn't it?

他没有通过入学考试使得他的父母十分生气，是吗？

What I said is that you should study hard, isn't it?

我说的是你应该努力学习，是吧？

四、反义疑问句的回答

对反义疑问句的回答，无论问题的提法如何，如果事实是肯定的，就用 yes，事实是否定的，就要用 no。要特别注意陈述句部分是否定结构，反义疑问句部分用肯定式提问时，回答 yes 或 no 与汉语正好相反。这种省略回答的 yes 要译成"不"，no 要译成"是"。例如：

——He likes playing football, doesn't he?

——Yes, he does. / No, he doesn't.

——他喜欢踢足球，是吗？

——是的。/ 不是。

—His sister didn't attend the meeting, did she?

—Yes, she did. / No, she didn't.

——他妹妹没有参加会议，是吗？

——不，她参加了。/ 是的，她没参加

—They don't work hard, do they?

—Yes, they do. / No, they don't.

——他们没有努力工作，是吗？

——不，他们工作努力。/ 是的，他们工作不努力。

易错盘点

1. 陈述部分主谓是 I am，反义疑问句用 aren't。 例如：

I am an adult, aren't I?

我是成人了，不是吗？

I am doing what you want me to do, aren't I?

我正在做你想要我做的事，不是吗？

2. 当陈述部分含有以下这些含有否定意义的词时：few, little, seldom, hardly, never, not, no, neither 等，其反义疑问句需用肯定结构。 例如：

He is never late for school, is he?

他上学从来不迟到，是吗？

Few students are in the classroom, are they?

教室里有少数几个学生，是吗？

She hardly goes to see her grandparents, does she?

她很少去看望她的祖父母，是吗？

3. 当陈述部分所含的否定词是通过加前缀或后缀构成的，其后的反义疑问句依然用否定结构。 例如：

It is unfair, isn't it?

这不公平，是吗？

This medicine is unhelpful, isn't it?

这药不起作用，是吗？

4. 当 must 用来表示对过去的情况进行"推测"（must ＋ have done）时，如强调对过去情况的推测（一般句中有过去的时间状语），反义疑问句部分要用"didn't ＋ 主语"；如果强调动作的完成（一般没有过去时间状语），反义疑问句部分要用"haven't / hasn't ＋ 主语"。 例如：

She must have read the novel last week, didn't she?

她上星期一定读了这本小说了，是吗？

You must have told her about it, haven't you?

你一定把这事告诉她了，是吗？

5. 反义疑问句中问句部分的动词在时态上应和陈述部分的时态一致。 例如：

Your mother likes cooking, doesn't she?

你妈妈喜欢烹饪，是吗？

The plane took off an hour ago, didn't it?

飞机 1 小时前起飞了，是吗？

He didn't go to school late this morning, did he?

他今早上学没有迟到，是吗？

They have known the matter，haven't they?

他们已经知道了这件事，是吗？

They will go to Beijing soon，won't they?

他们很快就要去北京了，是吗？

6. 变异祈使句，即句首为一呼语，后接第二人称代词引导的一个一般现在时的陈述句，这时，我们应视为无主语的祈使句结构，反义疑问句部分要用 **will you** 构成。例如：

Mike，you take all these tables out of the next room，will you?

迈克，你把这些桌子都搬出隔壁房间，好吗？

7. 陈述部分主语是动词不定式或动名词（To do/doing），反义疑问句主语是 **it**。例如：

Swimming is great fun，isn't it?

游泳很有趣，是吗？

To Succeed needs hard work，doesn't it?

成功需要付出努力，不是吗？

小试牛刀

Complete the following sentences.

1. Something is wrong with your computer，_____?

2. Somebody wants to see you，_____?

3. Those aren't your books，_____?

4. Kate has to help her mother at home，_____?

5. They had a good time in Beijing，_____?

6. We'd better stop talking，_____?

7. We need to arrive in Shanghai at 7：00，_____?

8. That man must be Mr. Wang，_____?

9. I'm right，_____?

10. Listen to me carefully，_____?

学以致用

Ⅰ. **Choose the best answer from the four choices A，B，C and D.**

1. I suppose the shoes will last you at least one year，_____?

　　A. won't they　　B. will they　　C. do I　　D. don't I

2. Everyone is surprised at the news，_____?

　　A. are you　　B. are they　　C. aren't they　　D. isn't she

3. You don't have to go to school on Sundays，_____ you?

　　A. have　　B. do　　C. should　　D. would

4. Tom isn't a hard working student，for it is the third time he has been late，_____?

　　A. wasn't it　　B. hasn't it　　C. isn't it　　D. hasn't he

5. Do pay attention to your work and keep your eyes open all the time，_____?

　　A. will you　　B. don't you　　C. shall we　　D. won't we

6. All the drivers dislike driving on the narrow roads，_____?

　　A. don't they　　B. don't each of them　　C. do I　　D. don't you

7. Let's go and have a walk，_____?

　　A. do we　　B. shall we　　C. haven't we　　D. shan't we

8. Go and fetch a chair for him, _____?

    A. don't you   B. shall you   C. won't you   D. will you

9. There used to be a shop behind the factory, _____?

    A. didn't there   B. used there   C. usedn't it   C. didn't it

10. I'm sure he must have been sleeping at the moment, _____?

    A. wasn't I   B. mustn't he   C. aren't I   D. hasn't he

11. I had to tell the truth, _____?

    A. hadn't I   B. wouldn't I   C. didn't I   D. shouldn't I

12. — Why is Tom absent now?

    —He must be sick, _____?

    A. isn't he   B. must he   C. is he   D. mustn't he

13. He'd like to have a look at your picture, _____ he?

    A. hadn't   B. didn't   C. couldn't   D. wouldn't

14. Jack had dinner with his mother at home yesterday, _____?

    A. did he   B. does he   C. didn't he   D. hadn't he

15. Let John finish the work all by himself, _____?

    A. shall we   B. will you   C. do you   D. do we

16. Nothing the boy did was right, _____ it?

    A. was   B. did   C. wasn't   C. didn't

17. It's the first time that she has been to the United States, _____?

    A. isn't she   B. isn't it   C. hasn't she   D. hasn't it

18. He was hardly able to stand on his feet after the car accident, _____ he?

    A. could   B. couldn't   C. was   D. wasn't

19. Jack seldom goes to the park, _____?

    A. does Jack   B. doesn't he   C. doesn't Jack   D. does he

20. People use tag question (反义疑问) because they are not sure of what they have said, _____ they?

    A. do   B. did   C. don't   D. didn't

21. Everyone wants to be chosen for the work, _____?

    A. don't they   B. does he   C. isn't he   D. do they

22. She is going to see you, _____ she?

    A. is   B. isn't   C. don't   D. doesn't

23. They used to live in these mountain areas, _____ they?

    A. didn't   B. did   C. used   D. weren't

24. He ought to go by plane, _____ he?

    A. wouldn't   B. shouldn't   C. should   D. would

25. Lovely weather! _____?

    A. isn't it   B. is it   C. are they   D. aren't they

26. We must start earlier, _____ we?

    A. needn't   B. mustn't   C. don't   D. mustn

27. You must have studied English for many years, _____ you?

    A. didn't   B. haven't   C. needn't   D. mustn

28. I needn't show her the keys to the question, _____ I?

A. can　　　　　B. must　　　　　C. needn't　　　　　D. do

29. We need to practice speaking English more often, _____ we?

A. mustn't　　　　B. needn't　　　　C. don't　　　　D. can't

30. I have to work this afternoon，_____ I?

A. haven't　　　　B. needn't　　　　C. don't　　　　D. do

Ⅱ．Translate the following sentences into English.

1. 他过去工作很努力，对吧？
2. 房间里什么也没有，是吗？
3. 孩子们从未去过重庆，对吧？
4. 我认为你不可能做这件事，对吧？
5. 我是个很诚实的人，不是吗？
6. 比赛中，每个人都已经尽了他们最大的努力，是吗？
7. 咱们一起回家吧，好吗？
8. 我们最好自己做它，是吧？
9. 他们过去是好朋友，是吗？
10. 他几乎没钱了，对吗？

第三节　强调句、倒装句和省略句

重点知识概览

强调句、倒装句和省略句重点知识概览

类别	形式	结构	备注
强调句	It is/was ＋…	It is/was＋强调部分＋that/who ＋句子其余部分	强调人称用 that/who，强调其他用 that
	用助动词 do	do/does/did ＋v.	
倒装句	全部倒装	方位副词＋vi.＋主语	谓语动词是不及物动词，主语是名词
		表示地点的介词短语＋vi.＋主语	
	部分倒装	否定词语（词组）＋do/does/did＋主语＋v.	
		Not until …；Not only … but also …；Neither … nor …	否定分句倒装
		No sooner… than …；Hardly/Scarcely … when …	否定从句倒装
		Only＋状语＋助动词＋主语＋…	
省略句	并列句	省略后一分句中相同的词语	
	复合句	省略宾语从句中第一个 that	
		状语从句中省略主语和 be 动词	从句主语和主句主语一致时

知识梳理

强调句(Emphatic Sentences)是一种修辞，是人们为了表达自己的意愿或情感而使用的一种形式。

倒装句(Inversion Sentences)分为完全倒装和部分倒装。把谓语全部放在主语之前，称为完全倒装。只把助动词、情态动词或连系动词等放到主语之前，称为部分倒装。

省略句(Elliptical Sentences)是将句子中一个或多个成分省去，避免重复，使语言简练紧凑的一种语法手段。

一、强调句(Emphatic Sentences)

1. 用助动词"do(does/did)＋动词原形"来表示强调。例如：

He does know the place well.

他的确很熟悉这个地方。

Do be careful when you cross the street.

过马路时千万要小心啊！

They do come tomorrow.

他们明天的确回来。

He did help me a lot.

他的确给了我许多帮助。

2. 用形容词 very, only, single, such, best, ever, even 等修饰名词或形容词来加强语气。例如：

You are the only person here who can speak Chinese.

你是这里唯一一会讲汉语的人。

At that very moment the policemen came.

就在那时，警察来了。

Not a single person has been in the shop this morning.

今天上午这个商店里连一个人都没有。

War and Peace is the best novel that I have ever read.

《战争与和平》是我读过的最好的小说。

3. 用 in the world(究竟)，on earth(究竟)，at all(究竟)，not in the least(一点儿也不)等介词短语可以表达更强的语气(常用于疑问句)。例如：

Where in the world did you go just now?

刚才你究竟去哪儿了？

What on earth are you doing?

你究竟在做什么？

Do you know at all?

你到底知不知道？

She's not in the least angry with me.

她一点也不生我的气。

4. It is/was…that…句型

Be 动词：is /was，be 动词的选择要视谓语动词的时态而定。

注意：It 无词义，that 没有实际意义，只起语法连接作用。

一般来说，如果把句子的 It is/was…that 去掉，稍加语序调整，句子结构完整，不缺成分，则是强调句型。

(1)陈述句的强调句型：It is/ was ＋被强调部分(通常是主语、宾语或状语)＋that/ who＋其他部

> **重点点拨**
>
> ★ 强调句的两个主要用法：
>
> 1. 助动词 do/does/did 强调谓语动词。对过去动作的强调用 did，一般现在时第三人称单数用 does，其余情况用 do。其后的谓语动词用原形。
>
> 2. It is/was ＋ 强调部分 ＋ that/who ＋ 句子其余部分。
>
> 当强调人物时，用 who/that 都可以，强调其他成分时，用 that。
>
> 强调部分不能是谓语动词。

分。例如：

It is she that/ who will go abroad to study. （强调主语）

是她要出国学习。

It was her that/ who I saw on the street last night. （强调宾语）

我昨天在街上看到的是她。

It was on the street that I saw her last night. （强调地点状语）

昨天晚上我是在街上看见她的。

It is on Oct 1st that we will celebrate the National Day. （强调时间状语）

在十月一日我们庆祝国庆节。

(2)一般疑问句的强调句为"Is（Was）it ＋ … that … ?"例如：

Was it ten years ago that his mother died?

他的母亲是 10 年前去世的吗？

Is it Prof. Yang who will give us a talk on employment?

是杨教授要给我们做关于就业的讲座吗？

(3)特殊疑问句为："特殊疑问词＋ is（was）it ＋ that … ?"结构。表示"究竟是谁……，到底在哪里……"等。例如：

When is it that you can finish your homework?

你到底什么时候才能完成你的作业？

Who was it that you wanted to see?

你究竟想见的是谁？

Why is it that you want to change your mind?

你究竟为什么要改变主意？

(4)"not … until …"句型的强调结构为"It is not until … that … "应注意把否定词 not 转移到 until 前面。例如：

It was not until 7:00 p. m. last night that I went home.

直到晚上 7 点钟我才回家。

It was not until she took off her dark glasses that I realized she was a famous film star.

直到她取下墨镜我才认出她是位著名的电影明星。

(5)强调句型中，也可以用情态动词＋be 。例如：

It may be＋ 被强调部分＋ that …

It must have been＋被强调部分＋that …

Would/ Could it be ＋被强调部分＋that … ?

It may be next week that she leaves for Hongkong.

或许下周她要出发去香港。

It must have been John who bought a new book for Mary yesterday.

昨天一定是约翰买了一本新书给玛丽。

Could it be yesterday that you lost your handbag?

你的手提包会是在昨天丢的吗？

(6)It is/was … that … 强调句型的被强调部分如果是原因状语从句，只能由 because 引导，不能由 since、as 或 why 引导。例如：

It was because the water had risen that they could not cross the river.

正是由于水位上涨，他们没能渡过河去。

It is because our country has become powerful that we can live a happy life.

正是因为我们的国家变得强大了，我们才能过上幸福的生活。

(7)强调句型的反义疑问句形式

句式特征为：It is/was＋被强调部分＋that…，isn't / wasn't it? 例如：

It was Alice and her boyfriend who sent the old man to the hospital，wasn't it?

是爱丽丝和她男朋友把那位老人送往医院的，不是吗？

It is on May 5th of lunar month that the Chinese celebrate the Dragon-Boat Festival，isn't it?

中国人庆祝端午节是在农历的五月五日，不是吗？

5. 用倒装句型表示强调，也就是将要强调的句子或被强调的部分置于句首。例如：

On the table were some fresh flowers. （强调地点）

桌上摆着一些鲜花。

Only in this way，can we solve this problem. （强调方式）

只有这样，我们才能解决这个问题。

Many a time have he climbed that hill. （强调时间）

他多次翻过那座山。

Not until she had arrived home did she remember her appointment with the doctor. （强调时间）

直到她到家了才想起她和医生的约定。

6. What（What… is/was…）引导的主语从句表示强调。例如：

What I did last weekend was (to) visit an old friend. （强调谓语）

我上周末所做的事就是去拜访了一位老朋友。

What he wishes most is to become a scientist. （强调宾语）

他最大的愿望是成为一名科学家。

What interested me most in Sichuan was various delicious food. （强调主语）

在四川最让我感兴趣的是各种各样的美食。

What I want to say is that you should study hard. （强调宾语）

我想说的是你应该努力学习。

What encouraged us to go ahead was the example he set for us. （强调主语）

鼓舞我们前进的是他为我们树立的榜样。

📝 易错盘点

在强调句型"It is/was＋强调部分＋that/who＋句子其余部分"中，注意以下几点。

1. 当被强调部分指人时，可用 that，也可用 who；指物时，只能用 that。例如：

It was Mary that/who I came across yesterday.

我昨天遇到的是玛丽。

It is she who/that often helps those old men who live alone.

是她经常帮助那些独居的老人。

2. 强调状语时，只用 that，不用 when、where、which。例如：

It is 8:20 that we begin to have classes.

我们是 8:20 开始上课。

It was in Beijing that the 2008 Summer Olympic Games was held.

2008 年夏季奥运会是在北京举办的。

3. 被强调的部分是主语时，注意句子的谓语动词和被强调的主语保持一致。例如：

It is he who is often late.

是他经常迟到。

It is they that are often late.
是他们经常迟到。

4. 被强调成分是作主语的代词，用主格，是作宾语的代词，用宾格。例如：

It was he that helped me yesterday. （强调主语）
昨天是他帮助了我。

It was me that he helped yesterday. （强调宾语）
昨天他帮助的是我。

5. 强调句可强调主语、宾语、状语等，不能用来强调谓语动词、表语、补语、让步状语、条件状语等。例如：

Could it be in the restaurant _____ you had dinner with me yesterday _____ you lost your handbag?

    A. that；which   B. which；that   C. where；that   D. that；where

解析："you had dinner with me yesterday"是 where 引导的定语从句修饰"the restaurant"，整个"in the restaurant where you had dinner with me yesterday"是强调部分，强调地点状语，本句的意思是"你可能是在昨天与我一起吃晚饭的那家餐厅弄丢的手提袋吗?"所以答案为 C。

6. 强调句型的省略形式。例如：

句式特征为：在一定的上下文中，强调句型的某个部分可以省略。做题时要特别注意将其复原并加以比较。

—Who is making so much noise in the garden?

—_____ the children.

    A. It is   B. They are   C. That is   D. There are

解析：本题选 A。根据上文意思，完整回答应是"It is children that are making so much noise in the garden."本句意思是"是孩子们在花园里发出如此大的吵闹声。"

7. 强调句型的时态要以原句的时态为依据。原句用现在时，强调句用 is；若原句为过去时，强调句中则要用 was。例如：

I met him in the street yesterday. （原句）
→It was him that I met in the street yesterday. （强调句）
我昨天在街上见到的是他。

I like Chinese culture best. （原句）
→It is Chinese culture that I like best. （强调句）
我最喜欢的是中国文化。

二、倒装句(Inversion Sentences)

英语句子的正常语序(Natural Order)是主语在前，谓语在后(主＋谓＋宾＋状)。但有时为了语法或修辞上的需要，也可以将谓语置于主语之前，这样的语序就叫作倒装语序(Inverted Order)。倒装语序分为全部倒装(Full Inversion)和部分倒装(Partial Inversion)。全部倒装是将整个谓语置于主语之前；部分倒装只将谓语的一部分(通常是助动词或情态动词)置于主语之前。例如：

There is a table in the dinning-room. （全部倒装）
客厅里有一张桌子。

Only in this way can we do the work better. （部分倒装）
只有这样我们才能把工作做得更好。

1. 全部倒装

(1)"介词短语(地点状语)＋不及物动词＋主语"完全倒装句，谓语动词常是 be, stand, sit, lie, come 等，主语是名词。例如：

Under the tree sits a beautiful girl. ＝A beautiful girl sits under the tree.

树下坐着一位漂亮的女孩。

On the floor were piles of old books, magazines and newspapers.

地板上是一堆堆旧的书报杂志。

In the front of the lecture hall sits a professor.

演讲厅的前面坐着一位教授。

From the distance came a policeman.

远处来了一个警察。

(2)以方位副词开头的倒装句：以 ahead, away, back, down, in, off, out, up, over, below, upstairs, downstairs, outside 等表示方位的副词开头的倒装(方位副词＋不及物动词＋主语)，其谓语动词通常为 come, go, fly, rush 等表示移动的动词，主语是名词。例如：

Back fought our soldiers.

我们的士兵还击了。

Out rushed the children.

孩子们冲了出来。

Away flew the bird.

鸟儿飞走了。

The door opened and in came Mr. Smith, our headmaster.

门开了，史密斯先生——我们的校长走了进来。

(3)在语气词 There, Here 引导的句子(There/Here＋不及物动词＋主语)，谓语动词用不及物动词 come, go 等，主语是名词。例如：

Here comes the bus.

公交车来了。

There goes the bell.

铃响了。

(4)时间副词 Then, Now, Next 等开头的倒装句(Then/Now/Next＋不及物动词＋主语)，其谓语动词通常是 be, come, go, follow, begin, end 等，主语是名词。例如：

Now comes your turn!

该你了!

Then followed a shot of gun.

接着是一声枪响。

Thus ended the meeting.

会议就这样结束了。

(5)以引导词 there 开头的倒装句：表示存在的 there be 句型，主语在 be 之后。除 be 外，还可以使用 appear, exist, lie, remain, seem, stand, live, rise, happen, come, go, occur, follow 等半系动词，或 seem to be, happen to be, is likely to be 等，主语是名词。例如：

There is a pen and some books on the desk.

桌上有一支钢笔和一些书。

There are many people dancing on the square every evening.

广场上每晚都有许多人在跳舞。

There stands an ancient temple in this mountain, which attracts visitors.

重点点拨

★完全倒装；

1. 表地点的介词或方位副词开头的倒装结构："方位副词/表地点的介词短语＋不及物动词(vi.)＋主语(名词)"。

2. "there, here"引导的句子结构为"There/Here＋不及物动词＋主语(名词)"。

3. "表＋系＋主"结构中，表语可以是形容词、-ing 分词、-ed 分词。

4. There be 句型中，be 动词或其他动词的单复数形式由其后的主语单复数确定。

这座山里矗立着一座古庙，它吸引着许多游客。

There lives an old fisherman in the village.

村里住着一位老渔夫。

There seems something wrong with my radio.

我这台收音机好像有什么毛病。

There exist different opinions on this question.

关于这个问题还有不同的意见。

(6)"表+系+主"(表语通常为形容词、现在分词和过去分词)的全部倒装句，谓语是 be，表语提前时，整个句子需倒装。例如：

Happy is he who devoted himself to the cause of communism.

投身于共产主义事业的他很幸福。

Lucky is she who was admitted to a famous university last year.

她很幸运，去年被一所名牌大学录取。

Gone are the days when they could do what they liked to the Chinese people.

他们对中国人民为所欲为的日子一去不复返了。

Present at the meeting are some well-known scientists.

一些知名的科学家出席了会议。

Lying on the floor was a litter boy.

地上躺着一位小男孩。

Sitting in the front are the leaders of our college.

坐在前面的是我们学校的领导。

(7)若直接引语的部分或全部放在句首，并且说话人是名词时，将 say 或 ask 置于说话人之前，就是完全倒装。例如：

"You've made great progress this term." said the teacher.

老师说："你这学期取得了巨大进步。"

"Tom", said his father, " You shouldn't make friends with such boys!"

"汤姆"，他的父亲说，"你不应该跟这样的男孩子们交朋友！"

(8)such 置于句首时，此句型中的 such 多被认为是表语，所以 such 后的 be 动词应与其后的"真正主语"保持一致。例如：

Such are the facts; no one can deny them.

事实就是如此，没有人能否认它们。

2. 部分倒装

(1)否定词语放在句首，句子部分倒装。常见否定词：no, not, never, few, little, seldom(几乎不), hardly(几乎不), rarely(几乎不), scarcely(几乎不), seldom(几乎不), nowhere(无处，哪儿也找不到)等，例如：

Not a penny will I lend you.

我一分钱也不会借给你。

Little did she know that the police were around.

她一点也不知道警察就在旁边。

Hardly could she believe her own eyes.

她几乎不敢相信自己的眼睛。

Nowhere else could you find such beautiful scenery.

哪儿也找不到这样美丽的景色。

Never before in all my life have I felt so happy!

我一生中从未这么开心过!

Seldom had he seen such beauty.

他以前很少见过这样的美景。

(2)否定词组放在句首,句子部分倒装。

常见否定词组:by no means = in/under no circumstances = on no account = in no case = on no consideration 表示"绝不",in no way(一点也不),at no time(无论在什么时候都不),on no condition (无论如何也不),no longer(不再)等。例如:

By no means shall I change the plan.

我绝不会改变计划。

No longer will I believe a word he says.

我再也不信他说的任何话了。

In no case are you to leave your post.

你决不可以离开你的岗位。

Under no circumstances should we give up our dream.

我们绝不放弃我们的梦想。

At no time do you give up hope.

无论什么时候你都不要放弃希望。

(3)否定句型放句首,句子部分倒装。常见句型:not until(直到 ……才),not only…but also(不仅……而且),neither … nor …(既不 ……也不),no longer(不再),no sooner…than(刚……就……), hardly/scarcely…when(刚……就……),例如:

Hardly had he arrived home when he began to do his homework.

他一到家就开始做作业了。

Not only is this young man clever but he is also hard working.

这个年轻人不仅聪明,而且勤奋。

Not until a month later did she learn the news.

直到一个月后她才听到那个消息。

No sooner had we got home than it began to rain.

我们刚到家就开始下雨。

Neither has he called her, nor will he do so.

他既没有给她打过电话,将来也不会给她打。

(4)"only+状语"式部分倒装(only+状语从句,从句不倒装,主句倒装),Only 后加副词/介词短语/状语从句时,后面的主句需要部分倒装。

句式:only + 状语 + 助动词/系动词/情态动词 + 主语 + 动词原形。例如:

Only then did I see life was not easy.

只有那时我才知道生活是不易的。

Only in this way can you use the computer well.

只有用这种方法你才能把计算机用好。

Only when one loses freedom does one know its value.

只有当人们失去自由时,方知其珍贵。(修饰状语从句)

Only by working hard can we succeed.

重点点拨

★不完全倒装:

1.否定词语或词组放在句首,其结构形式为"否定词/否定词组+助动词+主语+谓语动词+…"。助动词由谓语动词的时态确定。

2.only+状语从句,从句不倒装,主句倒装。

3.not until(直到……才……)置于句首,从句不倒装,主句倒装。

4.not only…but also…(不但……而且……),neither … nor …(既不……也不……)连接两个分句,两个分句都要倒装。

5.no sooner … than(刚……就……),hardly/scarcely … when(刚……就……)句型中,主句是过去完成时,采用倒装,than 和 when 后的从句不倒装,用一般过去时。

6.so,nor,neither 开头的句子里。表示前面说的话也适用于另一人或物,其倒装句型为:"so/neither/nor + be/助动词/情态动词+主语"。

7.as/though 引导的让步状语从句倒装结构句式:"形容词/副词/动词/名词 + as/though+主语+ 动词"。

只有努力工作我们才能成功。

（5）so/such＋部分倒装＋that 从句。so 或 such 位于句首加强语气时，构成部分倒装句，例如：

Such a good boy is he that we all love him.

他是如此好的一个孩子以至于我们所有人都喜欢他。

So attentively was he working that he didn't notice me come in.

他如此聚精会神地工作以至于没有注意到我进来了。

So angry was he that he couldn't speak.

他是如此生气以至于说不出话来。

Such was his anger that he lost control of himself.

他是如此生气，以至于控制不了自己了。

（6）在以 so, nor, neither 开头的句子里，表示前面说的话也适用于另一人或物，其倒装句型为："so/neither/nor＋be/助动词/情态动词＋主语"。So 与前面的肯定句呼应，neither/nor 与前面的否定句呼应，意为"……也是，/……也不是"，例如：

She is a teacher. So is her mother.

她是教师，她母亲也是。

He has been to Beijing. So have I.

他去过北京，我也去过。

He can send emails to his former classmates. So can she.

他能发电子邮件给以前的同学，她也能。

I didn't go to the cinema last night. Nor did he.

昨晚我没有去看电影，他也没有去。

I have never been abroad. Neither has he.

我从未出过国，他也没有出过。

I am not interested in maths. Neither is he.

我对数学不感兴趣，他也不感兴趣。

（7）as/though 引导的让步状语从句倒装结构

句式："形容词/副词/动词/名词＋as/though＋主语＋ 动词"。

①表语提前，构成倒装。例如：

Pretty though she is, she is not clever.

虽然她很漂亮，但是她不聪明。

Disabled as he was，he tried his best to serve the people.

虽然他残疾了，但他仍尽力为人民服务。

Child as she is, she knows several foreign languages.

虽然她还是个孩子，但她懂几门外语。（child 作表语，提至句首，其前不加冠词）

②动词提前，构成倒装。例如：

Search as they did, they could not find anything in the house.

虽然他们搜遍了整个屋子，却没找到任何东西。

Fail as she did, she would try again.

尽管她失败了，但她还要再试。

③副词提前，构成倒装。例如：

Hard as he tried, he couldn't pass the exam.

尽管他努力了，还是没有通过考试。

Attentively as I listened，I still couldn't understand what he said at the meeting.

尽管我专心听了，还是听不懂他在会议上说的话。

(8)省略 if 的虚拟条件句，将这些词"were，had，should"移至主语之前，例如：

Should he be interested in this subject, he might work hard at it.

如果他对这一科目感兴趣的话，他或许会努力学习它。

Were I you（＝ If I were you），I would go.

如果我是你，我就会去。

Had I time（＝ If I had time），I would go and help you.

如果我有时间，我会去帮你。

(9)一些表示频率的副词位于句首时，句子部分倒装。常用词有：often，always，once，many a time，now and then，every other day，every two hours，thus，then 等，例如：

Many a time has he helped me with my lessons.

他多次帮助我学习功课。

Every weekend do I go to see my grandparents.

我每周末都去看望我的爷爷奶奶。

Often did she come to my house in the past.

过去她常到我家来。

Thus was it stolen.

它就是这样被偷的。

注意：这些词如不提前，仍在原位置，则不用倒装。例如：

I often spoke of him before.

我以前经常说起他。

(10)表示方式、程度的副词位于句首时。例如：

Well do I remember the day when I joined the Party.

我对入党的那一天还记忆犹新。

Gladly would I accept his proposal.

我会很高兴地接受他的建议。

3. 常见的其他形式的倒装结构

(1)the …more… the more …结构中的倒装，例如：

The harder you work, the happier you feel.

你越努力工作，就越觉得快乐。（表语提前）

The more you study, the more you know.

你学得越多，就明白得越多。（宾语提前）

注意：有时从句倒装，主句不倒装。例如：

I like the painting better the more I look at it.

我越看这幅画，就越喜欢它。

(2) 感叹句(What 感叹名词，How 感叹形容词/副词)

What ＋ a/ an ＋ *adj*. ＋ 可数名词单数 ＋ 主语 ＋ 谓语!

What ＋ *adj*. ＋ 可数名词复数 / 不可数名词 ＋ 主语 ＋ 谓语!

How ＋ *adj*. / *adv*. ＋ 主语 ＋ 谓语! 例如：

What exciting news it is!

多么激动人心的消息啊!

How beautiful the scenery is!

多么美丽的风景啊!

(3)宾语位于句首表示强调，例如：

The past one can know，but the future one can only feel.

一个人可以知道过去，但只能感悟未来。

What you did I cannot imagine.

我想象不出你做了什么。

(4)一些习惯说法使用倒装语序，例如：

How goes it with you?

你好吗？

What care I?

关我什么事？

What matters it?

这有什么关系？

(5)一些表祝愿的句子用部分倒装，例如：

Long live China!

中国万岁！

Long live our friendship!

我们的友谊万岁！

注意：在"Long live…!"句型中live要用原形动词。

易错盘点

1. 完全倒装易错点

(1)完全倒装构成条件有3个。

①表方位的副词或介词短语放句首。

②主语是名词，不是代词。

③谓语动词是不及物动词。

试比较：

Here it is.	Here is the book.
In he comes.	In comes the boy.
Here you are.	Here are the students.

注意：当主语是代词时，不构成倒装。

(2)在完全倒装句中，谓语动词的数要与后面主语的数一致。例如：

There seems to be many people in the room.（误）

There seem to be many people in the room.（正）

房间里似乎有许多人。

In front of the house stand a tall tree.（误）

In front of the house stands a tall tree.（正）

房前有一棵高大的树。

(3)直接引语倒装注意以下两点。

①主语是代词时，倒装不倒装都可以。例如：

"What are you doing?" asked he.（He asked）

他问："你在干什么？"

②引用动词另有宾语时，即使主语是名词也不倒装。例如：

"Why were you late again?" the teacher asked him.

老师问他："你为什么又迟到了?"

2. 部分倒装句易错点

(1)部分倒装的结构形式：助动词＋主语＋谓语动词＋其他。助动词由谓语动词时态确定，谓语动词是一般现在时，助动词用 do/does；谓语动词是一般过去时，助动词用 did；其余时态则是把助动词提到主语之前。例如：

Seldom does she care about her clothes.

她几乎不在意她的穿着。

Only then did I realize the importance of love.

只有在那时，我才意识到了爱的重要。

If you don't go to the party, nor / neither will I.

如果你不去参加晚会，我也不去了。(主将从现)

At no time should a Party member put his personal interest first.

一名共产党员绝不应该把个人利益放在首位。

Never have I heard such a big lie.

我从来没有听过如此大的谎言。

Hardly had we arrived home when it began to rain.

我们一到家就开始下雨。

(2)如句首含有否定意义的词在句中作主语，或起修饰、连接主语的作用，则不倒装。例如：

Not only the students but also all the teachers will take part in the school sports meeting.

不仅是学生还有全体教师都会参加校运会。

Not a single word that she said was true.

她说的话没有一句是真的。

Little difficulties cannot prevent me from carrying out the plan.

这些小困难不能阻止我实施这个计划。

Not all countries celebrate the New Year on the same day.

不是所有国家都在同一天庆祝新年。

Few classmates haven't handed in their homework.

少数几位同学没有交作业。

注意：如否定词语或词组不提前时，则句子不倒装。

I seldom read newspaper before.

我以前几乎不看报纸。

(3)not until... 置于句首时，句型中前面的从句不倒装，后面的主句用部分倒装。

句型：Not until ＋ 状语(/从句) ＋ 主句(部分倒装)，例如：

Not until the villagers realize how serious the pollution was did all the fish die in the river.

直到村民们意识到污染有多严重时，河里的鱼都死了。

Not until the child fell asleep did the mother leave the room.

直到孩子睡着了，妈妈才离开房间。

(4)no sooner... than...；hardly... when...；scarcely... when... 意思是"一……就……"置于句首时，句型后面的从句不倒装，前面的主句采用部分倒装并且要用过去完成时。而 than 和 when 后的从句要用一般过去式。例如：

No sooner had he come back home than he went to see his sick mother.

他一回到家就去看他生病的母亲。

Hardly had he arrived home when he began to do his homework.

他一到家就开始做作业了。

He had hardly finished his homework when the light went out.

他一完成作业灯就熄灭了。

(5)Neither…nor 连接的两个句子时，两个句子都要倒装。例如：

Neither do I know where he is，nor do I care.

我既不知道也不关心他在哪里。

(6)not only…but also 连接的两个句子时，not only 后面的句子要倒装，but also 后的句子不倒装。例如：

Not only shall we learn from books，but also we should learn from practice.

我们不但要从书本上学习，还要从实践中学习。

(7)only 修饰状语从句时，主句倒装，从句不倒装；only 修饰的不是状语时，则不用倒装语序。例如：

Only when he is seriously ill does he ever stay in bed.

只有病重时，他才待在床上。

Only you are allowed to come in.

只许可你进入。（非倒装句）

(8)当 however，no matter how 引导让步状语从句，常把"however / no matter how ＋ 形容词 / 副词"放在句首，此时主谓不倒装。例如：

No matter how well a poem is translated，something of the spirit of the original work is lost.

无论一首诗翻译得多么好，原作品中的一些神韵还是会失去。

No matter how difficult the work is，he will try his best to finish it.

无论这项工作有多困难，他都会尽全力去完成。

(9)so，neither/nor 引导的倒装，前后两句的时态及谓语动词必须一致。例如：

I loved this movie and so did all my friends.

我喜欢这部电影，我所有的朋友也喜欢。

I hadn't been to New York before and neither had Jane.

我以前没有去过纽约，简也没去过。

She can hardly drive a car. Neither/Nor can I.

她几乎不会开车，我也不会。

注意1：表示对前面或对方所说情况的赞同或证实，意思是"的确如此"句式是："So＋主语＋助动词/be/情态动词"，这种结构中的主谓是正常语序。例如：

—It's very cold today.　　今天很冷。

—So it is.　　的确很冷。

注意2：如果前面所说的内容既有肯定又有否定，或前后的谓语动词形式不一致时，用"It is the same with ＋主语"结构或用"So it is with ＋主语"结构。例如：

He worked hard，but didn't pass the exam. So it was with his sister.

他很努力，但没有通过考试。他妹妹也是这样。（既有肯定又有否定）

She is a teacher and she enjoys teaching. So it is the same with Mr. Li.

她是老师，热爱教书。李先生也是这样。（谓语一个是系动词，一个是行为动词）

(10)as/though 引导的让步状语从句倒装结构中，放在句首的名词不用冠词，形容词或副词最高级前不用 the。例如：

Though he ran the fastest，he still didn't catch the train. → Fastest as he ran，he still didn't catch the train.（副词最高级前不用定冠词 the）

尽管他跑得最快，仍没有赶上火车。

Although he is a child，he speaks fluent English. →Child as he is，he speaks fluent English.（名词单数前不用不定冠词 a）

虽然他是个孩子，但能讲流利的英语。

三、省略句(Elliptical Sentences)

在英语中，凡是能省去的词语通常都应省去，省略后的结果不仅能使句子更加精炼，而且还可起到连接上下文使相邻词语得到强调的作用。

1. 简单句中的省略

(1)省略主语，通常多用在祈使句或口语中的固定表述中。例如：

Not at all! (＝ You needn't thank me at all)

不客气。

(I'm) Sorry.

对不起。

(You) Never mind.

没关系。

(That's) Enough!

够了!

(I) Thank you.

谢谢你。

Have (you) a good time.

祝(你)过得愉快。

(You) Open the door，please.

请(你)开门。

(It) Doesn't matter.

(它)没关系。

(2)省略谓语或谓语的一部分。例如：

(Does) Anybody need help?

谁需要帮忙吗?

(Is there) Anything you want?

你要什么东西吗?

Who (comes) next?

该谁了?

(3)省略主语和谓语的一部分。例如：

Why (do you) not say hello to him?

为什么你不跟他打招呼?

What (do you think) about a cup of tea?

来杯茶怎么样?

(Do you) Understand?

明白了吗?

(I am) Afraid I can't come.

恐怕不能来了。

(It) Sounds nice.

重点点拨

★简单句中的省略：

1."have trouble/difficulty (in) doing, be busy (in) doing sth, prevent/ stop …(from) doing …, spend time (in) doing"等固定短语中介词往往省略。

2.要注意不定式的省略的几种情况。

3.感官动词和使役动词"feel, hear, listen to, let, have make, see, watch, notice, observe"后省略 to 的动词或动词短语作宾语补语，当变为被动语态时，to 不能省掉。

★并列句中的省略：

and，but，or 连接的两个并列句中，后一个分句常省略与前一分句中相同的部分。

听起来很好。

(4)省略表语和宾语的一部分。例如：

—Are you thirsty?

—Yes，I am（thirsty）.

——你口渴吗？

——是的，我口渴。

—Where should we go?

—I don't care（where you go）. Anywhere you want.

——我们该去哪里？

——我不在乎你要去哪里。你想去哪里都行。

(5)固定短语中介词的省略：have trouble/difficulty（in）doing，be busy（in）doing sth.，prevent/ stop…（from）doing…，spend time（in）doing… 例如：

They spent a large sum of money（in）building the tower.

他们花费大量钱财用于建造那座塔。

He has difficulty（in）studying English.

他学习英语有困难。

注意：当 spend money（time）in doing sth. 结构用于被动语态时，in 不能省略。

A large sum of money was spent in building the tower.

建造那座塔花费了大量的钱财。

(6)一些句子中介词的省略。例如：

You will never manage successful（in）that way.

你用那种做法是永远不会成功的。

It's no use（in）crying.

哭也没用。

We have lived here（for）ten years.

我们在这儿已经住了 10 年了。

注意：在否定句中，此类 for 不能省略。

I haven't seen you for three months.

我已经 3 个月没有见到你了。

(7)不定式的省略。

①为避免重复，常省略上文已提到的动词原形，只保留不定式符号 to，这类动词有：expect，forget，hope，intend，mean，prefer，refuse，try，want，wish，would like 等。例如：

She asked me to dance with her，but I didn't want to（dance with her）.

她叫我和她一起跳舞，但我不想。

My mother asked me to buy some fruit after work，but I forgot to（buy some fruit）.

妈妈叫我下班后买些水果，但我忘了。

②在某些情态动词短语或助动词短语 have to，need，ought to，be going to，used to 等后省略动词。例如：

I really didn't want to go there with him，but I had to（go there with him）.

我真的不想和他一起去，但又不得不和他一起去。

③在某些形容词 delighted，glad，happy，pleased 等后省略 to 后面的动词。例如：

—Will you join in our discussion?

—I'll be glad to（join in your discussion）.

——你愿意加入我们的讨论吗？

——我很乐意。

④两个或两个以上的动词不定式并列在一起时，第一个不定式带 to，后面的不定式可省去 to。例如：

Her job is to take care of the children and（to）wash clothes.

她的工作是照看孩子和洗衣服。

(8)所有格之后的名词如为住宅、商店、矿、教堂等可以省略。例如：

She is going to her uncle's（house）.

她要去她的叔叔家。

Today I met her at the tailor's（shop）.

今天我在裁缝店遇到了她。

2. 并列句中的省略

and，but，or 连接的两个并列句中，后一个分句常省略与前一分句中相同的部分。

(1)当并列的主语相同时，后面的主语被省略。例如：

The machine was quite old but（it）was in excellent condition.

这台机器相当旧了，但性能还是非常好。

They shook hands and（they）began to talk at once.

他们握了手后立刻开始谈话。

(2)当并列的谓语动词相同时，动词(包括助动词、不定式等)可省略。例如：

Reading makes a full man；conference（makes）a ready man；writing an exact man.

读书使人充实；讨论使人机智；写作使人准确。

Some of us study English，others（study）Japanese.

我们中有的学英语，有的学日语。

John won the first race and Jimmy（won）the second.

约翰跑步第一名，吉米第二名。

(3)当并列的宾语相同时，省略动词宾语或介词宾语。例如：

Let's do some washing. I'll wash（the clothes）and you hang up（the clothes）.

咱们洗衣服吧。我来洗，你来晾晒。

(4)当并列的定语相同时，省略定语。例如：

A group of young boys and（young）girls are dancing on the meadow below the hill.

一群少男少女在山下的草地上跳舞。

He spent part of the money，and he saved the rest（of the money）.

他花掉一部分钱，把剩余的钱存起来了。

(5)省略主谓部分。

We tried to persuade her but（we tried）in vain.

我们想法子说服她，但没用。

Miss Li is easy in conversation and（she is）graceful in manner.

李小姐谈吐从容，举止优雅。

3. 复合句中的省略

(1)状语从句中的省略。当主句的主语和从句的主语一致时且谓语动词为 be，常省略从句的主语和 be 动词。

①由 when/while/as/once/whenever/as soon as 引导的时间状语从句。例如：

Please come here as soon as（it is）possible.

一有可能，她就来这里。

While (I was) walking in the rain, I heard my name called.

我在雨中漫步时，听到有人叫我的名字。

When (ice is) heated, ice can be turned into water.

当冰加热的时候，冰能变成水。

②由 if/unless 引导的条件状语从句，如果从句中含有"It＋be＋形容词/过去分词"结构，将 it 和 be 省略。例如：

She won't come to party unless (she is) invited.

除非她受到邀请，否则她不会来参加派对。

If (it is) sunny tomorrow, we will go for an outing.

如果明天出太阳，我们就去郊游。

③由 though/although/even if/even though 引导的让步状语从句。例如：

He is very good at painting, though(he is) very young.

虽然很年轻，但他非常擅长绘画。

Even if (he was) exhausted, he stayed up late.

即使疲惫不堪，他仍很晚才睡。

④由 because 引导的原因状语从句。

He was praised because(he was) brave.

因为勇敢，他受到了称赞。

Because ill, she didn't go to school yesterday.

因为生病，她昨天没去上学。

⑤由 wherever/where 引导的地点状语从句。例如：

Fill in the blanks with articles where (it is) necessary.

在需要的地方填上冠词。

⑥由 as if/as though/as 引导的方式状语从句。例如：

The boy looked as if(he was) afraid of nothing.

这个男孩看起来似乎什么都不怕。

Lucy hurriedly left the room as if (she was) angry.

露西急匆匆地走出房去，好像很生气的样子。

⑦比较状语从句中的省略。

She likes reading better than (she likes) going to parties.

比起参加舞会，她更喜欢读书。

He has lived here longer than I (have lived).

他比我在这里住得久。

In winter it is colder in Beijing than(it is) in Guangzhou.

冬天，北京比广东冷。

She is taller than I (am).

她比我高。

(2)定语从句中的省略。

①关系代词 who(m)，which 或 that 作宾语时可省略关系代词。例如：

I'll give you all (that) I have.

我会给你我所拥有的一切。

重点点拨

★复合句中的省略：

1.状语从句中：当主句的主语和从句的主语一致时且谓语动词为 be，常省略从句的主语和 be 动词。

2.定语从句中：

(1)关系代词 that/which，who(m)作宾语、表语时，可省去。

(2)省略定语从句中的关系代词和 be 动词，过去分词、-ing 分词短语作定语。

3.宾语从句中：

(1)动词后面接的宾语从句中，连词 that 可省略，若带有多个宾语从句，则只能省略第一个 that，第二个不能省略。

(2)在 I'm afraid, I think, I believe, I hope, I guess 等开头的作答句中，后面跟 so 与 not 分别用于肯定或否定宾语，宾语从句可省去。

He read the book（which）I got yesterday.

他读了我昨天得到的那本书。

The mobile phone（which）I wanted to buy was sold out.

我想买的那种手机卖完了。

②在以 the same…as/such…as 引导的定语从句中，可以省略与主句相同的部分。

David is such a good boy as all the teachers like（a good boy）.

大卫是一个如此好的孩子，所有老师都喜欢好孩子。

I have the same trouble as you（have）.

我和你有同样的困难。

③direction（方向），distance（距离），time（时间），times（倍数），the way（方式）等后面所接的定语从句中，可省略 that/in which/which。例如：

I don't like the way（that/which）she treats me.

我不喜欢她对待我的方式。

The distance（which/ that）light travels in one second is 300,000 kilometers.

光每秒走的距离是 30 万千米。

④that 在定语从句中作表语时可以省略。例如：

He is no longer the man（that）he used to be.

他不再是过去的那个人了。

My hometown is not a poor place（that）you think it to be.

我的家乡不是像你认为的那样，是一个贫穷的地方。

⑤过去分词、-ing 分词短语作定语。省略定语从句中的关系代词和 be 动词。例如：

Any body（which is）born in America naturally has American nationality.

在美国出生的人自然就拥有了美国国籍。

Fill in the blanks with the words（which are）given below.

用下列所给的词语填空。

The little girl（who was）selling matches was dying.

卖火柴的小女孩快要死了。

(3)宾语从句中的省略。

①在 know/think/consider/suppose/find/believe/say/decide 等动词后面接的宾语从句中，连词可省略，若带有多个宾语从句，则只能省略第一个 that。例如：

I believe（that）he will pass the national college entrance examination this year.

我相信他能通过今年的高考。

Our teacher said（that）the text was very important and that we should learn it by heart.

老师说这篇课文很重要且我们应该熟记于心。

②以 which/when/where/how 和 why 引导的宾语从句在其谓语与主句谓语相同时，可省略全部谓语，甚至主语也省略，仅保留一个 wh-词。例如：

She will go to Chengdu, but I don't know when（she will go to Chengdu.）

她将去成都但我不知道她何时去。

She can't attend the meeting, but I don't know why（she can't come）.

她不能出席会议，但我不知道为什么她不能。

You were late again, and I hope you will explain why（you were late again）.

你又迟到了，我希望你能解释一下为什么。

③在 I'm afraid，I think，I believe，I hope，I guess 等开头的作答句中，后面跟 so 与 not 分别用于

肯定或否定宾语，宾语从句可省去。例如：

—Do you think it will rain?

—I hope not（that it will not rain）.

——你认为要下雨了吗？

——我希望不。

—Are you leaving for Beijing this Sunday?

—I think so.（I'm leaving for Beijing this Sunday.）

——这个星期天你要去北京吗？

——我想是的。

4. 虚拟语气中的省略

(1)If 引导的虚拟条件从句中含 had/were/should，可以把 had/were/should 提到主语之前前，省略 if。例如：

Had he worked hard（If he had worked hard），he would have got through the examinations.

如果他努力学习，他就通过这次考试了。

Were I you，I would go to her birthday party.

如果我是你，我会去参加她的生日派对。

(2)在与 suggest/request/order/advise 等表示建议、请求（要求），命令等有关的名词性从句须用虚拟语气形式"主语 ＋should＋动词原形"，其中 should 可以省略。例如：

We all agree on his suggestion that we（should）work on the project at once.

我们都赞成他的建议，立刻开始这个项目。

He insisted that everyone（should）come to his office at one o'clock.

他坚持要求大家一点钟就要到他的办公室。

5. 各类词语的省略

(1)名词(短语)的省略，例如：

One hour today is worth two（hours）tomorrow.

今天的一小时胜过明天的两小时。

She likes classical（music）and country music.

她喜欢古典音乐和乡村音乐。

(2)限定词或代词的省略，例如：

(A)Friend of my mother gave it to me.

我妈妈一位朋友给我的。

(The)Trouble is he can't afford a house.

问题是他买不起房子。

My teachers and（my）fellow students have never heard about it.

我的老师和同学们都未听说过这件事。

(3)介词的省略，例如：

(Of) Course that's only a beginning.

当然这只是一个开头。

Why don't you catch up on it（before）Friday?

为什么不想办法在星期五之前把它做完。

(4)分词的省略，例如：

The meeting（being）over，we all left the room.

会议结束以后，我们都离开了房间。

Our work（having been）finished，we went home.

工作完成之后，我们就回家了。

(5)存在句中 there 的省略，例如：

(There) Must be something wrong with the car.

汽车一定出了什么毛病。

(There) Appears to be an accident over there.

那边好像出了事故。

6. 省略的一些特殊用途

(1)用于成语、谚语。例如：

More haste，less speed.

欲速则不达。

A lazy youth，a louse age.

少壮不努力，老大徒伤悲。

First come，first served.

先来先卖。

Better late than never.

迟做总比不做好。

No pains，no gains.

不劳则无获。

One Man，no Man.

个人是渺小的。

(2)一些固定句型中，如："How/what about ＋*n.* /*pron.* /*v.* ing，Why not ＋*v.* "中。例如：

How about going to France for our holiday?

咱们到法国去度假好吗？

What about the weather tomorrow?

明天天气怎样呢？

Why not go?

为什么不去呢？

(3) 用于电报、广告、公共警示用语、笔记、摘要、日记、报纸标题以及一些固定的表格。例如：

Congratulations on Your Great Success in Exam for Ph. D. Degree!

祝贺你参加博士学位考试成绩优异！（电报）

Passed TOEFL Exam Marks 636.

通过托福考试成绩 636 分。（电报）

Wanted：a typist.

招聘：打字员一名。（广告）

Keep off the Grass（Lawn）!

勿踏草地！（警示）

No Unauthorized Photography!

未经准许，不准拍照！（警示）

Usher in the 21-st Century!

迎接 21 世纪的到来！（标题）

易错盘点

1. 固定短语中介词的省略

这两个结构 "prevent/ stop…（from）doing… , spend time（in）doing" 在被动语态中，from, in 不能省略。例如：

He was prevented from going out alone.

阻止他独自外出。

One year was spent in finishing this project.

这项工程花了一年时间才完成。

2. 使役动词和感官动词后接省略 to 的动词或动词短语作宾语补语，当变为被动语态时，to 不能省掉。这样的动词有：feel，hear，listen to，let，have make，see，watch，notice，observe 等。例如：

I saw him steal a mobile phone from that girl's handbag. → He was seen to steal a mobile phone from that girl's handbag.

发现他从那个女孩的手提包里偷了一部手机。

3. 不定式的省略情况中，若不定式中带有 be，have，have been 等，通常保留 be，have，have been。例如：

—Aren't you the manager?

—No, and I don't want to be.

——难道你不是经理吗？

——不是，而且我也不想当经理。

John didn't come, but he ought to have (come).

约翰没来，但他本应该来的。

4. 主(宾)语补足语中的 to be 往往省略。例如：

We found the problem (to be) serious.

我们发现问题严重。

He was thought(to be) the cleverest boy in the group.

大家认为在小组中他最聪明。

5. 独立主格结构中的分词如为 being 或 having been 时，则多省去不用，意义不受影响。例如：

The meeting (being) over, we all left the room.

会议结束后我们都离开了房间。

6. 状语从句中省略需要满足的条件

(1)从句中被省略的主语必须与主句的主语一致，或者是 it。

(2)谓语动词必须含有 be。

(3)从句必须是主语和 be 动词一起省去，不可只省略主语而保留整个谓语，也不可只保留主语而省略谓语。例如：

The little girl began to cry when (she was) asked by the police.

当小女孩被警察询问时，她开始哭了起来。

When (you are) crossing the road, you'd better look at both sides.

当你横穿马路时，你最好往两边看看。

小试牛刀

Ⅰ. Omit some part to make the sentence more simple.

1. John worked hard but his brother did not work hard.

2. It is well done.

3. —I haven't finished the homework yet.

　　—Well, you ought to have finished the homework.

4. You must not be late and you must not be absent.

5. If it is necessary, we will finish it ahead of time.

6. While he was doing so, he trembled a little.

7. He said that he wouldn't go shopping and that he would go swimming instead.

8. This is the book that I bought yesterday.

Ⅱ. Underline the emphasized part in each sentence.

1. It was on October 1st 1949 that the PRC was founded.

2. It was in Jiuquan that we succeeded in sending up Shenzhou-18.

3. It's not until he got off the bus that he realized his money was stolen.

4. It was two years ago that I joined the army.

5. Why is it that electricity plays an important part in our daily life?

6. It is such an interesting book that we all like it very much.

7. Was it in the street that I met him yesterday?

8. David said that it was because of his strong interest in literature that he chose the course.

Ⅲ. Rewrite the sentences into inversion sentences.

1. He was able to get back to work only when the war was over.

2. He not only liked reading stories, but also he could even write some.

3. The old woman knew little that she was seriously ill herself.

4. He had hardly sat down when the telephone rang.

5. Light travels so fast it is difficult to imagine its speed.

6. A man named Jackson lived in the next house.

7. A tiger rushed out from among the bushes.

8. I have rarely seen such a beautiful sunset.

学以致用

Ⅰ. Complete the sentences.

1. _____（必要时），I will turn to you for help.

2. The river was deep and _____（冰薄）.

3. Only when the school is over _____（我们才可以去）for a holiday.

4. _____（老师不只对我们严格），but also he cared for us.

5. Not until yesterday _____（才知道真相）.

6. He passed the exam. _____.（我也过了）

7. _____（虽然他很聪明），he is not proud.

8. She can't speak English. _____.（她们也不会）

9. It was _____（直到那个时候）that I realized what trouble he was in.

10. _____（她一回家）when he began to do his homework.

Ⅱ. Translate the Chinese sentences into English.

1. 在中国工作时，彼得交了很多朋友。

2. 有可能的话，我会参加会议的。

3. 环境变了，环境中的人也变了。

4. 任何时间任何情况下，中国都不会首先使用核武器。

5. 如果她更小心些，就会避免这场事故了。

6. 直到开始工作，我才意识到我已经浪费了多少时间。

7. 是他每天早上在操场上读英语。

8. 我们刚到车站，火车就走了。

9. 是因为交通事故他才迟到的。

10. 房前躺着一位小男孩。

Ⅲ. Choose the best answer from the four choices A, B, C and D.

1. _____ give your friend some flowers?

    A. Why don't   B. Why not you   C. Why not   D. Why you not

2. — Would you like some more tea?

    — _____, please.

    A. No more   B. Just a little   C. I've had enough   D. Yes, I would

3. —I would never come to this restaurant again. The food is terrible!

    — _____ .

    A. Nor am I   B. Neither would I   C. Same with me   D. So do I

4. —Has he finished it?

    —Well, he _____ .

    A. ought to   B. ought to have   C. ought have   D. oughtn't have

5. —Do you think it's going to rain over the weekend?

    — _____ .

    A. I don't believe   B. I don't believe it   C. I believe not so   D. I believe not

6. I dislike the way _____ he speaks to his mother.

    A. in that   B. Which   C. What   D. /

7. _____ with the size of the whole earth, the biggest ocean does not seem big at all.

    A. Compare   B. When comparing   C. Comparing   D. When compared

8. —Why didn't you come to Mike's birthday party yesterday?

    —Well, I _____, but I forgot it.

    A. would   B. must   C. should have   D. must have

9. I hear Mr. Smith was writing a story last year and he still _____ .

    A. do   B. does   C. is   D. am

10. Water, _____ enough, can change into vapor quickly.

    A. when heated   B. heating

    C. though to be heated   D. when is heated

11. Never in my life _____ such a thing.

    A. I have heard of or seen   B. I had heard of or seen

    C. have I heard of or seen   D. did I hear of or seen

12. Not only _____ a promise, but also he kept it.

    A. did he make   B. he made

    C. does he make   D. has he made

13. _____ his appearance that no one would like him.

    A. So was strange   B. Was so strange

    C. So strange was   D. Strange so was

14. _____ and the lesson began.

    A. In came Mr. Brown   B. Mr. Brown in came

    C. In came he   D. In did Mr. Brown come

15. —Was _____ that I saw last night at the concert?

    —No，it wasn't.

    A. it you   B. not you   C. you   D. that yourself

16. I really don't know _____ I had my money stolen.

    A. where is it that   B. when it is that

    C. where it was that   D. it was where that

17. It was the culture，rather than the language，_____ made it hard for him to adapt to the new environment abroad.

    A. that   B. when   C. what   D. which

18. It might have been John _____ bought a present for Mary yesterday.

    A. where   B. why   C. what   D. who

19. —What should I do with his passage?

    —_____ the main idea of each paragraph.

    A. Finding out   B. Found out   C. Find out   D. To find out

20. —What kind of food would you like to have?

    — _____ but Japanese.

    —How about Korean，then?

    A. Anything   B. Something   C. Everything   D. Nothing

模块三　语言综合运用

第一章
阅读

重点知识概览

阅读重点知识概览

文本类型	题型类别	解题技巧	选项易错盘点
应用文 （宣传推广）	主旨大意题	1. 寻找主题句，确定文章主题。 2. 紧抓段落大意，概括中心思想。 3. 隐性主题，归纳要点。	张冠李戴
记叙文 （借景抒情）	细节理解题	1. 直接信息题：确定关键词，扫读找细节。 2. 语义转换题：同义转换、概念解析、归纳事实。 3. 数字信息题：理逻辑、算数字。	偷换概念 正误参半
议论文 （观点态度）	词意猜测题	1. 通过上下文语境猜词义。 2. 通过逻辑关系（同位、转折、比较、因果关系等）猜词义。 3. 根据已给解释猜词义（标点、定义、例子、代词、构词法等）。	以偏概全 望文生义
说明文 （特征用途）	推理判断题	1. 推断隐含意义（切忌片面思考、脱离原文、仅提取表层信息）。 2. 推理观点态度（积极、中立、消极）。 3. 推断文章出处（报纸、广告、网站、杂志、旅行指南等）。 4. 推断篇章结构（时间顺序、空间顺序、举例论证、对比、解释、分析、描述等）。	范围扩缩

阅读技巧

一、体裁详解

阅读理解是英语试题的重点，是考查学生语篇阅读能力、语言意识、英语语感的重要题型。阅读理解的核心是"理解"。"理解"既包括能准确把握所读材料的表层（字面意思）内容，理解内在含义；又包括能概括文章的主旨大意，能对语篇、文段的内部结构进行逻辑分析，推断出段落大意、文章主旨、作者的观点意图及文中未表达的事实、结论。

阅读理解材料内容真实，选材生活，贴近时代，渗透文化意识，强调实际应用。主要涉及人物趣事、中外交流、社会文化、语言习惯、历史事件、日常生活、新闻广告、科普知识等。在体裁上，记叙文、说明文、议论文和应用文各占一定的比例。阅读理解主要考查学生对语篇的主旨要义、特定细节、深层含义以及对篇章结构等的把握，大致包括主旨大意题、细节理解题、词义猜测题、推理判断题这几种题型。

(一)说明文

在阅读理解题中，说明文所占比重尤为突出。它既要求考生能熟练运用词汇和语法知识、理解文章语句、把握语篇整体结构，还要求学生有大量的阅读积累和知识储备，熟悉不同的话题和不同的题目考查方式。

1. 文体特点

说明文通常是使用平实的语言客观地解说事物、阐明事理，给人以知识的文体。它通常运用举例、对比、分类、引用、演绎、归纳等方法，按照时间、空间或事物发展的逻辑顺序进行介绍和说明。通过对实体事物(如仪器、产品、自然环境)的解说，或对抽象事理(如概念、原理、定律)的阐释，使人们对事物的形态、特征、构造、性能、种类、成因、功能等有所了解，或对事理的特点、来源、演变、异同等有所认识，从而获得相关的知识。说明文实用性很强，它包括广告、说明书、内容提要、规则章程、解说词、操作指南等。

2. 命题特点

阅读理解主要考查考生理解主旨与要义、理解文中具体信息、根据上下文推断单词和短语的含义、做出判断和推理、理解文章的基本结构、理解作者的意图、观点和态度等的能力。

(二)应用文

应用文是阅读理解命题的重要体裁，也是最贴近日常生活的文体，它通常以实用性为目的，以真实性为基础，以时效性为根本，以规则性为准则，形式多样，题材各异。

1. 文体特点

应用文不同于其他文体的文章，其目的是向读者传输信息，信息量大，文句简练，形式灵活，力求用最少的篇幅表达最多的信息。文章中会包含较多的人名、地名、专有名词，缩略词等，多祈使句和省略句。一般会采用醒目的标题突出重点，用粗体字或各类符号标识使文章结构鲜明，条理清晰。文章内容生活化，多样化，实用性强，目的都是向读者传输信息。共包括两大类：一类是说明性应用文，包括广告、启示、海报、守则、公告、指南、个人简历、备忘录、摘要等；另一类是叙事性应用文，如书信、日记、便条、报告、请帖等。

2. 命题特点

应用文主要考查学生提取信息和处理信息的能力，既注重特定细节的筛选、类比、综合，又注重判断推理题的考查。

(三)议论文

议论文是英语中的重要文体，是一种作者通过陈述观点，试图说服读者接受其所给的观点的文体。议论文涉及的论题具有生活化的特征，与社会生活密切相关。相比其他文体，议论文阅读理解要更难一些，因此要多加重视。

1. 文体特点

议论文观点明确、论据充分、语言精练、论证合理，有严密的逻辑性，通常采用三段式的结构，即"提出问题(引论)—分析问题(本论)—解决问题(结论)"。一篇好的议论文，观点明确且正确，论据充分，论证合乎逻辑，结构、层次清晰。议论文题材多样化，包括社会科学的多个领域，涵盖文化、历史、文学、科学和教育等各个方面。

2. 命题特点

议论文阅读理解以考查细节理解和推理判断为主，也不乏对观点态度的考查。议论文阅读理解易错点往往在于事实与观点的区分以及观点本身，解题时谨防将引述的观点和作者的观点混为一谈。

(四)记叙文

记叙文通常描述的是一件具体事情的发生、发展和结局，通常包括时间、地点、人物、事件等信息。

1. 文体特点

记叙文是一种通过记载和叙述来描绘事物和人物情景状态、过程及发展的文体。英语阅读理解中的记叙类文章一般包括人物传记、哲理故事等。英语记叙文以描写叙述为主，主要描写人物、事件、地点或过程，主题往往隐藏在字里行间，文章主旨需要通过人物、事件来提炼。文章大多数按照时间顺序、空间顺序、事情发展顺序来展开。

2. 命题特点

记叙文的命题顺序都会按照文章脉络和故事发展的顺序层层推进。同时，记叙文需要事件的发展过程作支撑，一半以上的题目都会用来检测考生对故事的了解，因此，我们必须弄明白整件事情的发展脉络。此外，细节题是记叙文命题的主流题型。

二、阅读方法

针对阅读理解中不同类型的题目，解题的总体策略应定位于：单句入手，语篇突破，着眼整体，归纳推断。为了更好地获取和处理信息，也必须具备下列两种常用的阅读方法：略读(Skimming)和扫读(Scanning)。略读和扫读是两种最常见的阅读技巧，它们在目的、方法和应用场景上有所不同。

(一)略读

略读的主要目的是快速获取文章或材料的大意。它要求读者有选择性地进行阅读，跳过一些细节，以便快速抓住文章的主旨和要点。略读可以通过关注标题、副标题、小标题、粗体字、斜体词等文体特征来实现，这些特征往往能帮助读者预测文章的内容和结构。略读的关键在于文章的首段和尾段，因为英语国家的人在写文章时往往在首段就会开门见山地提出文章论点，然后在下文展开论述，尾段再照应前文，深化主题。所以对于以了解主旨大意为目的的题材类型，我们只需要在细读首尾段的基础上，略读正文的论述部分，就能快速抓住文章主题，了解文章大意。

例如：

◇ 我们浏览新闻网站了解全球每天发生的大事。

◇ 我们翻阅图书馆的书目看看最近有没有什么想看的书籍。

◇ 我们阅读学术文章了解学术研究的新成果。

略读的做法分为三步：

第一步，关注文章标题和首段。这可以使我们对文章的主题和内容有一个大概的了解。

第二步，快速浏览每段的首句和尾句。一般来说段落的主题句经常会出现在开头或者结尾，这可以使我们了解每段话的段落大意。不仅如此，段与段之间的逻辑关系也经常会出现在段落的开头或者结尾，这还可以帮我们理解文章的行文逻辑。

第三步，浏览故事结局或者文章结论。这可以使我们了解作者的观点、态度、目的和倾向。

From *big think*

People often have a hard time accepting new ideas. When computers were first introduced, some people were scared of them and thought they would take their jobs or hurt their health. But over time, people realized that computers were actually great and helped them learn new things, do creative work, play games, and connect with others. Scientists found that when an idea is really new, people disagree about whether it's good or not, which creates resistance to the new idea.

Defining value and newness is a challenge because different people judge them differently. Newness is about being different from what we're used to. For example, introducing a traditional Pakistani dish to someone in central Michigan who has never heard of it before would be considered new to them. When something is new, we wonder if it's brilliant or stupid because we don't have enough information yet.

New ideas have to be introduced multiple times before people start to like them. People often base their opinions on what other people think, so if lots of people disagree with an idea, it seems risky. However, disagreement doesn't necessarily mean the idea is bad. It might just mean that people don't know enough about it or have different standards for judging it.

Instead of giving up on an idea because of disagreement, we should come up with a checklist or criteria to evaluate ideas and have everyone use it. By using successful examples, people are more likely to see the potential in the new idea. So, even though people may initially resist new ideas, it's important to keep pushing forward and finding ways to show their value and potential.

> Read the first and last paragraphs attentively.

> Read the first sentence only and skip over the minor details.

上图展示了略读流程，我们可以一边略读，一边用笔将重要的部分高亮或者画线标记出来。

上图可以看出，在使用略读策略的时候，为了把握文章的大意和主要内容，需要重点阅读文章的第一段和最后一段，对于中间的段落则只阅读了每段的第一句，也就是段落的主题句。

(二)扫读

扫读则是一种更为具体的寻找信息的阅读技巧，主要用于查找特定的信息或数据。扫读过程中，读者会忽略与所需信息不相关的内容，专注于找到特定的事实、数字或其他关键词汇。它们可以是数字、日期、时间，专有名词和动词等。这种技巧特别适用于需要从大量文本中快速提取信息的场景。

例如：

◇ 我们扫读电话本去查询某个电话号码。

◇ 我们在一封邀请函里搜寻会议的时间和地点。

◇ 我们查询食物的原料表确认其中不含有使自己过敏的食材。

扫读的做法也分为三步：

第一步，理解并确认要查找的目标。这个目标往往出现在考试题目的题干中，也许是某个论点的论据，也许是某个具体的数据，也许是某件发生的事。

第二步，边读边勾画。带着需要查找的关键词扫读文章，一边读，一边用笔勾画出文章中出现的和考试题目目标相关的重点信息和词汇。

第三步，找到可能目标后，仔细阅读目标前后几句，甄别出正确目标。题目的设计者经常会在文章的篇章和文段中设计干扰内容，如果仅凭一两个目标词汇去答题，就很容易落入到陷阱之中。

From big think

People often have a hard time accepting new ideas. When computers were first introduced, some people were scared of them and thought they would take their jobs or hurt their health. But over time, people realized that computers were actually really great and helped them learn new things, do creative work, play games, and connect with others. Scientists found that when an idea is really new, people disagree about whether it's good or not, which creates resistance to the new idea.

Defining value and newness is a challenge because different people judge them differently. Newness is about being different from what we're used to. For example, introducing a taditional Pakistani dish to someone in central Michigan who has never heard of it before would be considered new to them. When something is new, we wonder if it's brilliant or stupid because we don't have enough information yet.

Locate specific key words

New ideas have to be introduced multiple times before people start to like them. People often base their opinions on what other people think, so if lots of people disagree with an idea, it seems risky. However, disagreement doesn't necessarily mean the idea is bad. It might just mean that people don't know enough about it or have different standards for judging it.

Instead of giving up on an idea because of disagreement, we should come up with a checklist or criteria to evaluate ideas and have everyone use it. By using successful examples, people are more likely to see the potential in the new idea. So, even though people may initially resist new ideas, it's important to keep pushing forward and finding ways to show their value and potential.

上图展示了扫读的流程，再次强调要一边扫读，一边去找寻目标进行勾画和标记。我们可以看到在这个案例中，读者将需要搜寻的重点词汇用笔勾画出来，然后着重阅读上下文去找寻相应的答案。

简而言之，略读侧重于整体理解，通过跳过细节快速把握文章主旨；而扫读则侧重于精确查找，通过细节分析快速定位所需信息。

三、题型分类

(一)主旨大意题

主旨大意题是阅读理解常考的题型之一，考查内容通常涉及短文的标题，以及选出短文或段落的主题、中心思想等形式。主旨大意题着重考查学生归纳总结和概括信息的能力。

1. 常见设问

(1) What would be the best title for the text?

(2) What is the second paragraph mainly about?

(3) What can be learned from the first paragraph?

(4) The text is mainly about_____ .

2. 解题技巧

(1)寻找主题句，确定文章主题

速读文章，抓住文章主题句或关键词。考生应抓住反复出现的中心词，即高频词，也叫主题词。

①主题句的特征

◇ 首段出现具体例子或假设时，例子或假设后面的内容往往体现文章主旨；

◇ 作者有意识地反复陈述的观点，通常是主旨；反复出现的词或短语，一般为体现文章主旨的关键词或短语，

◇ 段落中出现表转折的词或短语(如 however，but，in fact 等)时，该词或短语后的句子很可能是主题句。

②寻找主题句

◇ 主题句在段首：主题句在段首的文章结构是先点明主题，然后围绕这一主题进行分析，用演绎法阐述观点。在议论文、科技文献和新闻报道中多采用这种方式。

◇ 主题句在段中：当主题句被安排在段落中间时，通常前面只提出问题，文中的主题由随之陈述的细节或合乎逻辑的引申在文中导出，而后又作进一步的解释、论证或展开。

◇ 主题句在段尾：主题句也会出现在段尾。作者先摆出事实依据，层层推理论证，最后得出结论，即段落的主题。

(2)抓住文章段落大意，概括中心思想

每一段的前两句和最后一句最容易成为该段主题句。将首段的中心句与其他各段首句串联起来，往往可以得出文章的中心思想。此外，文章的逻辑结构也有助于定位中心句。比如，按时间先后顺序说明某一件事或某一理论的发展过程的文章，主题句通常在首段或末段；采用"分述——总说"结构的文章，前几段分述，末段总结，这类文章的主题句常在末段。

(3)主题隐于文章中，归纳要点抓大意

主旨大意题的另一类是文章中没有可概括全文的中心句，主题隐含在全文当中。读者必须根据文章内容，综合分析，找出有共同点的部分，归纳总结，从而推导出文章的主旨大意。这种类型的文章通常是叙述一件事的发展过程或是陈述一系列同等重要的细节或事实。

(二)细节理解题

细节理解题是英语阅读理解最重要的一类题型，旨在考查考生对事实细节的判断。设题一般针对文章某一个或若干个特定细节，分为直接细节类和隐含细节类。

◇ 直接细节类，其答案可以或几乎可以直接从原文中找出来，学生只要根据题干中的关键词与原文进行对照，就能找到答案；

◇ 隐含细节类，这类题虽然不能直接从原文中找到对应的词或短语，但学生可以根据文章的隐含意义，如原因、前提或结果等仔细推敲，得出正确答案。

1. 常见设问

(1) What can we learn from the passage?

(2) All of the following are mentioned except…

(3) Which of the following statements is true/right/false/wrong about…?

(4) The following statements are true, except…

2. 解题技巧

(1)直接信息题

该类试题的选项多根据原文中的信息直接进行考查。

考生可先从问题中找到关键词，然后以此为线索，运用略读及扫读的技巧在文中寻找细节，锁定与 who，what，when，where 等问题有关的细节关键词，再比较所给选项与文中细节的细微区别，从而确定最佳选项。

另外，广告、公告、演出信息、航班时间表等类别的文章常涉及快速寻找信息题。在解答这类试题时，考生要抓住题干中的文字信息，采用针对性方法进行阅读，因为这类试题的答案大都可以在文章中直接找到。

(2)语义转换题

该类试题的四个选项不出现原文中的直接信息，而是借助同义转换、概念解析、归纳事实等方法对原文信息进行适当变换。回答时，一定以文章所谈到的内容为依据，切忌凭自己的观点和经验去选择不符合文章内容的答案。

(3)数字信息题

此类试题分为直接考查和计算考查。

◇ 直接考查，可根据文中信息很容易地确定答案；

◇ 计算考查，在文章中虽有相关的事实细节，但一般要经过具体的计算才能得出正确的答案。这类计算比较简单，关键是要弄清数据间的逻辑关系，选准所需的数字，掌握单位换算关系，确定计算方法。

(三)词义猜测题

猜测词义是应用英语的重要能力,该题型也是阅读理解中必考的题型。因为猜测词义题涉及文章的题材背景、句子结构、文章主旨、作者的观点态度等,所以结合文章大意,整合上下文信息是解答该类题型的关键。

1. 常见设问

(1)What does the underlined word "…"in paragraph 4 mean?

(2)The underlined word "…" in paragraph 2 can be replaced by＿＿＿.

(3)As used in the passage, the phrase "…"suggests＿＿＿.

2. 解题技巧

(1)通过上下文语境猜测词义

任何一篇文章中的句子在内容上都不是孤立存在的,都与句子所在的段落及整篇文章相联系。所以要利用上下文提供的情景和线索,进行符合逻辑的综合分析,依此来推测词义。

(2)根据逻辑关系猜测词义

①通过同位关系猜测词义

该类型题目通常考查画线词句的同位语的词句。构成同位关系的两部分之间多用逗号连接,有时也使用破折号、冒号、分号、引号和括号等。

注意:同位语前还常有 or,similarly,that is to say,in other words,namely,or other,say 等词汇或短语出现。

②通过转折或对比关系猜测词义

如果一个句子或段落中有对两个事物或现象进行对比的描述,可以根据所考查部分的反义词猜测其含义。

表示转折关系的词汇主要有 but,however,otherwise,though 等;表示对比关系的标志性词汇或短语有 while,whereas,in contrast,unlike,on the other hand 等。

③通过比较关系来猜测词义

比较关系表示意义上的相似关系,如果一个句子或段落中有对两个事物或现象进行比较的描述,可以根据画线词的近义词或同义词来猜测其词义。

表示比较关系的词或短语主要有 similarly,like,just as,also,as well as 等。

④通过因果关系猜测词义

该方法是根据前后的因果关系来推断某个生词或短语的意思。可由表示原因的句意推测出表示结果的句子中的某个生词的意思,即由因推果;也可由表示结果的句意推测出表示原因的句子中的某个生词的意思,即由果推因。

表示因果关系的词汇、短语或句型有 because,since,so that,so/such…that… 等。

(3)根据针对性的解释猜测词义

①依据标点符号猜测词义

根据标点符号猜测词义是最直接、最简单的方式。比如,破折号、冒号、引号和括号常常起解释说明的作用。

②通过下定义、作解释猜测词义

在说明文和科技文中,运用下定义或作解释的方法来定义或诠释某一名词或概念是该类文体的一大特点。

在写作方法上常采用先总后分(即先定义后解释)或先分后总(即先说明后总结)的方式。常用于下定义的词或短语有:be(是),be called (被称为),mean/refer to (意指),be defined as/be termed as (被定义为)。

③通过文中举的例子猜测词义

文中的例子能够为猜测词义提供重要线索。通常由 such as/like，for example，for instance 等列举同类词汇引出例句。

④通过代词所指代的内容猜测词义

代词所指代的内容多在该句和前后句中。找到指代的内容后，把它放在代词位置上检查这句话是否合理，是否符合前后语境，然后确定正确答案。

⑤利用构词法猜测词义

学生可以依据构词法方面的知识，从生词本身出发猜测词义。最常见的是根据前缀和后缀来猜测词义。遇到合成词时，要在正确理解两词的基础上把握两词之间的关系，从而准确猜出其词义。对于转化而来的词，也要结合上下文来猜测其词义。

(四)推理判断题

阅读理解中的推理判断题属于层次较高的题目。所谓推理是指通过文章提供的信息得出文中没有明确提到的结论。因此在进行推理时必须以文中的有关内容作为前提和依据。判断是指对文章提供的事实进行分析，然后得出合理的结论。因此在进行判断时必须考虑文章的全部事实和信息。

1. 常见设问

(1)What does the quoted pat in the middle of the picture imply?

(2)What can be inferred from the passage?

(3)What is the tone of the author?

(4)It can be concluded from the passage that_____ .

(5)What will the author continue to talk about next?

2. 解题技巧

(1)推断隐含意义

此类试题的标志性词汇及短语有 infer，suggest，imply，conclude，indicate，intend，be likely to 等。

阅读文章的主要目的是获取信息，即作者所要传达的信息。有时读者需要根据文章提供的事实和线索，进行逻辑推理，推测作者未提到的事实或某事发生的可能性。

(2)推断作者的观点、态度或意图

此类试题是阅读理解中难度较大的试题，要求考生不仅理解文章的全部事实和细节，掌握全篇的主题，还要推测作者的观点、态度、写作意图等。做题时，考生要注意不要把自己的态度置入其中，也要区分开作者的态度和作者描述的别人的态度。当作者没有明确表达自己的态度时，要根据作者使用词语的褒贬性去判断。

◇ 观点态度题

寻找文中具有感情色彩的形容词、副词或动词，根据文章所用词语的褒贬性去判断作者的态度。常见的表达态度的词有：

表达积极态度的词	support(支持)，approve(赞同)，for(支持)，in favor of(支持)，optimistic(乐观的)，positive(积极的)，admiring(赞赏的)，interested(感兴趣的)，pleasant(愉快的)，impressive(给人印象深刻的)
表达消极态度的词	critical(批评的)，negative(消极的)，suspicious(怀疑的)，doubtful(怀疑的)，pessimistic(悲观的)，opposed(反对的)，disappointed(失望的)
表达中立态度的词	indifferent(漠不关心的)，objective(客观的)，impartial(不偏袒的)，neutral(中立的)

重点点拨

做题时要注意：

★全面分析所有相关信息，切忌片面思考，得出片面结论。

★忠实原文，切忌脱离原文，凭空臆断。

★切忌选择表层信息类的答案，应该立足于已知，推断未知。

◇ 写作意图题

如果是议论文，应该抓住文章的论点和论据；如果是记叙文，应该特别注意总结性的文字。

写作意图/目的通常有以下三种。

➤ 故事类：to entertain readers/ to describe an experience

➤ 广告类：to sell a product /to attract readers

➤ 科普类、新闻报道类：to inform readers/ to describe an event

（3）推断文章出处或写作类型

考生应根据文章的内容或结构来判断其出处或写作类型。例如：

➤ 有日期、地点或报社名称 —— 报纸(newspaper)

➤ 产品、活动介绍 —— 广告(advertisement)

➤ 有 click(点击)、online(在线)、internet(网络)、connect(连接)等词 —— 网站(website)

➤ 景点介绍 —— 旅行指南(travel guide)

➤ 时尚娱乐介绍——杂志/期刊(magazine/journal)

> **重点点拨**
> ★文章中直接陈述的内容不能选，要选根据文章推理出来的选项。
> ★一定要忠于原文的观点，不要主观臆断。
> ★推理要能从原文找到依据，不要凭空猜测。
> ★一定要多注意转折处，答案往往会在此处周围。
> ★题文同序，出题和文章段落顺序相同。

🖊 易错点拨

阅读理解中的正确选项是命题人员把阅读材料的内容或信息用不同的语言形式再现出来。一般而言，正确选项会选用原文中的词句，或与原文词句相似或相反的结构，抑或是对原文词句或段落的归纳、推理或演绎等。

阅读理解中的干扰项是用来干扰学生的注意力，使学生做出错误选择的选项。以下是几种学生容易混淆出错的情况。

一、张冠李戴

原文中有与干扰项相一致的细节，但与题干要求不符。一般干扰项会对原文中所涉及的甲和乙的信息进行转嫁，把本来属于甲的信息转嫁到乙的身上，反之亦然。此种类型的干扰项也有人称之为"混淆视听"。

例如：

【2022 四川省专升本大学英语阅读理解 A】

Dear Mr. Brown,

I know how disappointed you must be with my arriving late at our company's annual dinner last night. It is really unfortunate that it has happened and I offer you my most humble apologies.

Please understand that the last thing I wanted to do was to be late and offend you and the guests from the Head Office. My explanation is a simple one. I had left the key at home when I went to work in the morning. As you know, I live with my mother. To the best of my knowledge, she has no plans to go out in the afternoon. But when her friends called her to play bridge, she went completely forgetting that I had no key. Hence I was standing outside the apartment in despair and called her to come home quickly. But because of the traffic jam, she arrived home at about 7:30 p. m., when I should be at the dinner. You will understand that no matter how fast I was in dressing up, I was sure to be late. Mr. Brown, please be assured that such a thing will never happen to me again.

Yours sincerely,

Bob

33. Which of the following is true?

    A. The author lost the key.

    B. The author's mother lost the key.

    C. The author was held up in traffic jam.

    D. The author was locked outside the apartment.

【解析】这是一道细节理解题。快速浏览文章可知，这是一封 Bob 写给 Mr. Brown 的道歉信。昨天他把钥匙落家里了，而她的母亲临时和朋友相约出去打桥牌。他下班发现家里没人，急忙打电话让母亲快点回家。可因为堵车，她 7 点半才到家，所以 Bob 才在昨天的年会上迟到了。选项 A 和 B 与文章内容不符，钥匙并未丢失。选项 C 就是通过张冠李戴来干扰学生的。从文中得知，遭遇堵车的是 Bob 的妈妈，而非 Bob。选项 C 把 Bob 妈妈的经历，转嫁到 Bob 身上，就是试图通过张冠李戴来混淆视听。通过 "Hence I was standing outside the apartment in despair and called her to come home quickly." 可知，Bob 下班发现家里没人后，绝望地站在家门口打电话叫母亲回家。所以选项 D 是正确答案。

二、偷换概念

干扰项用了与原文相似的句型结构和大部分相似的词汇，却在不易引人注意的地方换了几个词汇，造成句意的改变。

例如：

【2022 四川省专升本大学英语阅读理解 B】

A retired postman from Turkey and a beautiful white swan have been inseparable for nearly four decades, and the story of their amazing friendship has melted the hearts of millions. When he spotted a wounded swan in a field, Recep had no idea that he was about to meet his best friend. He was in a car with a group of friends, when he noticed that the swan appeared to have a broken wing. He realized that leaving the bird there was the same as signing its death sentence, as it might be eaten by a predator（肉食动物）. So he took the bird home and started nursing it back to health.

After recovery, the swan didn't try to fly away. Instead, she befriended other animals on the farm, busy following her human friend around, either during his daily chores, or on his evening walks. Having no children, Recep regarded the swan as his child and named her Garip. Now she has been with him for the last 37 years.

"She comes when I call. She has never left me, not even during the river floods," the retired postman said, "She used to be more vigorous, but she has grown old now. If she dies, I will make her a nice grave here."

38. What can we learn from the text?

    A. The swan is treasured by Recep.

    B. Recep is working in the post office.

    C. The swan flew away after recovery.

    D. Recep met his best friend in the 1990s.

【解析】这是一道细节理解题。文章讲述了一位退休的邮递员 37 年前救助了一只白天鹅，之后相互陪伴近 40 年的动人故事。文中形容他是一名退休的邮递员 "a retired postman"，选项 B "Recep is working in the post office." 说 Recep 目前在邮局工作。"postman" 和 "work in the office" 乍一看属于同义替换，粗心的同学可能就会选择 B。但细看就发现出题人在干扰项中使用了现在进行时，偷换了概念，造成了句意的改变。从文章第二段首句可知，这只白天鹅在康复后并未试图离开，因此选项 C 错误。选项 D 所给的时间信息 "in the 1990s" 并未在文中出现。所以正确答案是选项 A。

三、正误参半

干扰项的前半部分表述是正确的，后半部分为错位联想，是我们一般把这种干扰项归为正误参半。

例如：

【2022 四川省专升本大学英语阅读理解 D】

…

Millions of primary and middle school students across China watched the 60-minute televised event hosted by the China Manned Space Agency, the Ministry of Education and other government departments. Groups of invited students in Beijing, Nanning in the Guangxi Zhuang autonomous region, Wenchuan in Sichuan province, and the Hong Kong and Macao special administrative regions were present at "ground class venues" and took part in video chats with the crew during the lecture.

More lectures will be held based on the country's manned spaceflights and will also be presented by Chinese astronauts, the manned space agency said, adding that such activities are intended to spread knowledge about manned spaceflights and spark enthusiasm for science among young people.

The agency said before the lecture that Chinese astronauts "sincerely invite young viewers to conduct similar experiments along with them to observe the physical disparities between space and land environments to experience the fun of exploration".

The Shenzhou XIII mission was launched on Oct 16 by a Long March 2F carrier rocket that blasted off from Jiuquan Satellite launch center in northwestern China's Gobi Desert, with the crew soon entering the Tiangong station. They are scheduled to spend six months working in the station, making it China's longest manned space mission.

50. Which of the following statements is TRUE?

A. Only students from Beijing, Nanning in the Guangxi Zhuang autonomous region, Wenchuan in Sichuan province, and the Hong Kong and Macao special administrative regions saw the lecture.

B. More lectures will be held based on the country's manned spaceflights and will also be presented by Major General Zhai Zhigang, Senior Colonel Wang Yaping and Senior Colonel Ye Guangfu.

C. Shenzhou XIII isn't designed to promote and spread science and technology knowledge.

D. Chinese astronauts will come back to the earth in April, 2022.

【解析】本题是一道细节理解题。选项 A 中 Only 一词过于绝对。选项 B 的前半部分 More lectures will be held based on the country's manned spaceflights 是正确的，是文章中的原句，但后半部分 will also be presented by Major General Zhai Zhigang, Senior Colonel Wang Yaping and Senior Colonel Ye Guangfu 则属于错误联想，因为文中说的是 will also be presented by Chinese astronauts，还会有宇航员来为大家开讲座，但并未具体说明是哪几位宇航员。所以干扰项 B 属于典型的正误参半。根据最后一段可知，飞船于 10 月发射升空，将在空间站开始为期 6 个月的工作，所以返回时间就在第二年的 4 月。所以选项 D 是正确答案。

四、以偏概全

考生在做猜测文章中心思想、给文章添加标题或推理判断题时，往往会犯以偏概全的错误。产生这类错误的原因是考生受思维定式的影响或考虑不周，以局部代替整体。

例如：

【文章选自 SUFERTODAY】

Ocean Ramsey is a marine biologist, professional freediver, scuba instructor, and marine and shark conservationist. She is probably one of the few people in the world who has swum underwater with great white sharks. Ramsey was born in 1987 in Oahu, Hawaii. She is 5-foot-9 and weighs approximately 128 pounds. And yes, Ocean Ramsey is her real name.

One late summer afternoon off the coast of Baja, Mexico, Ramsey entered her own unique kind of underwater petting zoo. With nothing but a dive suit and a snorkel mask as protection, she gracefully swam through the water toward a great white shark. "It was the most thrilling experience, touching the skin of a great white with my bare hands," she says. "There is a fear, but the beauty of the experience outweighs that for me." The videos have been seen online around the world, earning her the nickname "the shark whisperer". She says it's years of practice —like holding her breath for more than 6 minutes at a time — that has allowed her to successfully free dive with sharks. "I don't dive with any equipment that creates noise or bubbles that might scare them," she says. "And I've learned to read a shark's behavior. I try to stay calm, because a shark can sense fear and aggression."

Ramsey aims to use her fame to help the sharks out. She elaborated a list of things everyone could do, follow, and put into practice to defend and protect sharks such as ban shark fin soup, shark meat, shark liver oil, or other shark-related food product and speak up for sharks and help educate others by reposting shark conservation photos and posts on social media promoting hashtags #helpsavesharks.

1. The author's purpose in writing this passage is _____.

    A. to introduce a shark whisperer to us

    B. to call on humans to protect sharks

    C. to tell us that sharks are human's friends

    D. to tell us that sharks are important to the ecosystem

【解析】很多学生本题会选择 B 选项。以往我们在做类似文章的阅读理解时会发现，文章通过介绍个人经历，最终会上升到保护动物或保护环境的重要性上。根据惯性思维，加上文章倒数第二段有类似信息，学生很容易就误选了 B 选项。

实际上，学生在做主旨大意题的时候，容易忘记采用正确的做题方法。通常情况下，我们需要认真阅读首尾段和中间段开头部分，概括出每段大意，将一篇文章浓缩为几句话，然后再对比题目的选项，找到意思相近的表述。

本文一共三段。第一段是对 Ramsey 的个人简介。第二段描述了她潜水触摸大白鲨的视频实况和潜水的特点：需要多年练习，不带氧气罐，在水下试图保持镇定等；第三段介绍她潜水的目的：让人们关注和帮助鲨鱼。通过对这三段主旨大意的梳理可知，文章介绍了 Ramsey 这个 shark whisperer 的潜水实况、特点、目的和爱好，因此选项 A 是正确答案。而干扰项 B 潜水目的只是文章第三段的中心思想，属于典型的以偏概全。

五、望文生义

这种干扰方法常用于字句理解的备选选项中。考生往往仅凭字面或单从个别句子甚至若干句子的表面意思进行浅层理解，因而忽视了具体语境或一些特定修辞手法。

例如：

【文章选自 PIP MAGAZINE】

Farm My School is an initiative aiming to transform unused land within schools into regenerative market gardens, to grow community, educate youth and produce affordable nutrient-dense food.

Farm My School has gained the extraordinary enthusiasm of the locals, who answered an online shout-out（公开答谢）to buy tickets to the program's launch event at Bell Secondary School last October.

Called Build A Farm in a Day Festival, the event featured workshops by Ben and James to share the skills required to build what they say is the world's largest no-dig garden. "It was such a powerful event, and I think that comes down to people wanting to act now," says James.

We charged for the experience and 600 guys turned up! They didn't even need free drinks to get excited. We were gardening till midnight. It was amazing. We've got true community buy-in.

1. What does the underlined word "buy-in" mean in paragraph 3?

A. Competition.　　B. Investment.

C. Support.　　　　D. Protection.

【解析】本题为词意猜测题。根据"buy-in"所在的第三段的内容 We charged for the experience and 600 guys turned up! They didn't even need free drinks to get excited. We were gardening till midnight. 可知，我们组织的这次体验活动是收费的，结果依然来了 600 人。再结合第一段首句"Farm My School has gained the extraordinary enthusiasm of the locals"，可以看出此次活动得到了社区的热情回应和有力支持。与 C 选项意思一致。

"buy-in"本义"(证券或商品交易中的)空头购入；买进公司；买进(其他公司股份)；回购公司股票；对政策的同意"，所以学生很容易会犯望文生义的错误而选择答案 B。A 和 D 选项则是典型的无中生有。

六、范围扩缩

选项中的描述将原文内容扩大或缩小，与原文的内容极其相似，只是在程度上有些变动。干扰项使用了与文中某句话相似的句子结构和陈述，但在陈述中对某个细节的陈述有变动，关键地方换了单词，增加或删除了部分信息，从而改变了句意，而考生在答题时却没有注意到这一变化。

例如：

【2022 四川省专升本大学英语阅读理解 D】

Chinese astronauts aboard the country's Tiangong space station opened a science lecture on Thursday afternoon as they traveled with the gigantic spacecraft orbiting the Earth at an altitude of about 400 kilometers.

Major General Zhai Zhigang, Senior Colonel Wang Yaping and Senior Colonel Ye Guangfu, all members of the Shenzhou XIII mission crew, greeted students, teachers and other participants as the lecture began at 3:40 p.m.

The astronauts carried out experiments to display interesting physical phenomena in space such as "disappearing buoyancy"and a "water ball".

Millions of primary and middle school students across China watched the 60-minute televised event hosted by the China Manned Space Agency, the Ministry of Education and other government departments. Groups of invited students in Beijing, Nanning in the Guangxi Zhuang autonomous region, Wenchuan in Sichuan province, and the Hong Kong and Macao special administrative regions were present at"ground class venues" and took part in video chats with the crew during the lecture.

More lectures will be held based on the country's manned spaceflights and will also be presented by Chinese astronauts, the manned space agency said, adding that such activities are intended to spread knowledge about manned spaceflights and spark enthusiasm for science among young people.

The agency said before the lecture that Chinese astronauts "sincerely invite young viewers to conduct similar experiments along with them to observe the physical disparities between space and land environments to experience the fun of exploration".

The Shenzhou XIII mission was launched on Oct 16 by a Long March 2F carrier rocket that blasted off from Jiuquan Satellite launch center in northwestern China's Gobi Desert, with the crew soon entering the Tiangong station.

49. The purpose of the experiments is＿＿＿＿.

A. to show how they live and work inside the space station.

B. To answer the question about physical phenomena.

C. To prove the"disappearing buoyancy" and "water ball" do exist.

D. To show the fancy physical world and draw the students' interest towards science.

【解析】本题是推理判断题，要求读者判断实验的目的。通过关键词 experiment，扫读文章，首先定位第三段 The astronauts carried out experiments to display interesting physical phenomena in space such as "disappearing buoyancy" and a "water ball"。宇航员在太空做实验，展示了诸如"消失的浮力"和"水球"此类的有趣物理现象。其次继续扫读，定位倒数第二段"The agency said before the lecture that Chinese astronauts' sincerely invite young viewers to conduct similar experiments along with them to observe the physical disparities between space and land environments to experience the fun of exploration"。开讲座前，宇航员和他们一起做相似的实验观察陆地和太空实验的差异，来体验探索的乐趣。所以，答案应该包括这两方面的内容，即展示物理现象和体验探索乐趣。干扰项 B 说实验的目的是为了回答物理现象的相关问题，该选项范围只限定在物理现象的相关问题上，将原文两方面的内容缩小到一个方面，所以属于干扰项的扩缩范围。选项 D 既"展示物理现象，又吸引学生对科学的兴趣"正好对应文章中描述的两个方面，所以，正确答案是选项 D。

> **重点点拨**
>
> 文章表达的内容都相对客观理性，不会出现失之偏颇的观点和绝对肯定或绝对否定的表述。如果出现绝对化用词，一定要谨慎选择，除非原文有明确提及。
>
> 例如：absolutely, thoroughly, never, must, all, only 等类绝对概念的词汇一定要多加小心。反之，如果有一些类似比较温和的词语的出现，那么作为正确选项的概率也就大大增加了。比如：mildly, may, might, perhaps, partly 等。

小试牛刀

【2024 四川省专升本大学英语阅读理解】

阅读理解：本大题共 16 题，每小题 2.5 分，共 40 分。阅读下列短文，从每题所给的 A、B、C、D 四个选项中，选出最佳选项。

A

Teacher OF THE WEEK

Teacher's name：Mr. Scanlon

School：RGS WORCESTER,

Upper Tything，WoWORCESTERshire

"Mr. Scanlon is the best teacher because he is really supportive if we find things hard. I didn't use to enjoy maths but now it is my favorite subject because of him. He always has a laugh with us which makes the lesson fun."

James

If we pick your teacher as Teacher of the Week, we'll send your school three free issues of the Week Junior. Send your nominations, along with a picture of your teacher and your school's full name and address, to hello@theweekjunior.co.uk

1. What do we know about Mr. Scanlon?

   A．He's been given an honor.   B．He's on duty this week.

   C．He's a boring young teacher.   D．He teaches a new class.

2. James is Mr. Scanlon's _____ .

   A．colleague   B．student   C．friend   D．classmate

3. What does the quoted part in the middle of the poster imply?

   A．Mr. Scanlon dislikes maths.   B．Mr. Scanlon is good at teaching.

   C．Mr. Scanlon studies hard in school. D．Mr. Scanlon often laughs at students.

4. What is The Week Junior most likely to be?

   A．A magazine.   B．A dictionary.   C．An organization.   D．An award.

B

I recently had to give feedback（反馈）to a junior colleague after noticing some errors in a project we worked on together. My first thought was to fix them myself and move forward. But my manager said, "Well, Lucy, why not treat it as a teaching opportunity?"

It took more than a week to schedule the meeting, and even after I did, I kept moving it back. Delivering negative feedback to my team member sounded fearful. Minutes before the actual call, I felt heavy in my chest.

The reason these conversations feel so difficult for me is my social anxiety. When faced with the choice of argument or avoidance, I almost always choose the latter. While I understand objectively that feedback is necessary, my inner voice says that sharing anything negative will result in conflict. In this situation, I assumed my colleague would get upset or react defensively. I imagined us reaching a deadlock instead of a solution.

Here's what actually happened: I told my colleague I'd noticed some errors in our project and had corrected them. To avoid these kinds of errors in the future, I suggested we create a system to quality-check each other's work. Thankfully, my colleague listened calmly and told me they wished I had raised my concerns earlier so that we could have troubleshooted the issue together. It was a learning moment for both of us. We spent the next 30 minutes brainstorming solutions.

Giving tough feedback is an art — and a difficult one at that. Different people often require different approaches, depending on your relationship and the power dynamics involved. Despite these aspects, however, all feedback should be delivered thoughtfully and with the intention of helping others improve.

5. What did Lucy's manager do?

   A．The manager corrected the errors for her colleague.

   B．The manager asked her to correct the errors by herself.

   C．The manager taught her how to avoid making errors in the project.

   D．The manager advised her to help her colleague learn from the errors.

6. What is Lucy's problem?

   A．She has social anxiety.

   B．She often has conflict with people.

   C．She usually makes her colleagues upset.

   D．She has trouble finding solutions to problems.

7. What actually happened at their meeting?

   A．They discussed how to raise concerns in the project.

B. They communicated smoothly about their work.

C. They criticized each other for the errors.

D. They corrected the errors together.

8. The text is mainly about _____.

A. how to finish tough projects

B. how to give negative feedback

C. how to correct colleagues' errors

D. how to avoid conflict at workplace

C

For decades, not having a college degree has often been a barrier for workers seeking higher-level, better-paying job. But more employers are now saying they're willing to hire them.

College degrees were used by companies as an indicator of skills and competence when they evaluated potential hires — making it very difficult for non-degreed workers even to be considered. The majority of US workers have had to cope with that barrier. Only 37.7% of Americans aged 25 and up had a bachelor's degree (学士学位) in 2022, according to the US Census Bureau.

But employers are now — at least publicly — becoming more open to the idea of skills-based hiring, which focuses on the job candidates' competence and capacity to learn new skills rather than on their educational background.

Why the change of heart? There are several factors. But above all things is a population reality: The falling US birth rate will produce fewer workers in the years ahead to replace the number of workers to retire.

Additionally, employers are increasingly aware that the skills needed to do many jobs don't necessarily require a four-year degree, and that competent workers can be trained in needed skills as they arise.

Some companies are now investing billions of dollars to build new chip factories here — creating tens of thousands of jobs, many of them paying over $100,000 a year, and don't require a college degree. And businesses and high schools will be connected more closely so that students can get hands-on experience and a path to a good-paying job.

9. What can be inferred from paragraph 2?

A. Employers are willing to hire non-degreed workers.

B. The US Census Bureau has to cope with the barriers.

C. Most American workers don't have a bachelor's degree.

D. About 37.7% of Americans have no professional competence.

10. Employers used to focus on job candidates' _____.

A. creative skill

B. work experience

C. business capacity

D. educational background

11. What is the main factor for "the change of heart" in paragraph 4?

A. The retiring age.

B. The higher birth rate.

C. The population reality.

D. The better job training.

12. The cooperation between businesses and schools can_____.

    A．attract investment in new chips

    B．prepare students for a good college

    C．encourage factories to create more jobs

    D．help students acquire practical experience

D

After an online work meeting, nothing feels better than closing your laptop, stepping away from your desk, and slowly lowering yourself onto the floor. On TikTok, this practice has been named "floor time". With some videos under this tag reaching nearly 8 million views, floor time is good for anyone who's stressed, or sad, as well as for anyone who simply needs to relax.

Below, experts explain the reasons floor time feels so amazing, as well as how to make the most of it.

According to Brandt, a yoga teacher, floor time physically removes you from whatever stresses you out, like work or chores, just like an intentional savasana(休息术) at the end of a yoga practice. Lying flat on your back can release aches and tension in your muscles.

Feeling the hardness of the floor beneath you also sends a message to your body that you're safe and supported, which can help you feel more present — like the ground literally has your back. "You may feel connected to the earth," says Brandt. "This can calm the mind and reduce stress, making floor time appealing to many people."

Floor time may also help to reset your central nervous system, says therapist Janet. A moment of relaxation allows you to bring your breath back to normal, and your stress will gradually become weaker and your heart rate will lower.

13. What can be learned from paragraph 1?

    A．You need to use floor time videos to attract viewers.

    B．You'd better close your laptop after a work meeting.

    C．You may lower yourself onto the floor to be relaxed.

    D．You ought to step away from the desk when stressed.

14. Why does floor time feel so amazing?

    A．It can free you from work or chores.

    B．It can be used to strengthen your muscles.

    C．It can benefit you physically and mentally.

    D．It can be applied to heart disease treatment.

15. What does the underlined word "appealing" in paragraph 4 mean?

    A．Attractive.   B．Challenging.   C．Active.   D．Convincing.

16. What will the author continue to talk about next?

    A．Why a savasana can calm your mind.

    B．When you should lie flat on your back.

    C．Where to release your aches and tension.

    D．How to make the most use of your floor time.

第二章

翻　译

第一节　英译汉

🔍 重点知识概览

英译汉重点知识概览

题型类别	翻译方法	解题技巧	易错盘点
英译汉	增译法	1.英语有名词复数,翻译时可适当增加重叠词、数词或其他词来表达。 2.英语有时态,翻译时可通过适当增加表示时间的字词来体现,如"正、过、了、曾经、已经、一直、将要"等。 3.英语表达往往偏向于使用抽象名词,而汉语表达却常常以具体的形象表达抽象的内容,翻译时往往需要根据汉语的表达习惯增译一些范畴词,如"状态、工作、现象、局面"等。	一、词义的选择 1.根据语境分辨词义的广狭 2.根据语境分辨词义的褒贬 二、定语从句的翻译 1.前置法 2.拆分法 3.转换法
	省译法	1.省译代词 2.省译冠词 3.省译介词 4.省译连词 5.省译动词	
	转换法	1.词类转换 2.句子成分转换 3.语态转换	
	倒置法	在英语中,许多修饰语常常位于被修饰语之后,而在汉语中,定语修饰语和状语修饰语往往位于被修饰语之前。	
	拆译法	拆译法是把一个长而复杂的句子拆译成若干个较短、较简单的句子,使译文更加通顺。	

📖 知识梳理

英语和汉语两种语言在句法、词汇、修辞等方面均存在着很大的差异，因此在进行英汉互译时必然会遇到很多困难，需要有一定的翻译技巧作指导。常用英译汉技巧有增译法、省译法、转换法、倒置法和拆译法。

一、增译法

增译法指根据汉英两种语言不同的语言习惯和表达方式，翻译时增添一些词，以便更准确地表达出原文所表达的意思。

1. 英语有名词复数，翻译时可适当增加重叠词、数词或其他词。

例：In spite of *difficulties*, they managed to finish the task.

译文：尽管困难重重，他们还是设法完成了任务。

例：Available on various online platforms, short-form series transcend traditional media barriers.

译文：通过多个在线平台传播，这些短剧打破了传统媒体的界限。

2. 英语有时态，翻译时可通过适当增加表示时间的字词来体现，如"正、过、了、曾经、已经、一直、将要"等。

例：She *has already finished* washing.

译文：她已经洗完衣服了。

例：The reality is that EV sales *are growing* rapidly, the technology *is evolving* briskly, and everyone from policymakers to auto executives to consumers is putting EVs at the center of long-term planning.

译文：现实情况是，电动汽车销量正在迅速增长，技术正在迅速发展，从政策制定者到汽车高管再到消费者，每个人都把电动汽车放在长期规划的中心位置。

3. 英语表达往往偏向于使用抽象名词，而汉语表达却常常以具体的形象表达抽象的内容，翻译时往往需要根据汉语的表达习惯增译一些范畴词，如"状态、工作、现象、局面"等。

例：You'll need the insights and critical-thinking skills you gain in history and social studies to fight poverty and *homelessness*, crime and discrimination.

译文：你们将需要利用你们在历史学和社会学课堂上所获得的知识和批判性思考能力，来抗击贫困和解决无家可归问题，打击犯罪和消除歧视。

例：The Chinese government has always attached great importance to environmental *protection*.

译文：中国政府历来重视环境保护工作。

二、省译法

省译法，即省去不符合目标语思维习惯、语言习惯和表达方式的词，以避免译文累赘。省译法在英译汉时使用广泛。

1. 省译代词

例：It is not worthwhile to sacrifice one's dream for money.

译文：为了钱牺牲梦想是不值得的。

2. 省译冠词

例：Their brevity caters to the fast-paced digital age.

译文：它们的简短迎合了快节奏的数字时代。

3. 省译介词

例：By refusing to be defined by societal norms and material success, we can devote more time and energy to personal hobbies and spiritual pursuits.

译文：拒绝被社会规范和物质成功所定义，我们可以将更多的时间和精力投入到个人爱好和精神追求中。

4. 省译连词

例：If you come across a challenging question, stay positive.

译文：遇到难题，保持乐观。

5. 省译动词

例：When the pressure *gets* low, the boiling point *becomes* low.

译文：气压降低，沸点也随之降低。

三、转换法

转换法指翻译过程中为了使译文符合目标语的表述方式和习惯而对原句中的词类、句型和语态等进行转换。具体地说，就是在词性方面，把名词转换为代词、形容词、动词；把动词转换成名词、形容词、副词、介词；把形容词转换成副词和短语。在句子成分方面，把主语变成状语、定语、宾语、表语；把谓语变成主语、定语、表语；把定语变成状语、主语；把宾语变成主语。在语态方面，可以把被动语态变为主动语态。英译汉转换法的使用主要有以下几种情况。

1. 词类转换

例：We're all *for* your opinion.

译文：我们完全赞成你的意见。（介词转动词）

例：Accounting includes not only the maintenance of accounting records, but also *the design* of efficient accounting systems, *the planning* of income tax, and *the interpretation* of accounting information.

译文：会计不仅包括做好会计记录，还包括设计有效的会计制度，规划个人所得税，解释会计信息。（名词转动词）

2. 句子成分转换

例：Welcome to *Beijing*!

译文：北京欢迎你！（宾语变主语）

例：It is time *your girl* should be sent to school.

译文：该送你女儿上学了。（主语变宾语）

3. 语态转换

例：The new institutions of the open economy *have been steadily improved*.

译文：开放型经济新体制已经逐步健全。（被动语态变主动语态）

例：*Concerns have been raised* over the ability of Internet banking services to guarantee the security of customer transactions.

译文：人们高度关注网上银行服务是否有能力确保客户交易安全这一问题。（被动语态变主动语态）

四、倒置法

在英语中，许多修饰语常常位于被修饰语之后，而在汉语中，定语修饰语和状语修饰语往往位于被修饰语之前。主要情况有：修饰中心词时，英语中修饰语多置于中心词之后，而汉语中修饰语多置于中心词之前；英语多用被动句式和倒装句式，而汉语多采用主动句式和正常语序句；表达因果、假设等关系时，英语先果后因，先结论后假设，而汉语往往先因后果，先假设后结论；英语一般从小到大、从特殊到普遍，而汉语一般从大到小、从整体到个体。因此翻译时往往要把原文的语序颠倒过来，即对英语长句按照汉语的习惯表达法进行位置前后调换。

例：*People who cannot distinguish between colors* are said to be color-blinded.

译文：分不清颜色的人是色盲。

例：Much has been said *about the necessity of introducing foreign funds into Chinese enterprises*.

译文：有关中国企业引进外资的必要性已经谈得很多了。

例：Great changes have taken place in my hometown *since the introduction of the reform and opening policy*.

译文：改革开放以来，我的家乡发生了巨大的变化。

例：We will let you use the room *on condition that you keep it clean and tidy*.

译文：只要你们能保持整齐清洁，我们可以让你们使用这个房间。

五、拆译法

拆译法是把一个长而复杂的句子拆译成若干个较短、较简单的句子，使译文更加通顺。英语句子的主体结构虽然与汉语句子基本相同，大体上都呈现主语—谓语—宾语的格式，但是两者还是有着很大的差别。相比较而言，汉语的句式比较简单，句子的各个成分有相对固定的位置，而英语有众多性质的从句，其在句子中摆放的位置比较灵活，可以形成句中句结构。这就要求我们做翻译时，要基于英语句子的意思，对原句的成分进行拆分，重新组织汉语译句，使之符合汉语的表达方式。英译汉时，可以在原句的关系代词、关系副词、主谓连接处、并列或转折连接处、后续成分与主体的连接处，以及意群结束处将长句切断，译成汉语分句。这样可以顺应现代汉语长短句相替、单复句相间的句法修辞原则。

例：Overall, the human spine is designed to be on the move rather than static in one posture for long periods, *which* is why movement and changing your posture throughout the day is important to reduce fatigue and subsequent discomfort.

译文：总体而言，人类脊柱就是为了活动而设计的，而不是为了长时间保持一个静态姿势。这就是为什么在一天当中不时活动一下和变换姿势对于减少疲劳和久坐带来的不适很重要。

例：He shook his head *and* his eyes were wide, then narrowed in indignation.

译文：他摇了摇头，眼睛睁得溜圆，接着又眯成一条线，脸上露出愤怒的神色。

例：She had made several attempts to help them find other rental quarters *without* success.

译文：她已经试了好几次，要帮他们另找一所出租的房子，结果并没有成功。

例：Over the past 20 years the social media influencer industry has grown from nothing into a pervasive global force *that* has completely rearranged the way information and culture are conceived, produced, marketed, and shared.

译文：在过去的 20 年里，社交媒体网红行业从无到有，发展成为一股无处不在的全球力量，彻底改变了信息和文化的构思、生产、营销和共享方式。

易错盘点

一、词义的选择

英汉两种语言都有一词多类和一词多义的现象。一词多类就是指一个词往往属于几个词类，具有几个不同的意义；一词多义就是同一个词在同一词类中又往往有几个不同的词义。在英译汉的过程中，切忌望文生义，而是需要根据上下文或具体语境，弄清楚其确切的意思，而后才能选择相应的汉语来表达，以更好地表达出句子的意思。

1. 根据语境分辨词义的广狭

例：*Men* have traveled more widely than women in history.

译文：在人类历史上，男性比女性旅行的范围更广。

从以上例句中可以看出，单数名词"man"及其复数"men"的词义范围不定，有时泛指广义概念的"人类"，有时指狭义概念的"男性"。根据上下文的语言环境，确定其意义指狭义概念的"男性"，因此在翻译选词和表达时需要有所区分。

2. 根据语境分辨词义的褒贬

例：It is our belief that improvements in health care will *lead to* a stronger, more prosperous economy.

译文：我们坚信，改善医疗保健会使经济更加繁荣昌盛。

例：Both sides agreed that this incident should not *lead to* intensification of the contradictions between the two peoples.

译文：双方一致认为，此次事件不应导致两国国民之间的矛盾激化。

语言中的词语常常带有很多感情色彩，语言搭配和上下文语境都决定着词语的褒贬色彩。从以上例句中可以看出，"lead to"在这两句话中有不同的褒贬含义，应灵活翻译。

搭配不是约定俗成的，有很大的随意性，因此，给翻译造成了无数的陷阱。在翻译时，我们一定要注意词的搭配意义，所谓搭配意义是指适合用在某一个上下文中的意义。掌握词语的搭配意义对正确理解原文有重要的意义。英汉互译时，不能简单地用词典释义来替换。译者应该熟知两种语言的习惯搭配，同时也可以借助词典，来判断词的搭配意义。

二、定语从句的翻译

在英语中，定语从句很常见，一般起到修饰、限定和补充说明等作用。有些定语从句还具有让步、结果、原因、对比等意义，具体含义取决于语境。翻译时可根据其结构和含义采用不同的译法。

1. 前置法

前置法就是把定语从句译成带"的"的定语词组，放在被修饰词之前，从而将英语的复合句译成汉语的简单句。

例：A buyer has no choice but to pay more to obtain things *that* they cannot do without, such as food and fuel.

译文：买家别无选择，只能花更多的钱购买这些生活必需品，例如食物和燃料。

例：Perseverance is like a key *that* opens the door to success.

译文：毅力就像一把打开成功之门的钥匙。

例：Each failure was a lesson *that* brought him closer to success.

译文：每一次失败都是一个让他更接近成功的教训。

2. 拆分法

对于部分比较复杂的定语从句，需要按照汉语的表达习惯采用拆分法，使译文自然流畅、层次分明。

例：Social media platforms often require users to share personal information, *which* can be susceptible to data breaches and misuse by third parties.

译文：社交媒体平台通常要求用户分享个人信息，这些信息容易遭受数据泄露及第三方的不当使用。

例：Everyone has a unique light *that* does not have to be dimmed to fit in with others.

译文：每个人都有独特的光芒，不必为了迎合他人而黯淡。

例：Although he lacks experience, he has enterprise and creativity *which* are decisive in winning success.

译文：他虽然经验不足，但很有进取心和创造力，这正是获得成功的关键。

3. 转换法

转换法是将定语从句转译为原因状语从句、时间状语从句、地点状语从句、目的状语从句、条件状语从句、让步状语从句、结果状语从句等。

例：To the wind, *which* makes us understand that the beauty of life often lies in those unconscious moments.

译文：敬这风，因为它让我们懂得，生活的美好，往往在于那些不经意的瞬间。（表原因）

例：Our country has adopted opening up policy and carried out reforms, *which* has brought about great changes.

译文：我国采取开放政策，进行改革，因此，发生了巨大变化。（表结果）

例：The problem, *which* is very complicated, has been solved.

译文：这个问题虽然很复杂，但已经解决了。（表让步）

例：This company, *which* wants to make the product popular in the market, is trying to perfect its workmanship.

译文：为了使产品在市场上流行起来，这家公司正在尽力改进工艺。（表目的）

小试牛刀

Translate the following sentences into Chinese.

1. They are still reluctant to talk about unemployment.

2. In the past few years, the study of AI has made great progress.

3. Perseverance will see us through the tough times.

4. She wears a dress, a straw hat and a silk scarf.

5. As the match burns, heat and light are given off.

学以致用

Translate the following sentences into Chinese.

1. We'll come over to visit you on Wednesday if we have time.

2. You will find happiness when you adopt positive thinking into your daily routine.

3. The students should develop morally, intellectually and physically.

4. A large number of successful people have attested to the significance of career planning.

5. While the road ahead is tortuous, the future is bright.

第二节　汉译英

🔍 重点知识概览

汉译英重点知识概览

题型类别	翻译方法	解题技巧	易错盘点
汉译英	增译法	1.为了表达清晰自然而增词 2.为了语法需要而增词 3.为了增加背景文化知识而增词	逻辑重组 1.显性法 2.隐性法
	省译法	汉语中的重复现象多:为了表达得清晰、明确、生动,汉语经常采用原词复现的形式。而英语中的省略现象多:英语的用词造句讲究多样性,为了表达得简练、紧凑,避免原词复现。	
	转换法	1.动词转换 2.名词转换 3.形容词转换 4.副词转换	
	正反译法	从形式看,有时候汉语的"肯定",要根据英语表达习惯译成英语的"否定";而有时候则相反,汉语的"否定",要用英语的"肯定"形式来翻译。	
	顺译法	按照英语表达的层次顺序,依次翻译汉语句子,从而使英语译文与汉语原文的顺序基本一致。	
	合译法	根据需要注意利用连词、分词、介词、不定式、定语从句、独立结构等把汉语短句连成长句。	

☕ 知识梳理

英汉是两种不同的语言,有各自独立的系统,在形态和句法方面二者存在很大差异,所以在翻译实践中,我们需要确保原文的意思在翻译过程中得到准确且流畅的表达。常用汉译英技巧有增译法、省译法、转换法、正反译法、顺译法和合译法。

一、增译法

增译法是指根据原文上下文的意思、逻辑关系以及译文语言的句法特点和表达习惯,翻译时增加原文字面没有出现的词。由于汉英两种语言在词汇和句法等方面的显著差异,汉译英时,采用一对一地逐词翻译往往会使译文生硬晦涩,令人费解,有时甚至背离原文的意思。因此,翻译过程中,有时需要增加一些原文中无其形却有其意的词、词组或句子,补充一些必要的解释性信息,从而更准确地表达出原文的意思。增译法是汉译英时常用的方法之一,其主要的两个作用:一是保证译文语法结构完整，二是保证译文意思清晰、准确。

1. 为了表达清晰自然而增词

例：人与动物不同。

译文：Humans are different from *other* animals.（增译形容词）

2. 为了语法需要而增词

例：这是我们两国人民的又一个共同点。

译文：This is yet another common point *between* the people of our two countries.（增译介词）

3. 为了增加背景文化知识而增词

例：只许州官放火，不许百姓点灯。

译文：*While* the magistrates were free to burn down house, the common people were forbidden to light lamps.（增译连词）

例：剪纸最常用的颜色是红色，象征健康和兴旺。

译文：The color most frequently used in paper cutting is red, *which* symbolizes health and prosperity.（增译代词）

二、省译法

省译法是指在翻译过程中，省去不符合目标语思维习惯、语言习惯和表达方式的词，以避免译文累赘的一种翻译方法。汉语中的重复现象多：为了表达得清晰、明确、生动，汉语经常采用原词复现的形式。而英语中的省略现象多：英语的用词造句讲究多样性，为了表达得简练、紧凑，避免原词复现。鉴于汉英两种语言的表达差异，汉译英时可酌情使用省译法，以使译文更为地道、流畅。

例：读书使人充实，讨论使人机智，写作使人准确。

译文：Reading *makes* a full man; conference a ready man; writing an exact man.（省译动词）

例：中国人民历来是勇于探索，勇于创造，勇于革命的。

译文：The people of China have always been *courageous enough to* probe into things, to make inventions and to make revolution.（省译形容词）

三、转换法

词性转换不仅是重要的译词手段也是常用的句法转换变通手段，是一种常用的翻译技巧。汉译英时，将原文中的某个词的词性在译文里用其他词性表达出来。这种转换会使译文更加灵活变通，能更准确地传达出原文内涵。

1. 动词转换

汉语动词的使用频率远远高于英语，这是因为按照英语句法，受主谓关系的限制，一个简单句或分句大多只有一个谓语动词，而且，英语还可以通过谓语动词以外各种词性的词来体现动词意义。将汉语句子里的动词转换为英语里其他词性的词是汉译英的常用技巧之一。

例：这本书反映了60年代的中国社会。

译文：The book is *a flection of* Chinese society in the 1960s.（动词转换为名词）

2. 名词转换

英语中有很多由名词派生的动词，以及由名词转用的副词、形容词等。在汉译英时，汉语中的名词常常可以产生一些转换，从而更简洁有力地表达原文。

例：参加亚太经合组织对中国的影响是多方面的。

译文：The APEC membership has *influenced* China in several respects.（名词转换为动词）

3. 形容词转换

在汉译英时，汉语的形容词往往可以译成英语中的名词或副词，这些名词或副词通常具有抽象意义。

例：我们感到，解决这个复杂的问题是困难的。

译文：We found *difficulty* in solving this complicated problem.（形容词转换为名词）

4. 副词转换

有时出于修辞和句法结构的需要，往往把汉语中的副词用英语其他词性的词来表达，这也是汉译英时一个常用技巧。

例：独立思考对学习是绝对必需的。

译文：*Independent* thinking is an absolute necessity in study.（副词转换为形容词）

四、正反译法

在进行翻译时，为了确保译文的准确性，文化差异是我们不得不考虑的一个重要因素。语言的形成、发展和文化有着紧密的联系。由于文化差异，汉英两种语言在表达方式和思维习惯上大相径庭。因此，字对字的逐字翻译方法很多时候并不适用，会导致译文生硬不通顺。正反译法是常见的翻译技巧之一，包括正话反译和反话正译两种方式。在恰当的场合运用正反译法，能够确保译文语义明晰、文字通顺。从形式上看，有时候汉语的"肯定"，要根据英语表达习惯译成英语的"否定"；而有时候则相反，汉语的"否定"，要用英语的"肯定"形式来翻译。

例：有什么问题，尽管与我联系。

译文：If you have any questions, *don't hesitate to* contact me.（正话反译）

例：处理这件事，越谨慎越好。

译文：You *cannot be too* cautious in handling this matter.（正话反译）

例：他没有弄懂我的意思。

译文：He *failed to understand* me.（反话正译）

例：教室里有 5 位同学还没有走。

译文：Five students *remained* in the classroom.（反话正译）

例：遗憾的是，他愿望还没有实现，就去世了。

译文：Unfortunately, he died *before his wish could come true*.（反话正译）

五、顺译法

所谓顺译法，就是指把句子按照与译文相同的语序或表达方式进行翻译。汉译英时，适当地使用正译法可以使句子通顺流畅，符合所译语言习惯。按照英语表达的层次顺序，依次翻译汉语句子，从而使英语译文与汉语原文的顺序基本一致。

例：地震与断裂运动有密切的关系。

译文：Earthquakes are closely related to faulting.

例：由于我们实行了改革开放政策，我国的综合国力有了明显的增强。

译文：Thanks to the introduction of our reform and opening policy, our comprehensive national strength has greatly improved.

例：夜深了，风吹过树梢，他还在书桌前坚持工作。

译文：As the night deepened, the wind brushed through the treetops, and he remained at his desk, persisting in his work.

例：红色使人感到兴奋、充满活力；蓝色有助于减少压力和焦虑；而紫色则兼具红色和蓝色的特质，能激励运动员们发挥出最佳状态，帮他们创造好成绩。

译文：Red makes people feel excited and energetic; blue helps reduce stress and anxiety, while purple has some of the characteristics of both red and blue, which can motivate athletes to perform at their best and help them produce good results.

六、合译法

合译法是把若干个短句合并成一个长句，一般用于汉译英。汉语强调意合，结构较松散，因此简单句较多；英语强调形合，结构较严密，因此长句较多。所以汉译英时要根据需要注意利用连词、分词、介词、不定式、定语从句、独立结构等把汉语短句连成长句。

例：门口放着一堆箱子，大概有 15 个，五颜六色，大小不一。

译文：In the doorway lay about fifteen boxes *of* all sizes and colors.（介词）

例：中国是个大国，80％的人口从事农业，但耕地只占土地面积的1/10，其余为山脉、森林、城镇和其他用地。

译文：China is a large country with four-fifths of the population engaged in agriculture，but only one tenth of the land is farmland，the rest *being* mountains，forests and places for urban and other uses.（独立结构）

例：有时流到很狭窄的地段，两岸丛山叠岭，绝壁断崖，江河流于期间，回环曲折，极其险峻。

译文：Sometimes it comes up against a narrow section flanked by high mountains and steep cliffs，*winding* through a course with many a perilous twist and turn.（分词结构）

例：在读书的过程中，我们可能会遇到各种思想的碰撞，感受到不同文化的魅力，甚至会在书籍的海洋中迷失方向，但最终都会被带到一个新的认知境界。

译文：Through reading，we may encounter diverse ideas，appreciate cultural charms，and sometimes lose ourselves in the vast ocean of books，only *to be* led to new realms of understanding.（不定式结构）

例：他们片面地注重工业，忽视农业和轻工业，因而市场上货物不够，货币不稳定。

译文：Their lopsided stress on heavy industry *and* their neglect of agriculture and light industry results in a shortage of goods on the market *and* an unstable currency.（连词）

易错盘点

逻辑重组

逻辑重组指结合汉英思维模式的特点，适度调整译文信息的逻辑关系，加强译文信息的可读性和可接受性。汉语语言组织重意合，强调语义的内在连贯，语义逻辑的"隐含性"更明显。英语语言形式丰富，语法组织重形合，语义逻辑更多地表现为显性的语法关系。因此，翻译中，在确保充分传达原文语义信息和内涵的基础上，要考虑译文思维逻辑特点和逻辑在语法组织上的体现，提高译文表达的可读性。对汉语句子逻辑关系的理解是否正确、翻译处理是否恰当直接影响到翻译的质量。在翻译实践中，首先应对汉语句子进行逻辑分析，厘清意群之间的逻辑关系，再进行翻译。总的说来，汉语句子中的逻辑关系英译处理方式可以分为两大类：显性法（包含关联词语）和隐性法（不包含关联词语）。

1. 显性法

我们在翻译句子内容多、结构比较复杂的汉语长句时，一定要先搞清句子里各成分之间的主次关系和逻辑关系，然后按英语的表达习惯，采取不同的译法，把汉语句子译成准确、通顺、地道的英语。逻辑关系可以直接分为常见的几大类：并列、对比、选择、递进、承接、因果、让步、条件、假设、目的、转折。在汉译英时，对于汉语中隐性的逻辑关系，应先洞察其中的关系，然后选择英语中相对应的关联词语将原句译出。

例：人民有信仰，国家有力量，民族有希望。（隐含条件）

译文：*If* the people have ideals，their country will have strength，and their nation will have a bright future.

例：先发展的地区带动后发展的地区，最终达到共同富裕。（隐含时间）

译文：Those that develop faster can help those that are lagging，*until* all become prosperous.

例：人不犯我，我不犯人。（隐含假设）

译文：We will not attach *unless* we are attached.

例：虚心使人进步，骄傲使人落后。（隐含对照）

译文：Modesty helps one to go forward，*whereas* conceit makes one lag behind.

例：制造无人驾驶机的基本要求是体积小巧、结构简单、成本低廉、便于操作。（隐含并列）

译文：The basic demands for manufacturing non-pilot airplanes are small volume，simple structure, low cost *and* easy to operate.

例：我们必须加强企业管理，提高生产效率，改善劳动条件，增强竞争意识。（隐含并列）

译文：We must strengthen our business management, raise efficiency in production, improve working conditions, *and* enhance our sense of competition.

2. 隐性法

隐性法指不直接通过关联词语而通过其他语法形式或语言结构（动词或动词词组、名词性短语、形容词性短语、介词短语、非谓语动词形式等）来实现句子的衔接。事实上，英语当中存在大量的句子没有使用任何关联词语却传达了某种逻辑关系的现象。在翻译中，我们可以在特定的语境下灵活运用某些语言结构，使译文语言表达富于变化，符合英语的思维模式和表达习惯。

例：失之毫厘，谬以千里。

译文：A minimal error or deviation may *result in* wide divergence.（动词词组）

例：他受伤严重，不得已只好放弃工作。

译文：He suffered a serious injury that *obliged* him *to* give up work.（动词词组）

例：由于卫生条件不好，他生病了。

译文：Unhygienic conditions *gave rise to* his disease.（动词词组）

例：胃的功能是充分消化食物，以便让其进入肠道。

译文：The function of the stomach is to digest food sufficiently to *enable* it *to* pass into the intestine.（动词词组）

例：他们一听到这个消息，就立即出发去火车站了。

译文：*Hearing* the news, they immediately leave for the railway station.（非谓语动词形式）

例：由于不懂他们的语言，她没听懂他们在说些什么。

译文：*Not knowing* the language, she didn't understand what they were talking about.（非谓语动词形式）

小试牛刀

Translate the following sentences into English.

1. 机不可失，时不再来。
2. 我们要忠于党、忠于人民、忠于祖国。
3. 谦虚使人进步，骄傲使人落后。
4. 汉字的书写不仅是一种语言文字的表达方式，更是一种艺术的体现。
5. 不同颜色能够引发人们不同的情绪和感受。

学以致用

Translate the following sentences into English.

1. 加强基础研究，是实现高水平科技自立自强的迫切要求，是建设世界科技强国的必由之路。
2. 中医的养生之道深深影响了人们的饮食习惯。
3. 推进粤港澳大湾区建设，支持香港、澳门更好融入国家发展大局，为实现中华民族伟大复兴更好地发挥作用。
4. 这些文化元素在中国社会发展中扮演着重要角色，同时也深刻地影响着人们的思维方式、道德观念以及社会行为。
5. 随着全球化的发展和信息交流日益频繁，中国传统文化正以其独特的魅力在全球舞台上绽放光彩。

第三章

写 作

第一节　应用文写作

🔍 重点知识概览

应用文写作重点知识概览

类别	基本要素	常见类型	注意事项
信函类	写信日期； 信内地址； 称呼； 正文； 信尾敬语； 署名。	邀请信	称呼后用逗号","，不用冒号":"或句点"."。 通常为三段式结构。 电子邮件可以采用齐头式。
		感谢信	
		祝贺信	
		道歉信	
		求职信	
		投诉信	
		申请信	
		电子邮件	
通知类	标题； 正文； 发布者； 发布日期。	通知	通知标题可用"NOTICE"或通知的主要内容。 "通知的发布者在右下角,通知的日期位于右下角,发布者下方。"
		启事	
		海报	

☕ 写作技巧

　　应用文是人类在长期社会实践活动中形成的，在处理公私事务时经常使用的实用性文体，是人们日常生活、工作，以及人际交往中的重要载体。在高职英语写作考试中，信函类和通知类写作题型考查频率较高。本章重点介绍两类常见应用文体：信函类和通知类。

一、信函类

信函，又称书信或信件，是一种用于交流信息、表达情感或讨论事务的沟通形式。

英语信函的基本要素包括：写信日期(Date)、信内地址(Inside address)、称呼(Salutation)、正文(Body)、信尾敬语(Complimentary close)和署名(Signature)。写作考试常常只要求包含称呼、正文、信尾敬语和署名这几个要素即可。

(一)英文信函基本要素

写信日期(Date)：信函的开头，通常写在信纸最上方。格式如下。

英式英语写法：21 December 2024

美式英语写法：December 21，2024

信内地址(Inside Address)：收信人的信内地址，地址按从小到大的顺序排列，即门牌号码和街名、城市、州/省份、邮编和国家，写在日期下方。

称呼(Salutation)：对收信人的称呼，如 Dear Mr. Smith, Dear Mrs. Johnson, Dear Sir/Madam。称呼写在收信人信内地址下方，顶格左侧对齐，通常以逗号结束。

正文(Body)：正文是书信的主要部分，包含写信的原因、目的、传递的信息等。正文的写作应遵循完整、清楚、连贯、礼貌的原则。正文写在称呼下方，通常分几个段落，每个段落有明确的主题或要点。

信尾敬语(Complementary Close)：信函的结尾，表示对收信人的尊重、感谢或祝福等。如：Sincerely, Yours truly, Regards 等。位于正文下方，右侧对齐，句末用逗号。信尾敬语应根据通信人之间关系的亲疏恰当选择。

署名(Signature)：署名指写信人的亲笔签名或电子签名，以确认信函的真实性。写在信尾敬语下方，用手写签名或电子签名，右侧对齐。

(二)英文信函常见格式

1. 齐头式(Block Form)：所有构成要素都顶格书写，包括信内地址、日期、签名等。段与段之间通常隔一行，使信函内容更加易读。例如：

Dear Mr. Smith,

As the Mid-Autumn Festival approaches, our class would like to invite you to join our special class party.

Mid-Autumn Festival is a symbol of reunion and harvest in China. Our class party is scheduled on September 20 at 7：00 p. m. in Classroom 306 of the Teaching Building. We plan to celebrate it by various traditional Chinese customs, such as enjoying the bright moon, eating moon-cakes and making lanterns. You can deeply understand Chinese Mid-Autumn culture by experiencing the traditional activities with us.

Your presence would greatly enrich our experience. We are looking forward to your coming.

Warm regards,
Li Hua

2. 缩进式(Indented Form)：正文每个部分通过缩进来区分，形成层次结构，段与段之间不空行。例如：

Dear Sir/Madam,

I hope this letter finds you well. I am a student in our college and I am writing to inquire some information about the library.

I am interested in learning more about our library's services and resources. Would you mind telling me the library's open hours? Specifically，I would like to know about the availability of books and study spaces，as well as any special events or workshops you offer. Additionally，I would appreciate any information on how to access online books and research tools.

I believe the library is an important resource for students and I am eager to take use of it. Thank you for your assistance.

Best regards，
Li Hua

(三)英文信函常见类型

高职英语写作考试常见的信函类型有以下几种。

类型	定义	基本格式
邀请信	邀请信是由个人或集体在举办某些活动时，向对方发出的，旨在邀请他们前来参加活动的书信。	称呼：对收件人的尊称。 正文：开头表明写信目的，发出邀请。主体部分详细交代活动的时间、地点、内容、邀请原因等；参加活动的细节安排等。结尾部分表达希望对方接受邀请的期待。 落款：写信人姓名、日期，可附上写信人联系方式。
感谢信	感谢信是向个人或集体表示感谢的一种书信，用于感谢对方给予的帮助、关心、支持和爱护等。感谢信在表达感激之情同时，可增进双方情感联系。	称呼：对收件人的尊称。 正文：开头表明写信目的，表达感谢。主体部分具体说明对方在何时、何地、由于什么原因、做了什么事、表现了什么品德、对写信人产生了什么影响等。结尾部分再次向对方表达感谢。 落款：写信人姓名、日期。
祝贺信	祝贺信是用于向收件人表达祝贺、祝福和祝愿的书面信件。通常用于庆祝某人的成就、生日、婚礼、毕业等喜事。	称呼：对收件人的尊称。 正文：开头表明写信目的，表达祝贺。主体部分具体说明祝贺的原因，表达祝贺及喜悦之情。结尾再次向对方表达祝贺。 落款：写信人姓名、日期。
道歉信	道歉信是写信人就某事向某人表示歉意的信件。道歉信通过承认写信人的错误，表达愿意采取措施纠正错误或弥补损失，有助于关系修复和信任重建。	称呼：对收件人的尊称。 正文：开头表明写信目的，表达歉意。主体部分具体说明写信人出现差错的原因、差错所带来的后果、提出弥补措施等。结尾部分再次表达歉意，请求原谅。 落款：写信人姓名、日期。
求职信	求职信是个人向用人单位提出的工作申请信件。求职信通过介绍写信人的个人情况和求职意愿，希望得到某项工作或面试机会，通常与简历一起提交。	称呼：对收件人的尊称。 正文：开头表明写信目的，表达求职意愿。主体部分详细写明个人情况，如学历背景、能力、经验等，表明自我价值。结尾部分再次表达求职意愿，请求给予面试或工作机会。 附件：可附上简历或其他相关材料。 落款：写信人姓名、日期。
投诉信	投诉信是因个人不满某项产品或服务而撰写的一种正式书面沟通方式。投诉信的主要目的是表达不满、提出问题、要求改进或寻求解决方案等。	称呼：对收件人的尊称。 正文：开头说明写信目的，表达不满。主体部分客观阐述问题，包括时间、地点、涉及人员、事件经过、事件影响等。结尾部分明确表达自己的诉求，如希望得到的解决方案、补偿方式等。 落款：写信人姓名、日期。

类型	定义	基本格式
申请信	申请信是个人向收件人提出的某种请求,如申请奖学金、参与活动、访问权限等。申请信通过阐述申请事项,使对方了解情况并作出决定,以此达到申请目的。	称呼:对收件人的尊称。 正文:开头说明写信目的,简要介绍自己并表达申请目的。主体部分具体说明申请事项,阐述与申请事项相关的背景、能力、经验等,表达对申请事项的热爱、期望和承诺等。结尾部分再次表达申请目的和期望,请求收件人给予考虑和回复。 落款:写信人姓名、日期。
电子邮件	电子邮件是一种通过电子传输的文本消息,可包含文字、图像、声音等多种形式。因其方便快捷的特点在现代生活中被广泛使用,也是高职英语写作考试中常考的文体。	常见的电子邮件包括邮件头和正文两大部分。 邮件头一般包含: From:发件人邮箱地址; To:收件人邮箱地址; Date:发送邮件的日期; Subject:邮件主题。 电子邮件正文格式与英文书信相同,均包括称呼、主体、结尾敬语和署名部分。

(四)信函类写作题型

信函类写作一般为限制性命题,常见命题要素包含:限定情景、内容要点、写作提纲和注意事项。各命题要素可组合出题,考生应注意理解限定情景,明确写作目的,注意不要遗漏内容要点,按照写作提纲扩充内容,遵照注意事项进行写作。

Sample 1(四川省 2024 年普通高校专升本考试大学英语真题)

假如你是校学生会主席李夏,下星期学校将举办国际交流活动,给外教 Smith 写封电子邮件邀请他参加开幕式和一系列活动。

内容包括:活动简介、时间、地点和注意事项。

注意:

(1)词数 100 词左右;

(2)可以适当增加细节,使行文连贯;

(3)文章开头已为你写好,不计入总词数。

参考词汇:international,exchange,Opening Ceremony

Dear Dr. Smith,

    How are you? _____

参考范文:

Dear Dr. Smith,

    How are you? I am Li Xia, a student from Sichuan vocational school. Our college is going to organize an international exchange meeting, which aims to enhance the cultural communication and build the bridge between Chinese and foreign friends. I am writing this letter to invite you to attend the Opening Ceremony and participate in this wonderful activity.

    The event will start with an Opening Ceremony on April 17, followed by a series of engaging activities such as cultural performances, workshops, and interactive discussions. The Opening Ceremony will be held at 9:00 a. m. in our college stadium. We have invited some outstanding professors and students from all over the world to share their cultures and customs, aiming to promote cross-cultural understanding and friendship. We believe that your participation would greatly enrich the event and offer our students a unique opportunity to engage with a native English speaker.

With all mentioned above, I hope that my invitation will get your kind consideration. I'm looking forward to your early reply.

Yours sincerely,

Li Xia

Sample 2

Directions：Suppose you are Li Ming, a foreign friend of yours has written to inquire about the possibility of making a ten-day visit in China. Write a reply to give him some suggestions. You should write at least 100 words according to the outline given below.

(1)建议出行城市；

(2)提出建议的理由或根据；

(3)提醒注意事项。

Dear John，

_____

参考范文：

Dear John，

I'm delighted to learn that you plan to take a visit to China soon. In my opinion, visiting Beijing is your best choice. Here are the reasons.

On the one hand, since there are just ten days available, I suggest you visit the most valuable city in China. Beijing is definitely the most ideal choice for you. As you know, Beijing is both the political and cultural center of China. There are many historical and natural attractions worth viewing. On the other hand, I suggest you visit the most famous sites in Beijing, such as the Great Wall, the Forbidden City and Tian'anmen Square. It is strongly recommended that you climb the Great Wall to enjoy the wonderful bird-view there, which may provide you a different perspective to understand our culture.

It isn't necessary for you to bring anything except your comfortable shoes. In addition, I would advise you to taste delicious Chinese food. I'm sure you'll have a good holiday here. Please inform me of the time of your arrival. I am looking forward to seeing you soon.

Sincerely yours,

Li Ming

Sample 3(2016年6月大学英语四级考试作文真题)

Directions：For this part, you are allowed 30 minutes to write a letter to express your thanks to your parents or any other family member upon making a memorable achievement. You should write at least 120 words but no more than 180 words.

参考范文：

Dear parents，

This letter is written to tell you how much I love you and thank you for all the things you have done for me.

Firstly, thank you so much for bringing me up. I know how hard you have being working and I can imagine how many difficulties and obstacles you have conquered. Secondly, I want to thank you for your good education on me. There is an old saying "parents are the first teachers to their children". Both of you have taught me how to be a real man, a kind man. The most important thing that I want to say thanks is your respect on my pursuit. You say that you will always support me in pursuing my own dreams.

I really feel that words can not express my thanks. The only thing I want from you is to take good care of yourselves. And I hope you will be always proud of me.

Yours beloved,
Son

二、通知类

通知类文体是向特定对象告知或转达有关事项，让对象知道或执行的公文。通知、海报与启事都是常见的告知性应用文，具有语言简洁、篇幅短小的特点。

(一)通知类文体基本要素

通知类应用文通常包含：标题、正文、发布者和发布日期。

标题：位于页面顶部居中位置。

正文：位于标题正下方。通知的核心内容，包括通知的对象、事由、时间、地点等关键信息。写作时，应确保正文内容简洁明了、条理清晰。

发布者：通常位于正文结束后的右下角，右侧对齐。

发布日期：一般写在右下角，位于发布者下方，右侧对齐。

注：发布者和发布日期两项可以省略。

Sample

Notice

The English Department takes pleasure in announcing that an English Corner is to be held in Room 201, Building 2 at 6：30 p. m. on May 22. Activities include singing songs, recitation and storytelling.

All are welcome!

English Department
May 22，2024

(二)通知类文体常见类型

通知类文体常见的类型有：活动/会议通知、影视/球赛海报、招聘/寻物/招领启事等。

通知	通知主要用于信息的准确传达和执行。通知通常包括标题、正文、发布者和发布日期。有时可附加信息，如联系方式、地址等，以便接收者有疑问时进一步联系。
海报	海报主要用于广告、宣传和信息传达。海报的设计通常包括文字、图片、色彩等元素，通过这些元素的有机结合，能够以直观、生动的方式吸引公众的注意力，达到传达信息的目的。
启事	启事是一种公开声明某事的告知性应用文，种类多样，用途广泛，可包括寻人、寻物、招聘、征婚等多个领域。

Sample

For this part, you are allowed 30 minutes to write a passage under the title *Lost and Found*. You should write at least 100 words and base your writing on the outline given below.

你丢失了一部手机。请写一则寻物启事，包括以下信息。

(1)遗失的时间和地点。

(2)手机的特征。

(3)你的联系方式。

参考范文：

Last and Found

On the evening of June 9, I lost a Huawei cellphone. The place is in the English reading room on the 4th floor of the new library. The cellphone can be generally described as follows.

It is brand-new and silver gray in color. The cellphone is of the similar size as a small notebook and there is a blue phone case wrapped around it.

This cellphone is a birthday present from my parents. The one who found it please contact me at 783 214 21. He or she is sure to be given a gift in return.

Thank you very much!

Yours sincerely,

Li Ming

常用表达

一、信函类常用表达

(一)对收件人的称呼

给认识的人写信：可用 Dear Mr. ＋姓氏、Dear Mrs. /Miss. /Ms. ＋姓氏。如果知道收信人的职位或头衔，可以使用职位或头衔加上姓氏，如 Dear Director /Professor＋姓氏。

给陌生人写信：可以使用 Dear Sir or Madam、To Whom It May Concern 等。

给亲密的人写信：可以直接使用 Dear＋名字，如 Dear Mary。

(二)正文部分常用表达

1. 寒暄语：

Excuse me of not writing you for such a long time.

Words can't express my delight of receiving your letter.

I hope this email finds you well.

2. 写信目的：

I am writing to…

I wanted to let you know that…

The following is to inform you of…

I am very much delighted to inform that…

3. 回复邮件：

Thank you for your email regarding…

Thank you for getting back to me so quickly.

Thanks so much for your feedback on…

I appreciate your email and…

4. 礼貌请求：

Would you mind doing…

Can you possibly…

If possible, could you send me…

It would be greatly appreciated if you could…

Would you kindly respond by…

5. 提出问题：

Would you please clarify…

Could you please send me further details regarding…

Would you mind explaining that again?

6. 附件：

Please see the following attachments.

Please review the attachments below.

I've enclosed the… below.

Here are the documents we discussed earlier.

7. 感谢：

I sincerely appreciate your time.

Many thanks for your kind invitation.

It's very kind of you to have us over.

Thank you so much for your present/help/time/consideration/good wishes…

Thank you again from the bottom of my heart.

8. 道歉：

I sincerely apologize for…

I am sorry for…

Once again，I appreciate your understanding…

9. 表达期望：

I am looking forward to your early reply.

Your early reply would be much appreciated.

Thank you in advance for your help with this.

I appreciate your cooperation in this matter.

I'm excited to work with you.

10. 祝愿祝福：

We send you our best wishes.

With best regards.

Love to all of you.

Please give my best regards to your family/parents.

Good luck to you.

(三)信尾敬语表达

Best regards，

Sincerely，

Yours sincerely，

Yours truly，

Respectfully，

Cordially，

Yours respectfully，

Best wishes，

Warm regards，

二、通知类常用表达

1. 正式通知：

We hereby notify you that…

Please be informed that…

2. 说明事件或活动：

There will be… held on….

… is organizing… on…

3. 提供详细信息：

It will begin at… and last about…

The… will include…

There will be a party/speech/contest held by… on…

The… will arrange/provide…

4. 强调参与：

All staff/students are expected to attend.

Everybody is expected to attend it.

We encourage everyone to participate in…

Be sure to attend it on time.

All are welcome!

5. 联系方式或后续信息：

For more information，please contact…

Further updates will be posted on…

6. 结束语：

Thank you for your attention.

We look forward to seeing you there.

小试牛刀

Ⅰ. 下列问题可以在电子邮件的哪个部分找到？请找出最佳选项并连线。

1. To whom is the email written?　　　　　A. The opening paragraph.

2. Who write the email?　　　　　　　　　B. The subject.

3. What is the email mainly about?　　　　C. Salutation.

4. Why does the writer write the email?　　D. Signature.

Ⅱ. 根据邮件信息写出邮件主题。

1. Subject：_____

Dear John，

　　I am writing this email to apologize for the way I behaved to you yesterday.

2. Subject：_____

Dear Mr. Smith，

　　It is with great pleasure that I write to invite you to our class graduation party.

3. Subject：_____

Dear Sir，

　　I am writing to apply for the internship position in your company.

Ⅲ. 将下列句子按照逻辑顺序组织成一封信函正文，采用缩进式写在下面。

I can't wait to see you in the near future.

Congratulations! You make it after a year of hard work.

I am writing this letter to congratulate that you have been admitted to the college.

Now that you're starting this new chapter in your life，I want to offer you some advice.

Once again，congratulations on your acceptance to the college.

Don't be afraid to step outside your comfort zone and try new things.

And most importantly，don't forget to have fun!

These years will go by quickly，so make the most of them.

In my personal experience，university life may have some challenges，but it is also highly rewarding.

Join clubs，meet new people，and explore your passions.

Dear Zhang Xin，

_____

_____

_____

_____

_____

_____

_____

Yours sincerely，

Li Ming

学以致用

Ⅰ.(四川省 2022 年普通高校专升本考试大学英语真题)假设你是李夏，是第三十一届世界大学生运动会(Universiade)的一名志愿者，组委会安排你用英文为来自世界各地的运动员介绍四川一个知名景点。内容包括：景点简介、推荐理由、注意事项。

注意：

1. 词数 100 词左右；

2. 可以适当增加细节，使行文流畅；

3. 文章开头已为你写好，不计入总词数。

参考词汇：volunteer，recommend，scenic spot

Dear friends，

Welcome to Chengdu! _____

_____

_____

_____

_____

_____

Ⅱ.(四川省 2023 年普通高校专升本考试大学英语真题)假设你是李夏，请用英文写一封信，邀请外教 Smith 教授参加你班"世界地球日"(4 月 22 日)当天组织的登山活动。

内容包括：活动目的、时间、地点和注意事项。

注意：

1. 词数 100 词左右；

2. 可以适当增加细节，使行文连贯；

3. 文章开头已为你写好，不计入总词数。

参考词汇：the World Earth Day，mountain climbing，environment

Dear Professor Smith，

How are you? _____

_____

_____

_____

_____

_____

Ⅲ. 请以外国语学院的名义写一则通知，内容为史密斯教授将为全校师生举办一次名为 *How to Study English* 的讲座，时间为 3 月 10 日早上 9 点至 11 点，地点为会议室 401。词数 100 词左右。

_____

_____

_____

_____

_____

_____

第二节　提纲写作

🔍 重点知识概览

提纲写作重点知识概览

类型	段落结构	写作要点	注意事项
观点论述	三段式：开头段 主体段 结尾段	主要聚焦于某一问题或主题的独特见解和主张。	1. 开头结尾简略，中间段落详实。 2. 中间段落用 2—3 个连接词，使行文连贯。 3. 常采用"总—分—总"结构形式。
现象解释		旨在描述、分析和解释某一现象或问题的背景、特征、成因等。	
问题解决		主要关注某一具体问题的识别、分析和解决。	
对比选择		通过对两个或多个选项进行比较和分析，做出最佳选择。	
利弊评述		主要关注某一事物或现象的利弊进行分析和评价。	

✏️ 写作技巧

提纲写作通常考查议论文文体写作。议论文是一种通过摆事实、讲道理，直接表达作者观点和主张的文体。议论文通常由论点、论据、论证三部分构成，其中论点是作者对所议论的问题所持的见解和主张，论据是用来证明论点的材料和依据，而论证则是运用论据来证明论点的过程和方法。

在处理提纲写作时，建议使用三段式结构，即：**开头段、主体段**和**结尾段**。

开头段：对问题或现象等进行描述并提出观点。

主体段：围绕文章主题和观点展开论述。

结尾段：对全文进行总结和概括，呼应开头段，并提出建议/期望/反思等。

提纲写作类型主要有：**观点论述、现象阐释、问题解决、对比选择、利弊评述**。

观点论述：观点论述的论文主要聚焦于某一问题或主题的独特见解和主张。文章的结构通常包括引言(引出主题)、主体(论证观点)和结论(总结观点)三个部分。

现象阐释：现象阐释的论文旨在描述、分析和解释某一现象或问题的背景、特征、成因等。文章的结构可包括现象的描述、现象的分析(包括成因、影响等)以及结论等部分。

问题解决：问题解决的论文主要关注某一具体问题的识别、分析和解决。文章的结构可包括问题的提出、问题的分析(包括成因、影响等)、解决方案的提出以及结论等部分。

对比选择：对比选择的论文通过对两个或多个选项进行比较和分析，做出最佳选择。文章的结构可包括选项的描述、选项的比较(包括优缺点、适用条件等)以及结论(推荐最佳选项)等部分。

利弊评述：利弊评述的论文主要关注于某一事物或现象的利弊分析和评价。文章的结构可包括引言(引出主题)、利弊分析(包括正面影响和负面影响)以及结论(给出评价和建议)等部分。

Sample

Directions：In this part，you are allowed 30 minutes to write a composition entitled *Mobile Payment in China*. You should write at least 100 words according to the following outline.

Outline：

(1)移动支付越来越受欢迎；

(2)移动支付的好处；

(3)我的看法。

参考范文：

Mobile Payment in China

With the development of technology，mobile payment has been increasingly popular in China recently.

Mobile payment has many advantages. Firstly，when people go shopping，it can save time as customers don't need to bring their wallet for cash and cashiers don't need to count changes. Secondly，there is no need to worry about getting the fake cash. The customer just needs to scan the QR code to pay. No cash is needed during the whole process. Thirdly，mobile payment is much safer than traditional cash payment. Mobile payment can reduce the risk of losing money for people don't need to carry cash at all.

As mobile payment is so convenient，most of us are willing to pay with it. Nowadays，mobile payment in China has become a critical part of the digital economy. I believe it will drive more new business models and services in the near future.

常用表达

提纲写作常用表达

1. 解释现象：

It is true that…

It is universally acknowledged that…

There is no doubt that…

Everybody knows that…

2. 陈述观点：

As far as I'm concerned…

In fact，we have to admit that…

I am believed that…

In my opinion…

For my part，I agree with the… for the following reasons.

3. 表示原因：

The reasons for this are as follows.

The reason for this is that…

We have good reason to believe that…

4. 解决措施：

Prompt/proper measures must be taken to…

It's high time that…

We should take some effective measures to…

We should try our best to…

4. 举例：

for example/instance

take sth. as an example

In this case…

A case in point is…

5. 列举：

Firstly… Secondly… Lastly/Last but not least…

To start with… Next/ Furthermore /Moreover/Besides/ In addition… Finally…

On the one hand… on the other hand…

小试牛刀

根据下列写作题目草拟中文提纲。

1. Write a short essay on how to best handle the relationship among roommates.

开头段：_____

主体段：_____

结尾段：_____

2. Suppose a foreign friend of yours is coming to visit your hometown. What is the most interesting place you would like to take him/her to see and why?

开头段：_____

主体段：_____

结尾段：_____

3. Nowadays，our society advocates lifelong learning. Why we need lifelong learning? What are the benefits of lifelong learning?

开头段：_____

主体段：_____

结尾段：_____

学以致用

Directions：For this part，you are allowed 30 minutes to write a composition of no less than 100 words entitled *Find a Job or Study Further*. Write your composition according to the following outline.

Outline：

1. 大多数大学生毕业以后面临找工作和继续深造两种选择；
2. 你的看法。

第三节　图表写作

📝 重点知识概览

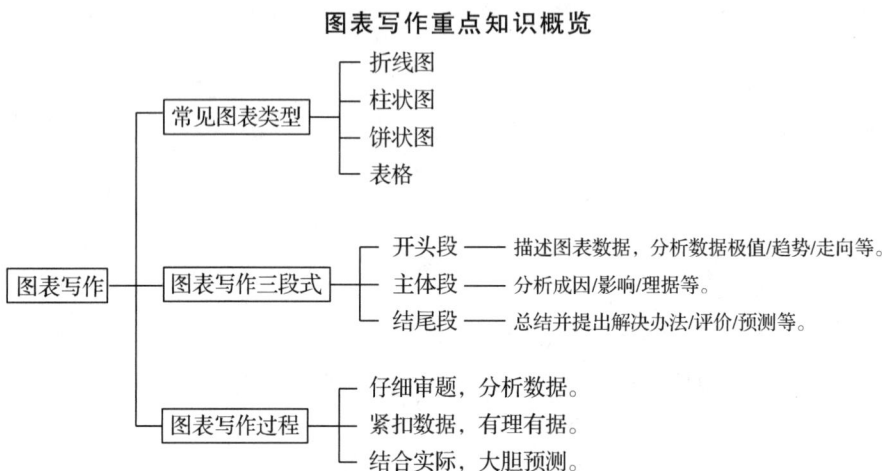

图表写作重点知识概览

```
                            ┌── 折线图
                ┌─ 常见图表类型 ┼── 柱状图
                │            ├── 饼状图
                │            └── 表格
                │
                │            ┌── 开头段 ── 描述图表数据，分析数据极值/趋势/走向等。
图表写作 ────────┼─ 图表写作三段式 ┼── 主体段 ── 分析成因/影响/理据等。
                │            └── 结尾段 ── 总结并提出解决办法/评价/预测等。
                │
                │            ┌── 仔细审题，分析数据。
                └─ 图表写作过程 ┼── 紧扣数据，有理有据。
                             └── 结合实际，大胆预测。
```

☕ 写作技巧

图表类作文是英语写作考试中常考题型。此类题型通常采用图或表等形式进行命题，考生必须要看懂图表反映出来的现象或问题，挖掘和阐述其深层次信息（原因、趋势、走向等）并做出相应的评述。

常见的图表类型有：折线图（Line Graph）、柱状图（Bar Chart）、饼状图（Pie Chart）和表格（Table）。

图表作文通常可采用三段式结构。

开头段：描述图表数据，分析数据极值/趋势/走向等；

主体段：分析成因/影响/根据等；

结尾段：总结并提出解决办法/评价/预测等。

图表作文写作过程如下：

首先，仔细审题、分析数据。在写作前，必须结合题目说明和图表（含图表中所有文字信息）认真审题。厘清图表数据的极值、趋势、走向等，分析图表数据所反映的主要问题和现象，提取文章主题，列出段落提纲，然后再进行写作。

其次，紧扣数据、有理有据。图表类写作经常要求考生分析可能的原因或影响。在写作过程中，考生可以结合生活实际分析原因或影响，做到有理有据。此外，还要注意数据描述的准确性。

最后，结合实际、大胆预测。在写作结尾，考生重新总结已表述的观点或成因，就图表反映出的问题或现象大胆进行评价、预测，或者结合实际生活提出解决办法，只要能做到自圆其说就是一篇合格的作文。

Sample［2020 年"外研社国才杯"全国英语写作大赛（高职组）复赛样题］

Directions：The following charts show the results of a survey on people's attitudes towards the impact of artificial intelligence（AI）on jobs. The number of people who participated in the survey is 2,000, and

among all the participants, 680 are AU users. Write a report to analyze the charts and give your possible reasons why half of AI users believe AI will create more jobs.

Impact of AI on Jobs

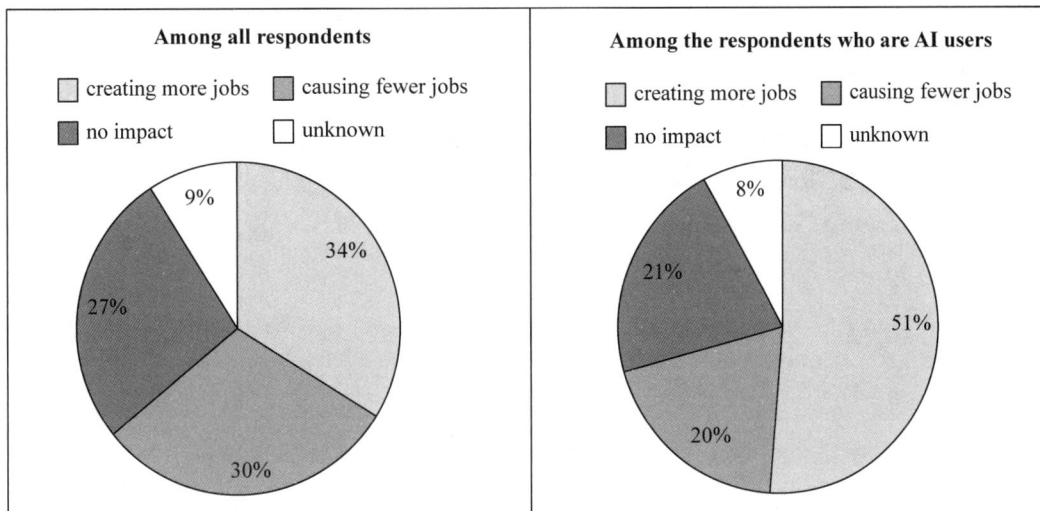

参考范文:

Impact of AI on Jobs

The pie chart shows people's different attitudes towards the impact of AI on jobs. Of the 2,000 respondents, 34% believe that AI will create more jobs, roughly the same as those standing against it. In comparison, among the 680 AI users, half of them hold a positive view on AI's job creation potential. Personally, there are three major reasons for the difference.

To begin with, AI users may recognize the potential of AI to drive innovation in us. In many industries, AI has been used to free human workers to focus on more valuable activities, saving people doing simple, repeated job. Moreover, with the access to AI, users can have a better chance to understand AI technology. Last but not least, having benefited from AI, users tend to hold greater expectations for the advancement of this new technology.

In conclusion, AI has brought mixed reactions among people. Due to differences in recognition, understanding and expectations of the new technology, AI users tend to believe that AI is favorable to job creation. It is believed that with greater access to AI, more people will realize the active role of AI in job creation.

常用表达

图表写作常用表达

1. 趋势变化:

increase/grow/rise/soar/jump/climb

fall/drop/decline/decrease

go down/slow down/remain/stand at

stable/unchanged/constant/fluctuating

an increase/a fall/a drop/a decline/a decrease

2. 占比:

70% of the students passed the exam.

Women make up 51% of the population in this country.

5 out of 10 people preferred the red shirt.

The southern region has a greater share of the country's natural resources.

As the data indicates，Project A is superior to others，accounting for 40%.

3. 比较：

There are more books in the first library than in the second.

This year's profit is three times as much as last year's.

The number of participants this year is five times more than last year.

Unemployment is 3% lower than the previous month.

In 2022，the average salary was 5,000 compared to 4,500 in 2021.

小试牛刀

一、图表匹配。

1. Line graph		A.	饼图
2. Pie chart		B.	柱状图
3. Table		C.	折线图
4. Bar chart		D.	表格

二、将下列句子翻译成中文。

1. The chart clearly depicts the fluctuating of oil prices.

2. The number of online users underwent a marked change，with a sharp rise in the last two years.

3. The chart reveals that the peak in monthly sales was reached in July.

4. The most notable observation from the chart is the unemployment rate，standing at 12%.

5. The chart depicts a clear trend in global temperatures，with a steady increase over the past century.

学以致用

Directions：For this part，you are allowed 30 minutes to write a composition on the topic *How People Spend Their Holidays*. You should write at least 100 words and base your composition on the table and the outline given below：

Year	2010	2015	2020
traveling	37%	51%	76%
Staying at home	63%	49%	24%

Outline：

1. 根据上表，简要描述某城市不同年份人们度假方式的情况及其变化；

2. 请说明发生这些变化的原因；

3. 得出结论。

参考答案

模块一　基础知识强化

第一章　词汇

第一节　名词和代词

小试牛刀

Correct errors in the following sentences.

1. brother 改为 brothers

Correct：She has two brothers.

2. he 改为 and he

Correct：This is my friend，and he is from Beijing.

3. they 改为 their

Correct：They don't like their teacher.

4. many 改为 much 或去掉 many，因为 homework 是不可数名词。

Correct：I have much homework to do. ／I have homework to do.

5. speak 后加 to，she 改为 her，作 speak to 的宾语。

Correct：I saw her in the street yesterday，but I didn't speak to her.

学以致用

I. Choose the right words to fill into the blanks.

1. J. Festival　2. B. China　3. A. history　4. G. moon　5. E. People

6. H. their　7. D. tradition　8. C. culture　9. F. us　10. I. family

II. Please mark and correct the 10 mistakes in the following passage.

1. he → his

2. museum → museums

3. was → were

4. Me → I

5. statue → statues

6. souvenir → souvenirs

7. it → them

8. real → really

229

9. can → can't   10. museums → museum

III. Translate the following sentences into English.

1. We should inherit and promote Chinese excellent traditional culture.

2. Socialist core values are our commonly pursued value goals.

3. He is always ready to help others and is a model for us to learn from.

4. Everyone should take their own responsibility.

5. This book is mine，not yours.

6. The Chinese nation has a five-thousand-year history of civilization.

7. We should respect everyone's choices and rights.

8. He has practiced the socialist core values through practical actions.

9. Students help each other and make progress together.

10. Chinese culture is profound and extensive，worthy of our in-depth study and inheritance.

第二节　动词

小试牛刀

Fill in the blanks with the correct forms of the verbs.

1. was built　2. visit　3. celebrate　4. promotes　5. have influenced

学以致用

I. Read the following passage and fill in the blanks with the correct forms of the verbs provided.

1. E. is celebrated　2. J. hold　3. D. can be traced　4. I. originated　5. B. drowned

6. G. threw　7. A. observed　8. F. serves　9. C. promotes　10. H. enjoying

II. Please mark and correct the 10 mistakes in the following passage.

1. decided go → decided to go   2. choose → chose

3. released → had been released   4. arrived to → arrived at

5. buy → bought   6. forget → forgot

7. begun → had begun   8. decided making → decided to make

9. buy → bought   10. forget → forgotten

III. Translate the following sentences into English，using the words provided.

1. We should respect traditional culture and inherit it.

2. The Chinese government is committed to promoting global economic development.

3. Teenagers should establish correct values and views on life.

4. China's aerospace industry has achieved tremendous accomplishments.

5. We should strive to study hard and contribute to realizing the Chinese Dream.

6. The Four Great Inventions of China have exerted a profound influence on world civilization.

7. We should adhere to the path of peaceful development and promote the building of a community with a shared future for mankind.

8. Chinese traditional culture is extensive and profound，deserving our in-depth study and inheritance.

9. We should promote patriotism and contribute to the prosperity of our country.

10. The Chinese government actively promotes green development and protects the ecological environment.

第三节　形容词和副词

小试牛刀

Fill in the blanks with the correct forms of the words.

1. highest　2. more beautifully　3. hardest　4. worse　5. happier　6. the smartest　7. earlier
8. the most boring　9. louder　10. more delicious

学以致用

Ⅰ. Read the following passage and fill in the blanks with the correct forms of the words provided.

1. B. through　2. I. richness　3. E. confused　4. G. friendly　5. J. patiently
6. H. attentively　7. D. impressed　8. A. profoundly　9. F. proud　10. C. helpful

Ⅱ. Please mark and correct the 10 mistakes in the following passage.

1. amazing → amazingly　　　　　2. beautifully → beautiful

3. perfectly → perfect　　　　　　4. neat → neatly

5. a interesting → an interesting　6. tast → tasty

7. real → really　　　　　　　　8. friendliness → friendly

9. greatly → great　　　　　　　10. happily → happy

Ⅲ. Translate the following sentences into English.

1. This book is so interesting that I have read it over and over again.

2. She sang so beautifully that everyone applauded for her.

3. He works very hard and often stays up late working overtime.

4. This dish tastes delicious, and I finished it quickly.

5. She performed exceptionally well in the competition, winning warm applause from the audience.

6. He greeted me very friendly.

7. This movie was quite boring, and I fell asleep halfway through.

8. She always arrives on time and never be late.

9. China's Chang'e-5 successfully returned to Earth, which is another major breakthrough in China's aerospace industry.

10. The Terracotta Warriors is one of the wonderful cultural relics in the world.

第四节　连词和介词

小试牛刀

Choose the appropriate preposition and fill in the blanks.

1. with　2. by　3. from　4. with; at　5. with　6. about　7. in; to　8. To　9. on　10. with
11. for; with　12. On　13. in; with　14. for; of　15. At; in　16. In; with　17. to; on　18. To; for　19. In; with; near　20. of

学以致用

Ⅰ. Choose the best answer from the four choices A, B, C and D.

1. C　2. D　3. D　4. D　5. D　6. A　7. D　8. B　9. A　10. C
11. B　12. A　13. B　14. C　15. A　16. B　17. D　18. A　19. B　20. C

Ⅱ. Please mark and correct the 10 mistakes in the following passage.

1. In → On　2. that → who　3. but → and　4. go → going　5. for → in
6. Because → Although　7. so → for　8. and → but also　9. in → at　10. help → to help

III. Translate the following sentences into Chinese.

1. 努力学习，否则你就赶不上你的同学了。

2. 我的祖母很老了，但她从不停止学习。

3. 即使你通过了期末考试，也应该继续努力学习。

4. 他们早早出发，以便能准时到达那里。

5. 我得待在这儿，直到我妈妈好起来。

6. 我们不能在公园的草地上走。

7. 超市在书店和图书馆的前面。

8. 因为下大雨，他们上学迟到了。

9. 除非你亲眼看到，否则你不会相信这场大火有多可怕。

10. 车祸发生在一个炎热的夏天下午。

IV. Translate the following sentences into English.

1. We won't be able to do the job well without your help.

2. I am really interested in English.

3. Finally we came up with an idea.

4. "Dust" is used as a noun here，which means old things in the past.

5. BYD's latest car is on display at the mall.

6. What TV series is on tonight?

7. The post office is down the street on the left.

8. We used vegetable oil instead of butter when making bread.

9. Someone took my admission ticket by mistake.

10. The air conditioner will be on sale here in winter.

第五节 冠词和数词

小试牛刀

I. Fill in the blanks with appropriate articles.

1. A；/   2. a；the   3. the；a   4. an   5. a   6. /；a   7. the；an；the   8. a；an
9. an；/   10. the；the

II. Fill in the blanks with appropriate numerals.

1. first   2. seven   3. eight   4. fifty；fiftieth   5. three times   6. Forty percent
7. ninth   8. Sixty percent；three fifths   9. fifties   10. eleven forty/ twenty to twelve

学以致用

I. Choose the best answer from the four choices A，B，C and D.

1. A   2. D   3. B   4. D   5. B   6. A   7. A   8. B   9. A   10. C
11. C   12. C   13. B   14. D   15. D   16. C   17. B   18. C   19. A   20. D

II. Please mark and correct the 10 mistakes in the following passage.

1. to → 删除   2. lot → a lot   3. Between → Among   4. the → a   5. a → 删除
6. them → it   7. note → a note   8. a → the   9. a → an   10. few → little

III. Translate the following sentences into Chinese.

1. 引进新技术后，这家工厂 2010 年的汽车产量是前一年的两倍。

2. 全世界数以百万计的人都患有咬指甲的痛苦瘾，这可能比吸烟更难戒掉。

3. 据报道，有大量的人被杀，死亡人数已达近 1 万人。

4. 日本的人口不是很多。但据报道，大约 25％的人口是老年人。

5. 那个国家大约 50％的人口以种田为生。

6. 老师经常告诉我们："今天做一个诚实的孩子，明天做一个有用的人。"

7. 物以类聚。

8. 那个时候小岛上的人们过着多么幸福的生活啊！

9. 欧洲和美洲被大西洋隔开。

10. 我想要一间窗户朝南的房间。

IV.　Translate the following sentences into English.

1. I felt someone patted me on the shoulder.

2. Chang'an was the starting point of the world famous "Silk Road".

3. Qingdao is a beautiful city，located in the east of China.

4. It is eleven o'clock in the morning but he is still in bed.

5. Hangzhou，an energetic city，has set up trade relations with lots of countries and areas.

6. We need two more chairs for the event. You can go to Room 102 and get two more.

7. The boy has been late for class four times this term.

8. Tens of millions of people connect via WeChat every day.

9. Leo was in his twenties when he got married.

10. There are sixty students in our class and three fourths of us like football.

第二章　句法

第一节　句子的基本成分及结构

小试牛刀

Analyze the following sentences and mark the names of the components.

1. She(主语) asked(谓语)me(宾语)to buy some food(宾语补足语).

2. To catch the plane(状语)，we(主语)got up(谓语)early(状语).

3. My dream(主语)is(系动词)to be a teacher(表语)in the future(状语).

4. I(主语)have(谓语)nothing(宾语)to say(定语)on this topic(状语).

5. The children(主语)were(系动词)surprised(主语补足语).

学以致用

I.　Choose the right words to fill into the blanks.

1. J. those　2. K. for　3. A. studied　4. D. who　5. L. less　6. C. by　7. G. truth　8. F. improve

9. I. recently　10. B. continuing

II.　Please mark and correct the 10 mistakes in the following passage.

1. fail → failed　2. sadly → sad　3. friends → friend　4. she → her　5. careful → carefully

6. more → much　7. am → 删除　8. progresses → progress　9. best → the best

10. moving → move

III.　Translate the following sentences into Chinese.

1. 去年他的爸爸为了奖励他给他买了一辆新车。

2. 他的弟弟从小就想成为一名军人。

3. 我的家乡盛产甘蔗，被称为"甜城"。

4. 这部电影非常精彩，我昨天已经和男朋友一起去看过了。

233

5. 你说话的时候要小心，隔墙有耳。

6. 他不喜欢和人交流，以至于他没什么朋友。

7. 上星期我们进行了一次针对阅读习惯的调查。

8. 互联网改变了我们的生活，使我们的生活变得越来越便利，人们的距离越来越近。

9. 你不能总是回避生活中的困难，而是应该勇敢面对并试图解决它们。

10. 我们不仅需要考虑学校的短期利益，也要考虑长期的发展。

IV. Translate the following sentences into English.

1. Your story sounds wonderful.

2. I think this dress is expensive.

3. I don't know when he left home yesterday.

4. She bought a very fashionable dress.

5. My brother told me how to use the camera.

6. I recommend this reference book to all my students.

7. He was elected head of the health association.

8. Eat to live，but not live to eat.

9. You students，please keep the class quiet.

10. You should let your parents know what you think.

第二节　句子的种类

小试牛刀

Combine each pair of sentences into one sentence using a proper conjunction.

1. Your nose is bleeding，so you'd better lie down immediately.

2. Leo could neither read nor write.

3. You can travel either by car or by plane.

4. As time goes on，it's getting warmer and warmer.

5. He works as hard as others，although he is in poor health.

6. The nurse could not decide what to do，so she asked the doctor for advice.

7. The tourist lost his way，so he had to ask the way.

8. If you know the rules traffic，you will be able to pass the examination.

9. Get up quickly，otherwise you will be late for school.

10. The doctor went into the clinic and began to work.

学以致用

I. Choose the best answer from the four choices A，B，C and D.

1. C　2. D　3. D　4. B　5. C　6. D　7. C　8. A　9. B　10. B
11. D　12. A　13. B　14. A　15. C　16. C　17. B　18. D　19. D　20. C

II. Please mark and correct the 10 mistakes in the following passage.

1. did → do　2. much → many　3. high → higher　4. don't → didn't　5. so → yet
6. shouldn't → can't　7. who → what　8. you → we　9. However → Moreover　10. must → can

III. Translate the following sentences into English.

1. He not only washed the clothes but also cleaned the room.

2. Neither I nor he likes this song.

3. She is either drunk or mad.

4. My room is small，however，it's very comfortable.

5. Does he work at school or in the hospital?

6. I get up early，but my brother gets up late.

7. Hold your dream，or you might regret someday.

8. He started the job soon after he left the university.

9. If anyone calls，tell them I'm not in.

10. We used the computer in order that we might save time.

模块二　　重点语法梳理

第一章　时态

小试牛刀

Choose the best answer from the four choices A、B、C and D.

1. D　2. C　3. D　4. D　5. B　6. C　7. A　8. A　9. A　10. D

学以致用

I. Choose the right words to fill in the blanks.

1. C. faster　2. J. working　3. E. difficult　4. D. to help　5. I. making　6. F. also　7. B. takes
8. H. loses　9. A. will be used　10. G. us

II. Please mark and correct the 10 mistakes in the following passage.

1. children → child　2. late → later　3. end → the end　4. was → were　5. have had → have

6. talking → talk.　7. chat → chatted　8. in → on　9. frightened → frightening

10. put → putting

III. Translation

1. Translate the following sentences into English.

1. The old man used to sit on a bench in a quiet park，watching other people.

2. He used to visit his mother once a week.

3. He went to New York one week ago.

4. When did you first meet him?

5. She told me she was going to visit me.

6. From 1983 to 1998，he was teaching at Yale University.

7. They were building a bridge last winter.

8. If we didn't do that，we would make a serious mistake.

9. Someone broke the window.

10. We have lived here for many years.

11. I've been waiting for your reply for a week.

12. My father always cycled to work.

13. Tom was involved in a serious car accident.

14. Tom has been in a serious car accident.

15. He is now a worker and has served in the military for five years.

2. Translate the following sentences into Chinese.

1. 他们去年参观了长城。

2. 我明年将去日本旅行。

3. 我给他打电话时，他正在看电视。

4. 我还没完成我的家庭作业。

5. 我到家时，我爸爸正在打电话。

6. 这个月月底我将去北京。

7. 她打电话给我时，我正在看电视。

8. 当我们到达时，他们已经离开了。

9. 她整个晚上都要学习。

10. 飞机 10 点起飞。

第二章　语态

小试牛刀

Choose the best answer from the four choices A，B，C and D.

1. B　2. A　3. B

学以致用

I. Choose the best one from the four choices A，B，C and D.

1. D　2. B　3. B　4. C　5. B　6. D　7. C　8. C　9. D　10. A　11. C　12. A　13. C　14. B　15. A
16. C　17. C　18. A　19. C　20. D

II. Choose the right words to fill into the blanks.

1. A. chocolate　2. E. because　3. G. grandfather　4. I. brought　5. K. make　6. L. before
7. J. loud　8. F. heard　9. D. quietly　10. C. but

第三章　主谓一致

小试牛刀

Choose the best answer from the four choices A，B，C and D.

1. D　2. A　3. D　4. C　5. A　6. A　7. C　8. B　9. C　10. B

学以致用

I. Fill in the blanks with the right forms of the words.

1. am　2. are　3. has　4. leads　5. makes　6. is　7. know　8. is　9. are　10. is

II. Please mark and correct the 10 mistakes in the following passage.

1. think → thought　　2. misses → miss　　3. countryside → the countryside

4. on → with　　5. have been shown → have shown

6. seriously → serious　　7. airs → air　　8. much → many

9. found → find　　10. much → more

III. Translate the following sentences into English.

1. Thanks to his colleagues' help，he quickly adapted to the new environment.

2. The news came that the women's tennis team won the world championship.

3. Although I am also busy，I will try my best to help.

4. A significant number of books have been lost in the library of this district.

5. Wearing masks is one of the effective methods to prevent the spread of diseases.

6. All these facts prove that you are just as capable of being a manager as I am.

7. He was the only freshman in our school to win the first prize in the English speech contest.

8. In recent years，reality shows have been very popular with viewers.

9. His son，although is usually naughty，knows what to do when guests visit.

10. With the development of science，we will live in cities that are very different from what they are now in the future.

第四章　非谓语动词

小试牛刀

Please fill in the blanks with the appropriate forms of the following verbs.

1. D. to learn　2. C. breaking　3. A. interested　4. G. seeing　5. B. to solve

6. H. to finish　7. J. been improved　8. E. teaching　9. F. surprised　10. I. satisfied

学以致用

I. Choose the best one from the four choices marked A，B，C and D.

1. D　2. B　3. B　4. A　5. B　6. B　7. C　8. A　9. B　10. A

II. Please mark and correct the 10 mistakes in the following passage.

1. should to → should　2. replacing → replaced　3. making → make　4. sets → set

5. wasting → wasted　6. used → using　7. been → be　8. distracting → distracted

9. work → working　10. take → taking

III. Translate the following sentences into English.

1. Seeing him working so hard，I was deeply inspired.

2. I enjoy taking a walk after dinner.

3. After completing all the tasks，he sat down relaxed.

4. I like the feeling of being surrounded by nature.

5. This issue has been properly handled.

6. In order to keep healthy，he insists on exercising every day.

7. To achieve our goals，we need to develop a detailed plan.

8. After all the preparatory work was done，the meeting began.

9. Standing on the top of the mountain，we can see the beautiful view of the whole city.

10. This building designed by a renowned architect is full of Chinese style.

第五章　从句

第一节　名词性从句

小试牛刀

Indicate the types of the following clauses.

1. 主语从句　2. 宾语从句　3. 表语从句　4. 同位语从句　5. 宾语从句

6. 主语从句　7. 表语从句　8. 同位语从句　9. 宾语从句　10. 主语从句

学以致用

I. Choose the best one from the four choices marked A，B，C and D.

1. B　2. A　3. A　4. B　5. B　6. B　7. A　8. B　9. C　10. B

II. Please mark and correct the 10 mistakes in the following passage.

1. Study → Studying　2. where → that　3. that → of

4. who → which   5. what → that   6. why → that   7. of → to

8. whether → although   9. to → that   10. a → an

III. Translate the following sentences into English.

1. Protecting the environment is everyone's responsibility.

2. I heard that traveling can broaden one's horizons and enrich life experiences.

3. The biggest question is what causes global warming.

4. She looks as if she is ready to face any challenge.

5. When the sports meeting will be held hasn't been decided yet.

6. We received the exciting news that our team had won the competition.

7. I firmly believe that an optimistic attitude can bring happiness and success.

8. Whether we should accept the proposal or not needs further discussion.

9. The teacher's advice that we should read every day is very helpful for our English learning.

10. The main point of this book is that we should cherish and protect our earth.

第二节　形容词性从句

小试牛刀

Please fill in the correct relative words.

1. that/which   2. who/that   3. that/which   4. when/on which   5. that/which

6. where/in which   7. who/that   8. whose   9. why   10. whose

学以致用

I. Choose the best answer from the four choices A, B, C and D.

1. A   2. A   3. C   4. A   5. B   6. A   7. B   8. B   9. B   10. B

II. Please mark and correct the 10 mistakes in the following passage.

1. a → an   2. that → where   3. is → are   4. who → that   5. avoiding → avoided   6. or → and

7. a → the   8. which → who   9. of → about   10. for → /

III. Translate the following sentences into English.

1. This is a book that introduces Chinese culture.

2. My dream school is a place full of love and joy, where everyone helps and respects each other.

3. She is the smartest student that I have ever seen.

4. Yesterday, I met a teacher who taught me a lot about English.

5. This is a film that tells a story about love and courage.

6. This is the most beautiful garden that I have ever seen.

7. The gift that my parents gave me is my favorite.

8. The advice that you gave me is very useful.

9. Our school has a big playground, where we can do sports.

10. I like this teacher, whose classes are always interesting.

第三节　副词性从句

小试牛刀

Indicate the types of the following clauses.

1. 方式状语从句   2. 原因状语从句   3. 条件状语从句   4. 目的状语从句

5. 时间状语从句   6. 结果状语从句   7. 比较状语从句   8. 让步状语从句

9. 地点状语从句 10. 结果状语从句

学以致用

I. Choose the best answer from the four choices A, B, C and D.

1. C 2. A 3. A 4. D 5. A 6. A 7. A 8. C 9. B 10. A

II. Please mark and correct the 10 mistakes in the following passage.

1. Although → Even though 2. resist it → resist 3. in → on 4. fail → fails

5. Unless → If 6. Because → As 7. crucial → crucial that 8. So → While

9. are → be 10. Provided that → As long as

III. Translate the following sentences into English.

1. Though he was tired, he continued to work.

2. Wherever I go, I will remember my hometown.

3. Because he was sick, he did not come to the meeting.

4. If you do not work hard, you will not succeed.

5. I brought an umbrella in case it rains.

6. He ran so fast that no one could catch up with him.

7. Despite the rain, the match went on as scheduled.

8. As you suggested, we adopted a new strategy.

9. As time goes by, she becomes more and more independent.

10. We trust him because he is honest.

第六章　虚拟语气

小试牛刀

Fill in blanks with correct forms of the words in brackets.

1. were 2. will hear 3. were 4. hadn't been 5. know

6. let 7. would feel 8. is 9. had rained 10. wouldn't get

学以致用

I. Choose the right answer to fill in the blank.

1. A 2. C 3. B 4. A 5. A 6. B 7. C 8. A 9. B 10. A

II. Choose the best answer from the four choices A, B, C and D.

1. D 2. C 3. A 4. D 5. B 6. B 7. A 8. C 9. B 10. A

III. Translate the following sentences into English.

1. Would you please give me a hand?

2. Long live friendship!

3. I would rather you hadn't told me about it.

4. If it were to rain tomorrow, the meeting would be put off.

5. Please remind me of it again tomorrow in case I (should) forget.

6. We are surprised that they (should) arrive at such a conclusion.

7. The teacher's demand is that we (should) finish the exercise in 3 hours.

8. If we hadn't been working hard in the past few years, things wouldn't be going so smoothly.

9. But for your help, I wouldn't have been successful.

10. I suggest that you start your work at once.

第七章　特殊句型

第一节　感叹句和祈使句

小试牛刀

Fill in blanks with"What (a/an)，How"．

1. How　2. What an　3. How　4. What　5. What a

6. What　7. How　8. How　9. How　10. What

学以致用

I．Choose the best answer from the four choices A，B，C and D.

1. D　2. B　3. A　4. B　5. D　6. A　7. C　8. C　9. A　10. A

II．Please mark and correct the mistake in each sentence.

1. How → What　2. a → an　3. the piano is → the piano　4. What → How　5. How → What

6. Taking → Take　7. To be → Be　8. Not → Don't　9. shall we → will you　10. Got → Get

III．Translate the following sentences into English.

1. Please take care of your luggage.

2. Let's go to the library to read.

3. How beautiful this city looks at night!

4. How well she plays the piano!

5. Please save water.

6. What exciting news!

7. Don't be late again，will you?

8. What a wonderful football match it was!

9. He is not honest，so don't believe him.

10. Boys and girls，put up your hands if you want to take part in the summer camp.

第二节　反义疑问句

小试牛刀

Complete the following sentences.

1. isn't it　2. doesn't he　3. are they　4. doesn't she　5. didn't they

6. hadn't we/shouldn't we　7. don't we　8. isn't he　9. aren't I　10. will you/won't you

学以致用

I．Choose the best answer from the four choices A，B，C and D.

1. A　2. C　3. B　4. C　5. A　6. A　7. B　8. D　9. A　10. C　11. C　12. A　13. D　14. C　15. B

16. A　17. B　18. C　19. D　20. C　21. A　22. B　23. A　24. B　25. A　26. B　27. B　28. B　29. C

30. C

II．Translate the following sentences into English.

1. He worked very hard，didn't he?

2. Nothing is in the room，is it?

3. The boys and girls have never been to Chongqing，have they?

4. I don't think that you can do it，can you?

5. I am a very honest man，aren't I?

6. Everyone has done their best in the game，haven't they? /shoudn't they?

7. Let's go home together，shall we?

8. We had better do it by ourselves，hadn't we?

9. They used to be good friends，didn't they? /usedn't they?

10. He has little money，has he? /does he?

第三节　强调句、倒装句和省略句

小试牛刀

I. Omit some part to make the sentence more simple.

1. 省略第二个 work hard　2. 省略 It is　3. 省略 ought to 后的 have finished the homework

4. 省略 and 后的 you must be not　5. 省略 it is　6. 省略 he was　7. 省略第一个 that

8. 省略 that

II. Underline the emphasized part in each sentence.

1. on October　2. in Jiuquan　3. not until he got off the bus　4. two years ago　5. Why

6. such an interesting book　7. in the street　8. because of his strong interest in literature

III. Rewrite the sentences into inversion sentences.

1. Only when the war was over was he able to get back to work.

2. Not only did he like reading stories，but also he could even write some.

3. Little did the old woman know that she was seriously ill herself.

4. Hardly had he sat down when the telephone rang.

5. So fast does light travel it is difficult to imagine its speed.

6. In the next house lived a man named Jackson.

7. Out rushed a tiger from among the bushes.

8. Rarely have I seen such a beautiful sunset.

学以致用

I. Complete the sentences.

1. When necessary　2. the ice thin　3. can we go　4. Not only was the teacher strict with us
5. did they find out/know the truth　6. So did I　7. Clever as he is　8. Nor can they　9. not until at that time　10. Hardly had she come home

II. Translate the Chinese sentences into English.

1. While working in China，Peter made many friends.

2. If possible，I will attend the meeting.

3. Surroundings have changed，and so have the people in them.

4. At no time，under no circumstances will China be the first to use nuclear weapon.

5. Had she been more careful，she would have avoid the accident.

6. Not until I began to work did I realize how much time I had wasted.

7. It is he who reads English on the playground every morning.

8. No sooner had we arrived at the station than the train left.

9. It was because of the traffic accident that he was late.

10. In front of the house lay a little boy.

III. Choose the best one from the four choices A, B, C and D.

1. C　2. B　3. B　4. B　5. D　6. D　7. D　8. C　9. C　10. A　11. C　12. A　13. C　14. A　15. A　16. C　17. A　18. D　19. C　20. C

模块三　阅读、翻译及写作能力提升

第一章　阅读

小试牛刀

阅读理解

1. A　2. B　3. B　4. A　5. D　6. A　7. D　8. B　9. C　10. D　11. C　12. D　13. C　14. C　15. A　16. D

详情解析：

1. 这是一道细节理解题。略读海报全文，可以看出，第一部分是教师简介，第二部分是学生评语，第三部分则是投稿指南。从海报的标题"Teacher of the Week"可知，"本周最佳教师"是 Mr. Scanlon 获得的一项荣誉。所以选项 A 是正确答案。

2. 这是一道细节理解题。海报第二部分的引用部分是学生对老师的评语，而这段评语则是出自 James 之口，由此可见，James 就是 Mr. Scanlon 的学生。所以选项 B 是正确答案。

3. 这是一道推理判断题。从海报第二部分引用的学生评语可以看出，Mr. Scanlon 是一位上课非常有趣的数学老师，他使数学从曾经 James 最不喜欢的学科变成了他最喜欢的学科。A 选项张冠李戴，把 James 曾经的喜好安在了 Mr. Scanlon 身上。C 选项说 Mr. Scanlon 在学校刻苦学习，属于无中生有。D 选项试图通过望文生义来干扰学生，让学生混淆"has a laugh with us"和"laugh at students"。所以选项 B"Mr. Scanlon 擅长教学"是正确答案，因为他让讨厌数学的学生爱上了学习数学，所以他一定有独特有效的教学方法，是一位擅长教学的优秀教师。

4. 这是一道推理判断题。从海报最后一部分"每周最佳教师"的投稿指南可以看出，投稿地址是 theweekjunior. co. uk。由此可以判断该活动就是由《周刊少年》杂志组织的。所以选项 A 是正确答案。

5. 这是一道细节理解题。询问 Lucy 的经理做了什么。从题文同序的规律入手，略读前两段可知，当下属在团队工作中出错时，Lucy 对于给他们负面反馈这个事一直有所忌惮，感到压力巨大。而经理的话"Well, Lucy, why not treat it as a teaching opportunity?"说明经理是在建议她以此为契机，教下属如何在犯错之后，吸取教训，吃一堑长一智。选项 A 属于张冠李戴，把 Lucy 的行为安在了经理身上，选项 B 和 C 是无中生有。所以，正确答案是选项 D。

6. 这是一道细节理解题。从第三段的段首可以看出，Lucy 之所以觉得给下属负面反馈让他有畏难情绪，是因为她患有社交焦虑。所以正确答案是 A 选项。

7. 这是一道细节理解题。从第四段可以看出，为了让下属日后不要再犯类似的错误，Lucy 建议大家以后对彼此的工作开展质量监督，而同事也平静地聆听了 Lucy 的建议，并且表示希望 Lucy 能早些把问题提出来，这样大家可以集中力量早些解决问题。选项 A 和 C 都属于无中生有，选项 D 说他们一起纠正了错误。但事实是，"We spent the next 30 minutes brainstorming solutions"（我们花了 30 分钟一起头脑风暴，思考解决方案），选项 D 存在偷换概念，所以，选项 B 是正确答案。

8. 这是一道主旨大意题。结合文章首段"I recently had to give feedback（反馈）to a junior colleague after noticing some errors in a project we worked on together."和结尾"Giving tough feedback is an art — and a difficult one at that"，可以肯定，正确答案为 B 选项。

9. 这是一道推理判断题。根据题意锁定第二段。第二段描述了过去企业在招聘员工时，把大学学位看作技术和能力的指标，这让没有大学学位的工人很难找到工作。"The majority of US workers have had to cope with that barrier". （大多数美国工人不得不应对这一障碍。）从这句话可以看出，大多数美国人因学位问题求职受阻，选项 C 是该句的同义替换，所以是正确选项。

10. 这是一道细节理解题。从文章前两段可以看出，美国的就业市场正在从过去看重教育背景 (education background) 转变为重视技能和学习能力。所以，正确答案是 D 选项。

11. 这是一道推理判断题。询问导致如今企业改变想法的主要因素。第四段 "The falling US birth rate will produce fewer workers in the years ahead to replace the number of workers to retire." 可以看出，未来几年，美国将因出生率不断降低造成劳动力与日俱减，甚至导致新增劳动力少于退休人口。选项 A 无中生有，文中没有提到退休年龄的变化。选项 B 与 the falling US birth rate 的事实不符。选项 D 提到的 "better job training" 与企业改变想法毫无关系。所以，正确选项是 C，导致企业改变想法的主要原因就是人口现状。

12. 这是一道细节理解题。通过 Scanning（扫读）的阅读方法，我们快速定位到文章最后一段的最后一句 "businesses and high schools will be connected more closely so that students can get hands-on experience and a path to a good-paying job."（企业和高中将会更紧密地联系起来，以便学生获得实践经验和通往高薪工作的途径。）由此可见，选项 D 是正确答案。

13. 这是一道细节理解题。文章第一段告诉我们什么样的行为被称为 "floor time"，即 "closing your laptop, stepping away from your desk, and slowly lowering yourself onto the floor"。选项 A 属于偷换概念，文中只提及了带有 "floor time" 标签的浏览量高，但并未提及利用 "floor time videos" 吸引观众。选项 B 和选项 D 都是以偏概全，只描述了 floor time 准备工作，而非具体做法。所以，正确答案是选项 C。

14. 这是一道细节理题，询问原因。从第二段 "Below, experts explain the reasons floor time feels so amazing" 可以看出，正确答案就在接下来的三段中。第三段的最后一句说 "Lying flat on your back can release aches and tension in your muscles."（仰卧可以释放肌肉中的疼痛和紧张），第四段的最后一句说 "This can calm the mind and reduce stress"（可以平心静气、减缓压力），第五段的最后一句则说 "your stress will gradually become weaker and your heart rate will lower"（减轻压力、降低心率）。综上所述，正确答案是 C 选项，全面地概括了 "floor time" 的好处。选项 A 和 D 属于偷换概念，选项 B 是无中生有，均不符合文章内容。

15. 这是一道词义猜测题。从 "appealing" 所在段落的上下文可以看出，第四段主要讲述 "floor time" 给人带来的好处，会让人放松身心，减少压力。所以正确答案是 A 选项，表明它的诸多好处对人产生很大的吸引力。

16. 这是一段推理判断题。从篇章结构可以看出，这是一篇总—分结构的文章。从第二段的 "Below, experts explain the reasons floor time feels so amazing, as well as how to make the most of it." 可以看出，作者要在文中探讨两方面的内容：1. the reasons floor time feels so amazing；2. how to make the most of it. 文章三四五段都着重描述了 "floor time" 的优点，那么显而易见，文章接下来将继续探讨第二方面，即如何充分利用 "floor time"。所以，选项 D 是正确答案。

第二章　翻译

第一节　英译汉

小试牛刀

Translate the following sentences into Chinese.

1. 他们仍然不愿意谈失业问题。

2. 近几年来，对人工智能的研究已经取得了巨大进展。

3. 坚持将会帮助我们渡过困境。

4. 她穿着一件长裙，戴着一顶草帽，系着一条丝巾。

5. 火柴燃烧时发出光和热。

学以致用

Translate the following sentences into Chinese.

1. 如果有空的话，我们星期三来看你。

2. 积极看待生活，你就会找到幸福。

3. 学生应该德、智、体全面发展。

4. 很多成功人士证明了职业规划的重要性。

5. 道路总是曲折的，前途总是光明的。

第二节　汉译英

小试牛刀

Translate the following sentences into English.

1. When an opportunity is neglected，it never comes back to you.

2. We should be loyal to our party，to our people and to our motherland.

3. Modesty helps one to go forward，whereas conceit makes one lag behind.

4. The writing of Chinese characters is not only a way of expressing language but also a manifestation of art.

5. Different colors can trigger different emotions and feelings.

学以致用

Translate the following sentences into English.

1. Strengthening basic research is an urgent requirement for achieving greater self-reliance and strength in science and technology，and it is the only way for building a world leader in science and technology.

2. Traditional Chinese Medicine deeply influence people's dietary habits.

3. We will continue to develop the Guangdong-Hong Kong-Macao Greater Bay Area and support Hong Kong and Macao in better integrating themselves into China's overall development and playing a greater role in realizing national rejuvenation.

4. These cultural elements play important roles in the development of Chinese society，deeply influencing people's ways of thinking，moral concepts，and social behaviors.

5. With the development of globalization and increasingly frequent information exchange，Chinese traditional culture is shining on the global stage with its unique charm.

第三章　写作

第一节　应用文写作

小试牛刀

Ⅰ. 下列问题可以在电子邮件的哪个部分找到答案？请找出最佳选项并连线。

1. C　2. D　3. B　4. A

Ⅱ. 根据邮件信息写出邮件主题。

1. Sorry for My Rude Behavior

2. Class Graduation Party Invitation

3. Internship Position Application

Ⅲ. 将下列句子按照逻辑顺序组织成一封信函正文，采用缩进式写在下面。

Dear Zhang Xin，

I am writing this letter to congratulate that you have been admitted to the college. Congratulations! You make it after a year of hard work.

Now that you're starting this new chapter in your life，I want to offer you some advice. In my personal experience，university life may have some challenges，but it is also highly rewarding. Don't be afraid to step outside your comfort zone and try new things. Join clubs，meet new people，and explore your passions. And most importantly，don't forget to have fun! These years will go by quickly，so make the most of them.

Once again，congratulations on your acceptance to the college. I can't wait to see you in the near future.

Yours sincerely，

Li Ming

学以致用

一、参考范文：

Dear friends，

Welcome to Chengdu! I am Li Xia，a volunteer for the 31st Universiade. There are many famous scenic spots in Sichuan. I recommend you visiting Dujiangyan，a beautiful city renowned for its ancient irrigation system.

For one thing，Dujiangyan，also known as the Dujiangyan Irrigation System，is one of the UNESCO World Heritage Sites. It is the ancient engineering system that still functions today. Do visit the museum to learn more about its history. You will find the wisdom of our ancient Chinese in water management. For the other，you can appreciate the harmony of nature and human civilization here. Dujiangyan offers breathtaking views of nature and wonderful cultural sites together，including the beautiful scenery of Minjiang River and Qingcheng Mountains. A visit to Dujiangyan is sure to leave you with lasting memories.

Please wear a pair of comfortable shoes and take an umbrella in case of rain or sun. I hope you enjoy your stay in Sichuan!

Yours sincerely，

Li Xia

二、参考范文：

Dear Professor Smith，

How are you? The World Earth Day is coming. In order to improve students' environmental protecting awareness，we have organized a mountain climbing activity. I'm writing this letter to invite you to join us.

The details about this activity are as follows. First of all，the climbing activity will take place in Mount Emei at 8:00 a. m. on April 22. Then we will climb to the top of mountain at about 12 o'clock and enjoy the beautiful scenery here. At last，we will take a big group photo on the mountain top，after which we go down the hill and get back to our school at around 6 p. m.

Please bring enough water and food, as well as comfortable shoes for the climbing. We are looking forward to seeing you on that day.

Best regards,

Li Xia

三、参考范文:

Notice

We are pleased to announce that a highly expected lecture entitled *How to Study English* will be presented by Professor Smith. This lecture is designed to provide valuable tips for all of us to enhance our English. Professor Smith will share his insights on effective study methods and strategies. It is a great opportunity to learn from an expert and to enhance our English language skills.

The lecture will be held on March 10, from 9:00 a. m. to 11:00 a. m. in Meeting Room 401. All the teachers and students are welcome to attend this lecture. We look forward to seeing you.

The Foreign Languages School

第二节　提纲写作

小试牛刀

根据下列写作题目草拟中文提纲。

1. 开头段:室友关系是大学生活中不可或缺的一部分,影响我们的生活和学习状态。

主体段:

相互尊重与理解;

建立明确的规则与界限;

学会宽容与包容。

结尾段:处理室友关系需要双方共同努力和相互理解。

2. 开头段:对外国朋友的即将来访表示高兴和欢迎,介绍家乡古镇。

主体段:

古镇的历史与文化;

丰富的民俗活动;

独特的美食体验。

结尾段:古镇之行可使外国朋友深入了解家乡文化、感受当地风情。

3. 开头段:随着科技的飞速发展和知识的不断更新,终身学习成为必须。

主体段:

适应社会发展的需求;

提升个人竞争力;

拓宽视野和丰富生活。

结尾段:树立终身学习的理念,不断追求知识、提升自我。

学以致用

参考范文:

Find a Job or Study Further

Upon graduation, college students are often faced two decisions: whether to embark on a career path or to pursue further education. This phenomenon is not uncommon.

On one hand, finding a job after graduation can be a rewarding experience. It allows graduates to apply their knowledge into practice immediately and employment can also provide a source of income. On the other hand，pursuing further education also holds lots of benefits. Advanced degrees often lead to more specialized knowledge，higher-paying jobs，and broader career choices.

In my opinion，the choice between finding a job and studying further depends on one's goals and financial situation. All in all，the decision should be made based on college students' personal interests and long-term plans.

第三节　图表写作

小试牛刀

Ⅰ．图表匹配。

1. C　2. A　3. D　4. B

Ⅱ．将下列句子翻译成中文。

1. 该图表清晰地描绘了油价的波动。

2. 在线用户的数量发生了显著变化，特别是在过去的两年里急剧增加。

3. 该图表显示，月销售额的峰值出现在 7 月。

4. 从图表来看，失业率的极值高达 12%。

5. 该图表描绘了全球气温的明显趋势，即过去一个世纪气温都在稳步上升。

学以致用

参考范文：

How People Spend Their Holidays

As is clearly shown in the table that there was a dramatic change in the way people spent their holidays between 2010 and 2020. In 2010，63% of people spent their holidays at home，while the figure decreased considerably to 24% in 2020. There are three reasons for this phenomenon.

To begin with，with the development of our economy，people earn more money than they used to，making it possible for them to afford traveling expenses. In addition，people increasingly realize the importance of going outside to develop themselves. For example，a traveler may encounter or talk with someone with different cultural background to broaden personal vision. Last but not least，by traveling outside，people are close to nature，which is not only beneficial to their body but also their spirit. In short，more and more people take the occasion of holidays to travel outside and relax themselves.

As far as I am concerned，I prefer to go traveling instead of staying at home during holidays. I love meeting different people and take in some fresh ideas. In brief，I have benefited a lot and will benefit more from traveling during the holidays.

附录一：词汇

A	adjust	allow
abandon	administration	alongside
abnormal	admire	alter
aboard	admit	alternative
abroad	adopt	amateur
absent	adult	amazing
absolute	advanced	ambition
absorb	advantage	ambulance
abstract	adventure	amendment
academic	advertise	amuse
accent	advertisement/ad	analyze
accept	advise	ancestor
access	advocate	ancient
accident	affair	angle
accommodation	affect	ankle
accompany	afford	announce
accomplish	afterwards	annoy
according	agency	annual
account	agenda	anticipate
accurate	agent	antique
accuse	agriculture	anxious
ache	aid	apart
achieve	aim	apartment
acknowledge	aircraft	apologise/apologize
acquire	airline	apparently
actually	airport	appeal
adapt	aisle	appearance
addict	alarm	appetite
addition	album	applaud
address	alcohol	apply
adequate	alert	appointment

appreciate	attain	bark
approach	attempt	barrier
appropriate	attend	baseball
approve	attitude	basic
arch	attractive	basin
architect	audience	basis
argue	authority	bathtub
arise	auto/automobile	battery
arrange	automatic	battle
arrest	available	bay
arrow	avenue	beach
article	average	bear
artificial	avoid	beard
ash	awake	beast
ashamed	award	beat
aspect	aware	beautiful
assess	awesome	beef
asset	awful	behalf
assign	awkward	behave
assist	B	behaviour/behavior
association	backache	belong
assume	background	below
assumption	bacon	belt
assure	badminton	bend
astonish	ban	beneath
astronaut	band	benefit
astronomer	bar	besides
athlete	barbecue	beyond
atmosphere	barber	billion
attach	barely	bind
attack	bargain	biology

birth	breathe	campaign
bite	brick	campus
bitter	bride/bridegroom	canal
blame	brief	cancel
blank	brilliant	cancer
blanket	broad	candidate
bleed	broadcast	candle
bless	brochure	canteen
blind	bubble	capable
block	bucket	capacity
blog	budget	capital
blood	buffet	capsule
board	bullet	captain
boil	bunch	capture
bomb	bundle	carbon
bond	burden	career
bonus	burger	cargo
bookshop	burn	carpenter
boost	burst	carpet
boot	bury	carriage
border	business	cart
bore	butcher	cartoon
bother	C	carve
bounce	cabbage	cash
bound	cabin	cashier
boundary	cable	cast
bow	café	castle
brake	cafeteria	casual
branch	calculate	category
brand	calendar	cattle
breast	calligraphy	cause

caution	chilli/chili	colleague
cave	chin	collect
cease	chip	column
ceiling	choke	comb
celebrate	chore	combination
celebrity	chorus	combine
centimetre/centimeter	cigarette	comedy
central	circuit	comfortable
century	circumstance	comic
cereal	circus	command
ceremony	cite	comment
certificate	citizen	commerce
challenge	civilization	commercial
champion	claim	commission
channel	clap	commit
chaos	clarify	committee
chapter	classical	communicate
character	clay	communist
charge	client	community
charity	cliff	companion
chart	climate	company
chase	clinic	compare
chat	clone	compass
cheerful	clown	compete
cheese	club	competence
chef	clue	complain
chemical	coach	complex
cheque/check	coal	complicated
chess	coast	component
chew	collapse	compose
chief	collar	comprehensive

comprise	contain	craft
concentrate	contemporary	crash
concept	content	crayon
concern	contest	crazy
conclude	context	create
concrete	continent	creature
condition	continuous	credit
conduct	contract	crew
conference	contradictory	crime
confident	contrary	crisis
confirm	contrast	crisp
conflict	contribute	criterion
Confucius	convenient	critical
confuse	conventional	criticise/criticize
congratulate	conversation	crucial
connect	convince	crude
conquer	cooperate	crystal
consequently	core	cube
conservation	corporation	cuisine
conservative	correct	culture
conserve	correspond	cure
considerable	costume	curiosity
considerate	cottage	current
consideration	count	curry
consist	counter	curtain
constant	couple	curve
constitution	coupon	customer
construct	courage	cycle
consult	court	D
consume	co-worker	dairy
contact	crack	dam

damage	dependent	directly
damp	deposit	director
dash	depress	directory
data	describe	disable
dawn	desert	disadvantage
deadline	deserve	disaster
deal	despair	discipline
debate	desperate	discount
debt	despite	discourage
decade	dessert	discrimination
decent	destination	distinct
declare	destroy	distinguish
decline	detail	distribute
decorate	detect	distribution
decrease	determine	district
defend	device	diverse
deficit	devil	document
define	devise	dolphin
definite	devote	domain
delete	diagram	domestic
delicate	diamond	dominate
delicious	dictation	donate
delighted	differ	doubt
deliver	digest	download
demand	digital	dozen
democratic	dignity	draft
demonstrate	dimension	drag
dentist	dinosaur	dragon
deny	dip	drama
department	diploma	dramatic
departure	direct	drawer

driveway	elevator	erupt
drought	eliminate	escape
drown	embarrassed	especially
duck	embrace	essay
due	emerge	essential
dull	emergency	establish
dumb	emotion	estate
dumpling	emperor	estimate
duration	emphasis	evaluate
dusk	employ	eventually
dynamic	enable	evidence
dynasty	encounter	exact
E	encourage	exceptional
earn	endure	executive
earring	engage	exhibition
earthquake	enhance	expand
ease	enormous	expect
echo	ensure	expense
ecology	enterprise	experience
economy	entertain	experiment
edge	enthusiastic	expert
editor	entitle	explode
educate	entry	explore
efficient	environment	export
effort	envy	expose
elect	episode	extend
electrical	equal	extensive
electricity	equator	extent
electronic	era	external
elegant	eraser	extinction
element	error	extra

extraordinary	filter	frequent
extremely	financial	fresh
F	firefighter	friction
fabric	fireman	fridge/refrigerator
facility	fireplace	frighten
factor	fireproof	frontier
fade	fireworks	frost
failure	firm	function
faint	fist	fund
faithful	flame	fundamental
false	flash	G
familiar	flashlight	gain
fancy	flat	gallery
fantasy	flavour/flavor	gap
fare	flexible	garage
farewell	flour	garbage
fasten	flow	garlic
fault	flowchart	gasoline
favour/favor	fluent	gender
favourite/favorite	fluid	gene
feather	folk	generate
feature	footstep	generation
federal	forbid	generous
fee	forecast	genius
festival	forehead	gentle
fetch	former	genuine
fibre/fiber	fortunate	geography
fiction	forum	geometry
fight	foundation	gesture
figure	fountain	ghost
file	fragile	giant

glance	hammer	housewife
global	handkerchief	hug
glorious	handle	humble
goal	handmade	humorous
golden	handsome	hurricane
golf	handwriting	hut
governor	harden	hydrogen
grab	hardware	I
graceful	harmony	ideal
gramme/gram	harvest	identify
grand	headteacher	identity
grant	health	idiom
grape	height	ignore
graph	helicopter	illegal
grasp	hell	illustrate
grave	hence	image
gravity	herb	imagination
greedy	hesitate	immigrant
greenhouse	highlight	impact
grilled	high-tech	implement
guarantee	highway	imply
guideline	hike	import
guilty	hint	impress
guitar	hip-hop	institution
gulf	historical	instruction
gym/gymnasium	hollow	instrument
gymnastics	homeland	insurance
H	hometown	incident
habitat	hook	include
hairdresser	horizon	income
hairdryer	household	increase

incredible	intend	joint
independent	intensive	journalist
indicate	intense	journey
individual	intension	jungle
indoor	interaction	junior
industrial	interesting	justice
infant	intermediate	justify
infect	internal	K
infer	Internet	keen
inferior	internship	keyboard
influence	interpret	kick
informal	interrupt	kindergarten
initial	intervention	kitchen
initiative	interview	knowledge
inner	invade	L
innocent	invention	lab/laboratory
innovation	inventor	label
input	invest	labour/labor
inquire	investigate	lack
insect	investment	ladder
insert	invisible	lamb
inspect	invoice	landlord
inspire	involve	landscape
install	inward	lane
institute	iron	language
island	J	lantern
issue	jealous	laptop
item	jeans	laser
integrate	jet	latter
integrity	jewel	launch
intelligence	jewellery/jewelry	laundry

leadership	logical	mention
leading	loyal	mercy
leaf	luggage	merely
league	lunar	merit
leak	luxurious	merry
lean	luxury	mess
leather	M	message
lecture	magic	metal
legal	mainland	method
leisure	maintain	microphone
liberal	major	microscope
liberation	manage	microwave
liberty	manual	military
librarian	manufacture	mineral
licence/license	marathon	minimum
lightning	march	minister
likewise	margin	minor
limb	mark	minority
limit	mask	minus
link	mass	miracle
liquid	massage	missile
literally	mature	mission
literary	maximum	mist
literature	meantime	mobile
litre/liter	meanwhile	mode
litter	measure	model
loan	measurement	monitor
lobby	medium	mood
local	memorial	moral
locate	memory	mosquito
logic	mental	motivate

motor	northwest	optimistic
motorbike	notion	option
motorway	novel	oral
motto	nowadays	orbit
mount	nowhere	ordinary
mug	nuclear	organic
multiple	numerous	organise/organize
multiply	nut	original
murder	nutrition	outcome
muscle	O	outdoor
mushroom	objective	outgoing
mutton	observe	outline
N	obtain	output
national	occasional	outstanding
nationality	occupation	outward
naughty	occupy	overall
navy	occur	overcome
neat	ocean	overseas
necessity	odd	overweight
necklace	offend	owe
needle	offer	P
negative	official	pace
neglect	Olympic	pack
negotiate	onion	package
neighbourhood/ neighborhood	online	pal
network	opera	panic
nevertheless	operate	paragraph
noble	opponent	parcel
nobody	opportunity	participate
nod	oppose	particular
normal	opposite	passenger

passion	pillow	precise
passive	pilot	predict
passport	pin	prefer
password	pioneer	prejudice
pasta	plane/aeroplane/airplane	premier
paste	planet	present
paten	plastic	preserve
patient	platform	pressure
pattern	plentiful	pretend
pause	plot	prevent
peaceful	plug	previous
peak	plumber	primary
peculiar	policy	prime
perceive	polish	primitive
percent	political	principal
perception	politician	principle
performance	popular	prior
permanent	population	private
permission	portion	procedure
permit	pose	proceed
persist	position	process
perspective	positive	production
persuade	possession	profession
pessimistic	potential	professional
petrol	pour	progressive
phase	poverty	prohibit
phenomenon	powder	project
philosophy	practical	promise
physical	pray	promote
physician	precaution	proper
physicist	precious	property

proposal	rap	reject
prospect	rarely	relationship
protein	rat	relative
protest	rate	relay
psychology	raw	release
punctual	ray	relevant
purchase	reaction	reliable
purpose	realistic	relief
purse	reality	relieve
pursue	realize	religious
pursuit	rear	remarkable
Q	reasonable	remind
qualify	recall	remote
quantity	receipt	remove
quarrel	reception	renew
quarter	recipe	rent
queue	recite	represent
quit	recognise/recognize	representative
quiz	recommend	reputation
quote	recreation	rescue
R	recycle	reserve
race	refer	residence
racial	reflect	resident
racket	reform	resign
radar	refresh	resist
radiation	refund	resolution
radium	regional	resolve
railway/railroad	register	resort
random	registration	resource
range	regular	respond
rank	regulation	responsible

restore	rust	sensitive
restrict	S	separate
resume	safeguard	series
retell	salesperson/salesman/saleswoman	session
retire	sample	severe
reunion	sandstorm	shade
reveal	sandwich	shadow
revenue	satellite	shake
review	scale	shallow
revise	scan	shame
revolution	scarce	shampoo
revolutionary	scarcely	shape
reward	scare	shark
rhyme	scarf	sharp
riddle	scene	shave
rigid	schedule	shed
roar	scholar	shelter
roast	scholarship	shield
robot	scissors	shift
rock	scold	shock
rocket	scope	shore
role	score	shortcoming
romance	scream	shortly
romantic	sculpture	shot
rough	seasoning	shower
roundabout	section	sidewalk
route	sector	sightseeing
routine	secure	sign
royal	seek	signal
ruin	selection	signature
rural	selfish	significant

silence	sow	stimulate
silver	spade	stir
similar	spare	stock
sincere	spark	straightforward
site	specialist	strait
situation	specialty	strategy
skateboard	species	stream
slice	specific	stress
slide	splendid	stretch
slight	spoil	strike
slip	sponsor	string
smart	sportswear	structure
smog	spot	struggle
sneaker	spray	studio
sneeze	spread	stuff
soccer	stable	style
social	stadium	subjective
socialist	staff	submarine
software	stage	submit
soil	standard	subscribe
solar	starve	subsequent
sole	stationery	substance
solid	statistic	substitute
solution	statue	suffer
solve	status	sufficient
sore	steady	suitable
sorrow	steak	suite
soul	steep	summary
sour	stem	superb
source	steward	superior
souvenir	stiff	surf

surface	temperature	towel
surgery	temple	tower
surname	temporary	trace
surround	tend	track
survey	tendency	tractor
survive	tender	trade
suspect	terminal	tradition
suspend	territory	traffic
sustain	theatre	trail
swallow	theft	transfer
sway	theme	transform
swear	theory	transition
swift	therapy	transmit
swipe	thorough	transport
switch	thread	trap
symbol	threat	tray
sympathy	thunderstorm	treasure
symphony	timid	treat
symptom	tiny	trend
system	tissue	trial
T	title	trick
tablet	toast	troop
tackle	tobacco	tube
tag	tolerate	tune
talent	tone	tunnel
target	toothache	turkey
technical	torch	tutor
technique	total	twist
technology	tough	typewriter
teenager	tour	typhoon
telegram	tournament	typical

tyre/tire	various	vocation
U	vary	volcano
ugly	vast	volume
ultimate	vegetarian	volunteer
uncomfortable	vehicle	vote
underground	venue	voyage
underline	version	vs/versus
undertake	vessel	W
uneasy	vet	wage
unforgettable	veteran	waist
unfortunately	via	wander
uniform	vice	ward
union	victim	washroom
unique	victory	waterproof
unite	video	wave
unity	view	wax
universe	village	wealth
university	violate	weapon
unknown	violent	website
update	violin	wedding
urban	virtual	weep
urge	virtue	weight
urgent	virus	weird
V	visa	welcome
vacation	visible	welfare
vacuum	vision	whale
vain	visual	whip
valley	vital	whisper
valuable	vitamin	whistle
variable	vivid	weed
variety	vocabulary	widespread

wipe	worthy	yield
wire	wound	yoghurt
wisdom	wrap	youth
wit	wrinkle	Z
withdraw	wrist	zero
witness	X	zone
workshop	x-ray	zoom
worship	Y	
worthwhile	yard	

附录二：短语

a series of 一系列	be fond of (doing) sth. 擅长,热衷于
adapt to 适应	be identical to 与……一样
add…to 把…加进……,增加	be in danger/despair 处于危险/绝望中
after all 毕竟	be inferior to 不如,逊于
apologize to sb. for sth. 因为……道歉	be interested in… 对……感兴趣
as a whole 总体上,总体来讲	be jealous of 嫉妒
as long as 只要	be keen on 热衷于,喜欢
as well as 以及	be located in /at 位于
ask for 索求	be new to 对……很陌生,不熟悉
at all times 一直,总是	be open about sth. 对于……看法很开放
at ease 自由自在	be popular with… 受……欢迎
at hand 即将来临	be similar to 与……相似
at least 至少	be superior to 超过,优于
at most 至多,最多	be taken as 被当作,视为
be absent from 缺席	be through with 干完
be accused of… 因……被指控	bound for 前往,决心做
be addicted to 沉迷于	burst into… 爆发,突然发生
be admitted to 被……录取	by accident 意外
be aware of 意识到	by contrast 相比之下
be charged with… 因……被指控	call upon 呼唤
be committed to… 致力于,投身于……	care about 关心
be composed of… 由……组成	catch up 赶上
be critical of… 对……挑剔	cheer for 为……加油
be critical to… 对……至关重要	cheer up 振作起来
be determined to 决心……	come across 偶然遇到,偶然发现
be different from… 和……不同	come to mind 想起;浮现在脑海
be engaged in 从事,参与	come up with 想到
be expert in 在……方面专业	comment on… 评论
be exposed to 接触到,暴露于	complain about 抱怨,投诉
be familiar with 对……熟悉	concentrate on 专注于
be filled with 充满	conform to 符合

consist of... 由……组成	in addition to... 除了……
cut out 剪出	in advance 提前
deal with 处理,应对	in contrast to 和……形成对比
depend on 依靠,取决于	in detail 详尽地
distinguish...from... 区分	in good/no mood 心情好/不好
do one's part 尽自己的一分力量	in most cases 在多数情况下
do research on 对……进行研究	in one's efforts 努力
dozens of 数十个,很多	in regard to 关于
due to 因为,由于	in spite of 尽管
dwell on 纠结于	in the future 今后,将来
fail to do 未能	in turn 反过来
fall into 陷入	instead of doing sth. 代替做某事
fall on/upon... 落到……身上	jot down 匆忙记下
feel free to 随便,可以随时……	keep away from 远离
find out 找出,弄清楚	keep in touch 保持联系
focus on 聚焦于	keep pace with... 与……保持同步
follow through 完成,进行到底	keep silent 保持沉默
for a while 一会儿	keep sth. from 防止某事……
function as 起……的作用	laugh to the last 笑到最后
get ahead(with) 取得成功,取得进展	lead /live a ... life 过着……的生活
get lost 迷路	lead to 导致
get on one's nerves 令某人心烦	lie in 在于
get used to 习惯	lighten up 高兴起来
give up 放弃	link...to... 把……关联起来
go up/down 上升/下降	long for 渴望
have a try 尝试	look forward to 期待
have an impact on 对……有影响	make a commitment to 向……承诺
have to do with 与……有关	make a difference 有影响,使……改变
have trouble doing sth. 做某事有困难	make an effort 努力
have... in common 共同拥有	make sure 务必,保证
head for 走向	make time 腾出时间

make...possible 使……成为可能	satisfy... with……使……满意
never ever 从未,从不	search for 搜寻
occur to 想到	send out 送出
odds and ends 零碎东西	serve as 充当,用作
on a...scale 以……的规模	set up 挂上
on display 展览中	set...on fire 点燃,放火
on duty 值日/值班	share...with... 与……分享……
on exhibition 展览中	show thanks to 对……表达谢意
on one's own 独自	show up 出现
on purpose 有意	shut down 关闭,倒闭
on the basis of 在……的基础上	speak up 大声讲出来
on the contrary 相反	stand for 代表
on the other hand 另一方面	start with 从……开始
on the spot 当场,立即	stay still 保持不动
on the way 在路上	stretch out 伸出
on time 准时	surprise...with... 使……吃惊
once or twice 一两次,偶尔	take...into account 考虑
or so 大约,左右	take...into consideration 考虑
owe to 归因于	take aback 感到吃惊
participate in 参加	take action 采取行动
pay back 偿还,报复	take advantage of 利用
peace of mind 安心	take off 脱下;起飞
play a...role 起着……的作用	take one's part 承担自己的那一部分
provide with 提供	take place 发生
range from...to... 从……到……	take sth. for granted 认为……理所当然
rather than 不是	take the opportunity to 借机
rather than 而非	take time 慢慢来,不着急
refer back to 回查	tell...from... 区分
rely on 依靠	tend to 倾向于,往往会
remind ... of 使想起,提醒	the majority of 大多数……
respond to 回应	to one's surprise/joy 令……吃惊/高兴

on schedule 按时	turn out to… 结果
act as 充当	upon departure 离开的时候
feel at home 感到自在,舒服	upon request 应要求
regard…as 把……看作	word for word 逐字逐句
to some extent 从某种程度	work for 适用于,对……有效
toward the end of 临近……之末	work out 算出
turn around 转过来	worry about 担心……
turn off 关掉	